Screen Tastes

In *Screen Tastes: Soap Opera to Satellite Dishes* Charlotte Brunsdon analyses a wide range of contemporary film and television programmes, from British soap operas and crime series to Hollywood movies such as *Working Girl* and *Pretty Woman*. As well as interpreting the pleasures and meanings that these texts offer – particularly for women viewers – the book is concerned with the language of criticism, particularly feminist criticism, and the aesthetics of popular culture. Why have feminist media critics been so interested in the soap opera viewer? What is meant by 'quality' in television? What are the 'race' politics of the television crime series? And was the fuss about the erection of satellite dishes on British homes really about architecture?

Screen Tastes brings together Charlotte Brunsdon's key writings on film and television criticism, with introductions which contextualise and update the arguments, and new work on the 'post-feminist girly' in recent Hollywood cinema. Brunsdon's focus is on the tastes and pleasures of the female consumer as she is produced by popular film and television – and by feminist criticism.

Screen Tastes documents an important contribution to the development of a feminist cultural studies in the 1980s and 1990s with concerns ranging from 'shopping films' to the deregulation of public service broadcasting, from feminist teaching to the aesthetics of television. While acknowledging debates about the female spectator which underpinned the defence of soap opera and women's films, Brunsdon argues against feminist criticism getting stuck for ever in a girly zone. In a period in which global television is undergoing radical transformation, the book responds to problems facing the cultural studies agenda in an age of aggressive de-regulation.

Charlotte Brunsdon teaches in the Department of Film and Television Studies at the University of Warwick. She edited the collection *Films for Women* (1986) and is the co-editor, with Julie D'Acci and Lynn Spigel, of *Feminist Television Criticism: A Reader* (1997).

Screen Tastes

Soap opera to satellite dishes

Charlotte Brunsdon

London and New York

First published 1997
by Routledge
11 New Fetter Lane, London EC4P 4EE

Simultaneously published in the USA and Canada
by Routledge
29 West 35th Street, New York, NY 10001

© 1997 Charlotte Brunsdon

Typeset in Times by
Ponting–Green Publishing Services, Chesham,
Buckinghamshire
Printed and bound in Great Britain by
Biddles Ltd, Guildford and King's Lynn

British Library Cataloguing in Publication Data
A catalogue record for this book is available from the
British Library

Library of Congress Cataloging in Publication Data
Brunsdon, Charlotte.
    Screen tastes: soap opera to satellite dishes / Charlotte
    Brunsdon.
        p.   cm.
Includes bibliographical references and index.
        1. Feminism and motion pictures. 2. Feminist film
    criticism.
        3. Women in motion pictures. 4. Television and women.
    I. Title.
PN1995.9.W6B78   1997
791.43'082–dc21   96–35327

ISBN   0–415–12154–X (hbk)
ISBN   0–415–12155–8 (pbk)

Contents

Illustrations

Acknowledgements

The author and publishers are grateful to the following for permission to reproduce visual material:
Hello Magazine; Margaret Duerden, Reference Librarian of Central Broadcasting for her advice and ATV Licensing for figures 1 and 2. BFI Stills, Posters and Designs and: Twentieth Century Fox for figures 5, 6, 7, 8, 13, 14, 15; Thames Television for figures 9, 10, 11, 12; Touchstone Pictures for figures 16, 17, 18. Figure 19 is courtesy of BBC, ITN/Channel 4, Picture Palace Productions and HMSO. Figure 20 with permission of *The Independent*. Figure 21 courtesy of Thames Television. Figure 22 courtesy of Young and Rubicam.

For permission to reprint articles, the author and publishers thank Oxford University Press, The Women's Press, Pandora, Indiana University Press and the British Film Institute.

It is impossible, in a collection of this type, to make proper acknowledgement to the many people who have made the work possible. My intellectual debts are obvious from the text, but there is a broader debt to the Centre for Contemporary Cultural Studies at the University of Birmingham under Stuart Hall's direction in the 1970s which it gives me pleasure to record. This is in many ways a Birmingham book, and it pleases me to recall my obligations to, and many arguments with, friends and colleagues there. I also wish to acknowledge the following who commissioned, provoked or edited the original papers and essays: Bobby Allen, Helen Baehr and Gillian Dyer, John Caughie, Pam Cook, John Corner, Peter Dahlgren; Kath Davies, Julienne Dickey and Teresa Stratford; Alan Durant; Larry Grossberg, James Hey and Ellen Wartella; Ann Kaplan, Len Masterman, Patricia Mellencamp, Mandy Merck, Mark Nash; Ellen Seiter, Hans Borchers, Eva-Maria Wrath and Gabriele Kreutzner; Judith Squires.

The University of Warwick, students on the Film/Lit degree and chairs of the Department of Film and Television Studies, Jose Arroyo, Richard Dyer,

V.F. Perkins and Ginette Vincendeau have offered material support and constant intellectual stimulation for which I am most grateful – as has Rebecca Barden. The final manuscript would not have seen light of day without the assistance of Rachel Moseley and I am most grateful to my friends Ien Ang, Erica Carter, Angela McRobbie and David Morley for good ideas and speed reading. I could persuade none of them to write it for me.

Every effort has been made to trace the copyright holders of material reproduced in this book. The author and publishers would be pleased to make further acknowledgement in any future editions.

General introduction

This is a book about television and film, but it is also a book about the criticism and study of these media. While I do analyse and discuss particular television programmes and films in detail, my repeated interest, in a period in which academic attention to the audiovisual has become more legitimate, is in how these texts and media are discussed. I am interested in who can speak about culture, within which constraints, drawing upon which repertoires. What produces particular texts as worthy of study, and why are others illegitimate? These questions are nearer the surface in the study of film and television than in some more established disciplines because the study of film and television is less legitimate, and has a much shorter academic existence. Knowledge about cinema and television is curated outside as well as inside the academy. People keep collections of favourite films or television series – but they also accumulate collections of facts and the lore of fans. As a young film teacher in the 1970s, I soon had to learn that many members of my evening class knew more than I would ever know about, for example, particular directors or the history of censorship in Britain. All I had to offer was greater familiarity with the conceptual frameworks within which the academic study of film was being legitimated. So in the class we would enact the contestation of how film should be known about and the terms in which it should be talked about. I found this sense of the constitution of the field of study enormously exciting – I liked the way in which we seemed to be making something new. This moment didn't last that long with film studies, and I think one could argue that the impenetrability of some film studies language is partly a shrouding of the youth and volatility of the field. But that same sense of *the edge* of the academic – the negotiation of what it is proper to address, and in what terms – accompanied the development of television studies, cultural studies and feminist intellectual work.

These essays were written, in different ways, in negotiation with this edge of the academic. Usually produced for a particular occasion, with little sense of longevity, they trace a continuing concern with issues of taste and audience in particular contexts: the women's movement, cultural studies and the classroom. They have been written over a period of very substantial change in higher education. Most relevant is the way in which two arenas which were intellectually and politically formative for me – the women's movement of the late 1960s and 1970s, and the emergent discipline of cultural studies in the 1970s – have, in this period gained recognisable toe-holds in the academy. The women's movement, in Nancy Miller's phrase, was textualised (Miller, 1993: 41). This is her term for the institutionalisation of feminism, in which she chooses to stress the productivity of the transformed location of feminism since the campaigning 1970s. Women's studies, feminist theory, feminist approaches and analyses became available – if often to ridicule – within a range of educational institutions in the anglophone world. Cultural studies too has changed status and multiplied location. In the 1990s it is an international, diverse discipline, able to sustain international conferences and journals, if still a favourite target for traditional educationalists. These essays can be best approached as formed in the interstices, overlaps and contradictions of the relationships between attention to film and television in cultural studies and that in feminism. They move, through the period, from the defence of women's genres such as soap opera and the 'independent woman' Hollywood films of the 1970s, to a more reflective engagement with the history and consequences of feminist cultural studies for pedagogic practice and the wider paradoxes of the successes of the cultural studies agenda.

While it would be foolish to attempt to weave a whole from a collection of essays published in different contexts over a considerable period, there are two kinds of continuity that I wish to address briefly here. The first category is that of the recurrence across the essays of certain issues and themes. This, most obviously, has been with issues of taste and audience. Because I have usually addressed this issue as a gendered issue, this means that the essays often worry at the distinction between public and private. Do soap operas colonise the world of work from the point of view of personal life? Can women be heroes? Why is the world of public service so resolutely masculinist? The other continuity is a more formal one. This is the issue of voice and location, thrown into high relief by the project of collecting together essays written over several years. For while it is possible to contextualise and update the arguments of the essays as I do in the introductions to each of the four sections below, it is more difficult to address the historical variation in the voice in which they were written. This I return to at the end of this introduction.

My first and motivating concern has been with women as audience for popular or mass culture. I have always been conscious of the way in which what women and girls like is somehow *worse* than the equivalent masculine pleasures. As a teenager I could never understand why songs by girls and girl groups were *worse* than endless unendurably boring guitar riffs, or, even more incomprehensible, drum solos. Why was it so uncool to listen to records about love with lyrics you could sing? Why was obsessively collecting bootleg tapes more worthy than buying earrings? Because you had to label them? Why does what girls like show that they are silly and frivolous, whereas what boys like shows seriousness and commitment? These questions recurred as I became involved with film studies and the academic study of popular culture. Why were westerns and gangster films somehow OK, whereas romances and melodrama were rubbish? Why was football serious but fashion frivolous? Why, as feminist questions began to be formulated, was the public sphere of production so much more important than the private sphere of reproduction? Why was politics in the news and current affairs programmes, but not in the taken-for-granted repetitive world of serial drama?

This concern appears in two ways in this collection. Firstly, in the choice of study texts, where I have been repeatedly drawn to programmes and films that have been made specifically for female audiences: soap opera, the 'independent woman' Hollywood cycle of the 1970s, crime series which attempt to draw in a female audience and the 'post-feminist' films of the late 1980s and 1990s. Secondly, in a repeated address to the theorisation of the female audience. My analyses investigate the way in which these texts address their audiences as feminine through the particular repertoires of knowledge they assume and deploy and the particular satisfactions they offer. So my first concern, analytically, has often been to show *how* these particular texts are gendered, as well as to suggest the historical specificity of this gendering. For it would be my argument that through these particular texts – and, of course, many others – we can trace various types of media settlement with the ideas and practices of second-wave feminism. The implied addressee of the lower-income housewife that we find in 1970s serial drama is no more gendered than the 'liberated woman' cinemagoer in the 1970s. The contours and axes of this gendering, are, though, slightly different, particularly in relation to mobility in the public sphere and the relation to reproduction. Essays in Part I of the book deal with the defence of soap opera, in Part II with the address to the post-second-wave new woman.

In each case though, the address to these clearly gendered texts entailed a defence of this very project. I felt compelled to justify myself, to argue that what I was doing was worth doing. Retrospectively, what is clear is the dual address of the polemic. On the one hand there was the challenge to the traditional, masculinist construction of the field, with its stress on production and the real world of work. Here the argument was that this sphere of love and romance and everyday life was also important. And I don't think, as Stevenson has recently suggested in relation to the work of Ien Ang, that this argument involved a confusion of political with consumerist identities (Stevenson 1995: 110). Rather, one of the projects was to challenge how 'the political' was constituted. On the other hand, it was often against a certain kind of feminism that the polemic was addressed. Difficult though it may be to believe in the 1990s, writing about soap opera, or saying that you quite enjoyed films like *Alice Doesn't Live Here Anymore* (directed by Martin

Scorsese, 1974) or *An Unmarried Woman* (directed by Paul Mazursky, 1977), was contentious for a feminist in the late 1970s. This was because these were texts that positioned their heroines within the feminine, and were seen by many feminists as key sites for the reproduction of conventional femininity. To like them was to collaborate. These issues are discussed at more length in the relevant sections below – here I want only to add that I had rather the same feeling in writing the new essay for the book, on *Working Girl* (directed by Mike Nichols, 1988) and *Pretty Woman* (directed by Garry Marshall, 1990). I enjoyed both these films, and was very interested in their dependence on, but disavowal of, second-wave feminism. I suggest that, although different in many ways, the films share an address to, and a representation of, a new kind of figure, the post-feminist girly. Like Helen Gurley Brown's 1960s single girl, the independent woman of the 1970s, Judith Williamson's 1980s Single Working Woman and Carol Clover's Final Girl, the post-feminist girly is a persona best understood as offering some kind of embodiment of, and engagement with, the changing status of women. And, on the whole, I think she is to be welcomed, perhaps most because she is an unpredicted outcome of certain shifts and struggles. But again, what feminists often found most difficult about her is that there is no repudiation of the conventional accoutrements of femininity. Indeed, as we find in a film like *Clueless* (directed by Amy Heckerling, 1995) in Cher's (Alicia Silverman) and Dionne's (Stacey Dash) obsession with clothes, there is often an exaggerated performance of femininity. It is precisely this tricky and ambivalent relation between feminism and femininity which structures the essays in Parts I and II of the book.

Part III of the book continues the concern with taste and audiences, but in a different context. The essays on feminine texts carry explicit or implicit interrogations of existing aesthetic hierarchies. The underlying question is about the relationship between the historical gendering of feminine genres like soap opera and the place of the genre in legitimate aesthetic hierarchy. Was the genre disregarded because it was seen as a woman's genre? The essays in Part III, which were all written in the late 1980s, begin to address the issue the other way round. Here the question is whether, and on what grounds, it is appropriate to make judgements of quality – aesthetic and otherwise – in relation to television. This is a particularly interesting question for television because of the novelty and popularity of the medium, and the essays trace the different ways in which judgements about television are made by different people, institutions and groups. These are essays written in a particular historical context – the deregulation of British television – which is discussed at more length in the introduction to Part III. Although the British context is specific, the issues raised are much more general, and in some sense mark the paradoxes of the success of the cultural studies or television studies agenda. For the issues of value, quality and judgement won't go away, even if these words, in the 1990s, have somehow come to sound rather like an advertiser's endorsement for life insurance or private health care. If much cultural studies work has established the complexity and multiplicity of tastes and audiences, this, properly, makes only more difficult the passage between the rock and the hard place which is the exercise of judgement in any particular instance of aesthetic and cultural practice. Whether the issue is the funding of a particular cultural project, going to a movie, the grading of student essays or the policy frameworks for the (de)regulation of broadcasting, choices are made – and have to be made – which consciously and unconsciously employ a range of repertoires of judgement which are differentially available to different people. Cultural studies has successfully insisted on the *politics* of aesthetics. The essays in this section ask what is at stake in trying to think about the judgements of aesthetics.

The final section of the book returns to the terrain of feminist criticism, with two essays which, in different ways, map the engagement with 'women's genres' in feminist film and television scholarship. This history is one in which most of this book is formed and so in some ways these final essays provide a retrospective view to counterpoint the earlier work as well as a certain stock-taking. The concern with taste and audience continues, but here focused through analysis of the sub-fields of academic study that have been produced through feminist research on women's genres. The contradictions of the perceived self-reproducing femininity of feminist media research are discussed in the introduction to Part IV – here I want to comment briefly on voice and location in relation to this work. These are teacher's essays. They are written in a quite different voice to the early soap opera work, and Chapter 11 in particular was motivated by concern at some of the effects of the new feminist orthodoxies in the classroom and seminar room. But they are also written with much greater self-consciousness of the exclusions of the feminist project, of the particular cultural context of the 'we' of feminism. And that is an appropriate way to end a book formed in, and ambivalent about, the heritages of 1970s feminism.

Leamington Spa, 1996

NOTE ON THE TEXT

The essays have been reprinted as they first appeared with the original source at the head of each chapter. I have, however, pruned the footnotes, and very occasionally added a later reference. The introductions to each section carry some updating of the arguments and new references.

Part I

The defence of soap opera

Introduction

This section reprints three short early articles on soap opera and one later historical piece, Chapter 4, which reflects on the feminist engagement with soap opera in the context of feminist television criticism more generally. In this introduction I want to offer some brief contextualisation to the short essays and the feminist defence of soap opera of the late 1970s and early 1980s, bearing in mind that Chapter 4 in some ways functions as a retrospective introduction to the section as a whole.

The most substantial of the short essays, '*Crossroads:* notes on soap opera', emerges from a period of research at the Centre for Contemporary Cultural Studies at the University of Birmingham in the late 1970s. In this period the Midlands-produced serial *Crossroads* was widely referred to within British culture in a metaphorical sense to refer to the worst of cheaply produced, under-rehearsed serial television drama. This reputation lives on, partly through a regular sketch, *Acorn Antiques*, by the British comedienne Victoria Wood with performers Celia Imrie and Julie Walters, in her television series *As Seen On TV*. In *Acorn Antiques* which was transparently based on *Crossroads*, actors repeatedly forgot their lines, doors stuck, walls shook and the narrative never seemed to progress, despite the fact that characters were always talking about what had just happened. It was partly this metaphorical significance of *Crossroads* – an extremely popular pro-gramme – that first interested me in it, although it was Dorothy Hobson (also at CCCS) who made the substantial populist defence of the programme in this period (1982). One of the positions argued in Chapter 1, that it is analytically necessary to distinguish between the address of a text – in the terminology of the time, the spectator (position) the text constructs – and the social readers of the text who may have various relations to this position, has on occasion been attributed to me alone. In fact it was very much a product of the collective work of the Centre for Contemporary Cultural Studies in the 1970s, and can be found, for example, with direct reference to media consumption in the contemporary work of Janice Winship (1981) and David Morley (1992) and more generally in other CCCS work of the period. The argument was fuelled in a particular way in Britain by the hegemony, within leftist intellectual work, of the positions associated with the film journal *Screen* in the mid-1970s. *Screen*, under the editorship of Sam Rohdie and then Ben Brewster, had been responsible for the translation into English of key structuralist and 'metapsychology of cinema' texts which theorised the operations on the cinematic spectator of the film text and the cinematic 'machine' (see, for example vol. 14, 1–2 (1973); 16, 2 (1975). Particularly significant in this argument came to be both Colin MacCabe's notion of the 'classic realist text' (1974) and texts displaying those features loosely described as Brechtian, which were understood to 'undo' the imaginary unity of the spectator produced by classic illusionist cinema. That is, this Althusserian/Lacanian theorisation of cinema in its turn valorised particular avant-garde practices which were argued to have particular effects on the spectator. The address of this genre of criticism was consistently political – the task of the critic was to reveal the ideological workings of the film text, while the radical film-maker had to struggle to find cinematic forms which were not complicit with existing modes of representation. These arguments led to the dominance in the magazine *Screen* and associated British film culture of the assumption that it was not the explicit politics of a film text that were significant, but its formal operations. Thus the radical modernism of Jean-Luc Godard was validated above, for example, the naturalism associated with the work of Ken Loach and Tony Garnett. (*The Days of Hope* debate reprinted in Bennett *et al.* 1981 provides a good example of the ferocity of debate in this area in the 1970s.)

It was from this context that an essay on a popular, cheaply produced soap opera was developed. The *Crossroads* piece was conceived as a double provocation in that I wanted to address the issue of the gendering of the spectator – both textually and contextually – and I wanted to play with assumptions about the progressive effects of texts which displayed Brechtian formal features. In arguing that a despised programme like *Crossroads* displayed – looked at in a certain way – formal features such as discontinuity, interruption and tableau-like spacing which were heralded as the acme of progressive practice in radical cinema, I wanted to suggest both that making sense of these formal devices is significantly dependent on what the viewer brings to the viewing, and that the cultural competences of femininity are largely unrecognised as such. This was then, like early essays by Tania Modleski (1979) and Ellen Seiter (1982a), an attempt to find a theoretical space for a female viewer, but was, significantly, articulated in relation to the less culturally prestigious form, television, while haunted by the theorisation of the spectator within film studies, and particularly Laura Mulvey's inaugural gendering of the spectator (1975).

Annette Kuhn (1984a), in what has become a canonical account, has subsequently pointed to the way in which this essay straddles the disciplinarily bounded address to audiovisual women's genres. She shows the way in which feminist work on television soap opera is formed within sociological paradigms, dominated by notions of the real and the social, while feminist work on film melodrama is shaped by literary and psychoanalytic models which privilege the text and textuality. The validity of her argument, and the persistence of this distinction is demonstrated by the extraordinary paucity of empirical work on film audiences. The outstanding exceptions here, the work of Jackie Stacey (1994) and Jacqueline Bobo (1995), serve to accentuate this point, while Stacey herself has also challenged the taken-for-granted status of textual analysis as method in cinema studies (1993). I suspect that there are institutional, as well as disciplinary, factors in play here, and in fact, the feminist attention to audiences has had an enormous impact when considered in relation to the very small amount of funding it has received. Here it is worth observing, as Lyn Thomas (1995) has pointd out, that a high proportion of this work, the studies by Ien Ang (1985), Helen Taylor (1989) and Jackie Stacey (1994), has in fact used letters as principal data. The empirical study of audiences is both time-consuming and expensive, usually requiring research grants – which in turn require the support of grant-giving bodies. 'Women as viewers' has not been a favoured topic in comparison with research in the sex/violence/young men axis. However, my own dis-inclination to pursue empirical audience work and to investigate whether the hypotheses advanced in the *Crossroads* piece were valid was more influenced by anxiety about occupying the position of empirical researcher. I just couldn't imagine how to do this. Instead I have chosen to focus on the discursive context in which meanings are made, the talk and writing about soap opera which provide the vocabulary and repertoire of attitudes through and from which individuals express their attitudes to these programmes. It is this with which Chapters 2 and 3 are concerned.

David Buckingham has recently argued that the study of soap opera is now 'normal science', no longer requiring the challenges to existing paradigms that characterised the opening-up of this area in the 1970s and early 1980s (1997). Buckingham wrote this in a review of Robert Allen's international collection on soap opera, *To Be Continued. . .* (1995) and Jostein Gripsrud's major case study of the reception of *Dynasty* in Norway (1995), and certainly, 'soap opera studies' seems an established topic for both publishers and students. In English there have recently been books by Martha Nochimson (1992), Mary Ellen Brown (1994) and Laura Stempel Mumford (1995) on US soap opera, and the study of the genre is now an established part of many syllabuses. In the context of this continuing flow of genre and programme studies, the short essays here reprinted document an earlier phase of soap opera studies, when there was considerable resistance to the notion that the genre might be worthy of attention (despite the long history of social science research into the effects of daytime serials on their viewers or listeners). It is for this reason that I have called the section 'The defence of soap opera', for I wanted to retain some sense of soap opera as a contested object of study. These essays offer traces of a different context, when the arguments for the study of soap opera, although they *were* arguments about the significance of the genre, were also carrying many other arguments. These involved the gendering of television and media studies and polemics about the validity of the study of popular forms. So 'soap opera' carried ideas of a female spectator, respect for women as audience and an assertion of the significance of the private sphere. Similarly, in its place near the bottom of the aesthetic hierarchy, the genre posed most vividly the issue of the value of the study of popular culture. I think partly because the validation of soap opera as an object of study did carry so many other issues, there has perhaps recently been a certain wallowing in the evident value of the genre as a central area of study. I'm not sure that much is gained by the repetition of what have now become the clichés of the field, such as that soap opera is a woman's genre, and I'm also not sure that these arguments are in fact any longer true of popular programmes such as *Neighbours* and *Brookside*. Indeed Buckingham (1997) goes on to urge academics who teach in this area to (re)consider, 'what do we expect our students to *learn* about soap opera that they do not already know – and what difference do we think this will make?' These seem to me appropriate questions in the 1990s, for while I do want to insist on the historical significance of the defence of soap opera in the late 1970s and early 1980s, the significance of this defence lies mainly in the challenge to aesthetic hierarchy and the canon, the gendering of the study of popular culture and the associated gendering of its consumer, rather than, beyond a certain point, the study of soap opera as such. Soap opera, as I argue at more length in Chapter 11, was just one of many women's genres addressed by feminist scholars in this period. Soap opera was a site on which particular struggles within a rather marginal part of the academy were carried out. These were significant arguments, and have generated new areas of study and a substantial body of knowledge about the genre. Now I think it might be time to do something else.

Chapter 1

Crossroads: notes on soap opera[†]

Husband to wife weeping as she watches TV: 'For heaven's sake, Emily! It's only a commercial for acid indigestion.'

(Joke on Bryant & May matchbox)

INTRODUCTION: A GENDERED AUDIENCE?

The audience for soap opera is usually assumed to be female.[1] In these notes I would like to examine this assumption, and the extent to which the notion of a gendered audience can be useful to us in the understanding of a British soap opera *Crossroads*.

Initially, I should like to make a distinction between the subject positions that a text constructs, and the social subject who may or may not take these positions up. We can usefully analyse the 'you' or 'yous' that the text as discourse constructs, but we cannot assume that any individual audience member will necessarily occupy these positions.[2] The relation of the audience to the text will be determined not solely by that text but also by positionalities in relation to a whole range of other discourses – discourses of motherhood, romance and sexuality for example. Thus it may well be that visual pleasure in narrative cinema is dependent on identification with male characters in their gaze at female characters, but it does not necessarily follow that any individual audience member will unproblematically occupy this masculine position. Indeed, feminist film criticism usefully deconstructs the gendering of this 'you'. As Janice Winship has recently argued: 'A feminist politics of representation . . . has then to engage with the social reader, as well as the social text' (Winship 1981: 25).

The interplay of social reader and social text can be considered by examining the extent to which a gendered audience is implied in programme publicity, scheduling and advertisements. The Independent Broadcasting

---

[†]Written for the conference 'Perspectives on Television and Video Art', organised by Ann Kaplan at Rutgers University, May 1981. First published in *Screen* 22, 4 (1981). The conference proceedings were published in Kaplan (1983b).

Authority, in its 1979 annual handbook, groups *Crossroads* with other Drama serials:

> TV drama serials have for many years been an essential ingredient in the programme diet of a large and devoted audience. Established favourites such as *Coronation Street* and *Crossroads* continue to develop themes and situations which often deal with the everyday problems and difficulties to which many viewers can relate. Occasionally the more adventurous type of serial is produced.
>
> (Independent Broadcasting Authority 1979: 92)

The femininity of the audience is specified, apart from the structuring dietary metaphor, in the opposition of 'devoted' and 'everyday' to 'adventurous'. There are a wide range of 'spin-off' materials associated with *Crossroads* – novels, special souvenir supplements, interview material, and a *Crossroads* cookbook. I will take up the question of the incoherence of *Crossroads* narratives below.

In terms of scheduling, although *Crossroads* is broadcast at different times in different regions (stripped across four evenings a week),[3] it is always broadcast within the 5.15 p.m. to 7.30 p.m. slot. That is, with early evening, weekday transmission the programme is definitely not scheduled in the prime time in which it is expected to maximise on a male audience. If we accept Richard Paterson's argument that notions of the family and the domestic dominate the scheduling of British television programmes, then fathers are not expected to control television choice at this point. Paterson also suggests a relationship between scheduling and programme structure:

> Its narrative is constructed of multiple short segments, with continual repetition of narrative information, but no overall dramatic coherence in any episode. In part this structure reflects its place in the schedule: continual viewing has to be ensured even though meal times and other domestic interruptions might make it impossible to follow a coherent narrative.
>
> (Paterson 1980: 82)

The broadcast slot of *Crossroads* is surrounded by magazine news programmes, panel games and other serials – all suitable for family, and interrupted, viewing. However, the advertising that frames, and erupts within, the programme is quite clearly addressed to a feminine consumer – beauty aids, breakfast cereals, instant 'man-appeal' meals and cleaning products: the viewer as sexual, as mother, as wife, as housewife, in contrast to the ads for lawn mowers, car gadgets, DIY equipment or large family purchases which dominate from 8.30 p.m. on. These 'extra textual' factors suggest that women are the target audience for *Crossroads*.

A DISCONTINUOUS TEXT

The ideological problematic of soap opera – the frame or field in which meanings are made, in which significance is constructed narratively – is that of 'personal life'. More particularly, personal life in its everyday realisation through personal relationships. This can be understood to be constituted primarily through the representations of romances, families and attendant rituals – births, engagements, marriages, divorces and deaths. In Marxist terms this is the sphere of the individual outside waged labour. In feminist terms it is the sphere of women's 'intimate oppression'. Ideologically constructed as the feminine sphere, it is within this realm of the domestic, the personal, the private, that feminine competence is recognised. However, the action of soap opera is not restricted to familial or quasi-familial institutions but, as it were, *colonises* the public masculine sphere, representing it from the point of view of the personal.

Thus in *Crossroads* we have a family run business, the Crossroads motel, with an attached garage. The motel is near a village, Kings Oak, which at various times has included a market garden, a doctor's surgery, a post office, an antique shop and so on. Regular characters are members of one of three groups – the Crossroads family, the motel/garage workforce or the village. The fictional community, clearly socially hierarchised through *mise-en-scène* and dialogue, is kept interacting through a series of interlocking economic relationships, but this business interaction is of diegetic importance only as the site of personal relationships. It is always emotionally significant personal interaction, often reported in dialogue, which is narratively foregrounded. This can be seen most clearly through the narrative construction of time and place.

There is no single linear time flow. The minimum three concurrent narratives proceed through a succession of short segments (rarely exceeding two and a half minutes). In contrast with classical narrative cinema, the temporal relationship between segments is rarely encoded. Time in general moves forward, although there is repetition at the beginning of episodes. Relationships between segments can be read as in most cases sequential or simultaneous. One continuous scene can be broken into several segments – notoriously over commercial breaks and between episodes, but this is a standard intra-episodic suspense device. The lack of any overarching time scheme permits the rise and fall of different narrative threads. As each narrative has only its time of exposition, there is no loss of 'real' or referential time if a narrative lapses. Similarly, the very simplicity of the use of 'interruption' as the major form of narrative delay, extending dramatic action, also works against the construction of a coherent referential time. The different present tenses of the narrative co-exist, temporally unhierarchised.

Space in *Crossroads* is also organised in a way which is quite distinct from the conventions of classical narrative cinema, conventions which are carried over to some other forms of television drama. The shoestring budgets mean very restricted sets (all internal, usually no more than five in one episode) and few available camera positions.[4] Generally, sets have two distinct spaces arranged laterally to each other – that is, there are two distinct camera fields, and it is the articulation of these fields which constructs the space.[5] Some sets allow only one camera position. These camera set-ups are not variable, and camera movement is limited. Most scenes are shot in mid-shot or medium close-up, opening with either a close-up or a longer shot. The narrative does not mobilise space within any particular set, nor is there any attempt to make the different spaces of the different sets cohere. We are instead presented with a series of tableau-like views, more theatrical than cinematic. The sets thus function very literally as setting or background, seen always from the same points of view, as familiar as the room in which the viewer has the television.

I am thus arguing that the diegetic world of *Crossroads* is temporally and spatially fragmented, and that this fragmentation, accompanied by repetitious spatial orientation, foregrounds that dialogue of emotional and moral dilemma which makes up the action. The coherence of the serial does not come from the subordination of space and time to linear narrativity, as it does in classical narrative cinema, but from the continuities of moral and ideological frameworks which inform the dialogue. It is these frameworks which are explored, rehearsed and made explicit for the viewer in the repeated mulling over of actions and possibilities. *Crossroads* is in the business not of creating narrative excitement, suspense, delay and resolution, but of constructing moral consensus about the conduct of personal life. There is an endless unsettling, discussion and resettling of acceptable modes of behaviour within the sphere of personal relationships.

There are two key elements in this. Firstly, structurally, the plurality of story lines, which allows the use of the narrative strategy of interruption, and secondly, diegetically, the plot importance accorded to forms of lying and deceit. Structurally, although the different physical spaces of narratives do not cohere, except in the meeting place of the motel lobby, the same set of events, or the same dilemma, will be discussed, by different characters in 'their own' environments. A range of different opinions and understandings of any one situation will thus be voiced. At the same time, the use of interruption, the consistent holding off of denouement and knowledge, invites the viewer to engage in exactly the same type of speculation and judgement. The viewer can, as it were, practise possible outcomes – join in the debate about how a particular event is to be understood.

The use of deceit in the narrative works slightly differently. By deceit I mean the development of a narrative line in which the audience knows that one character is consciously lying or misleading other characters. Here the viewer is in a position of privileged knowledge in relation to the protagonists, and can see clearly what and who is 'right'. The drama of morality is here produced by the tension between the fact that 'good' characters must continue to be trusting, to remain 'good', but that they will suffer unless they 'find out' about the true nature of another character, X.

In both cases what are being set in play, or exercised, are repertoires of understandings and assumptions about personal and familial relationships, in which the notion of individual character is central. Thus although soap opera narrative may seem to ask 'What will happen next?' as its dominant question, the terrain on which this question is posed is determined by a prior question – 'What kind of a person is this?'. And in the ineluctable posing of this question, of all characters, whatever their social position, soap opera poses a potential moral equality of all individuals.

A GENDERED AUDIENCE – 2

Recently Tania Modleski has argued for the textual inscription of a female (maternal) subject in American soap opera. She has suggested that the multiple narrative structure of soap opera demands multiple identification on the part of the viewer, and thus constitutes the viewer as a type of ideal mother, 'a person who possesses greater wisdom than all her children, whose sympathy is large enough to encompass the claims of all her family . . . and who has no demands of her own' (Modleski 1979: 15). I will consider the related question of the type of cultural competence that *Crossroads* as soap opera narrative(s) demands of its social reader.

Just as a Godard film requires the possession of certain forms of cultural capital on the part of its audience to 'make sense' – an extra-textual familiarity with certain artistic, linguistic, political and cinematic discourses – so too does *Crossroads* and soap opera. The particular competences demanded by soap opera fall into three categories:

1 Generic knowledge – familiarity with the conventions of soap opera as a genre. For example, expecting discontinuous and cliff-hanging narrative structures.
2 Serial-specific knowledge – knowledge of past narratives and of characters (in particular, who belongs to whom).
3 Cultural knowledge of the socially acceptable codes and conventions for the conduct of personal life.

I will comment only on the third category here. The argument is that the narrative strategies and concerns of *Crossroads* call on the traditionally feminine competencies associated with the responsibility for 'managing' the sphere of personal life. It is the culturally constructed skills of femininity – sensitivity, perception, intuition and the necessary privileging of the concerns of personal life – which are both called on and practised in the genre. The fact that these skills and competencies, this type of cultural capital, are ideologically constructed as natural does not mean, as many feminists have shown, that they are the *natural* attributes of femininity. However, under present cultural and political arrangements it is more likely that female viewers will possess this repertoire of both sexual and maternal femininities which is called on to fill out the range of narrative possibilities when, for example, the phone rings. That is, when Jill is talking to her mother about her marriage (17 January 1979), and the phone rings, the viewer needs to know not only that it is likely to be Stan (her nearly ex-husband) calling about custody of their daughter Sarah-Jane (serial-specific knowledge) and that we're unlikely to hear the content of the phone-call in that segment (generic knowledge) but also that the mother's 'right' to her children is no longer automatically assumed. These knowledges only have narrative resonance in relation to discourses of maternal femininity which are elaborated elsewhere, already in circulation and brought to the programme by the viewer. In the enigma that is then posed – will Jill or Stan get Sarah-Jane? – questions are also raised about who, generally and particularly *should* get custody. The question of what *should* happen is rarely posed 'openly' – in this instance it was quite clear that 'right' lay with Jill. But it is precisely the terms of the question, the way in which it relates to other already circulating discourses, if you like, the degree of its closure, which form the site of the construction of moral consensus, a construction which 'demands', seeks to implicate, a skilled viewer.

I am thus arguing that *Crossroads* textually implies a feminine viewer to the extent that its textual discontinuities require a viewer competent within the ideological and moral frameworks, the rules, of romance, marriage and family life to make sense of it.

Against critics who complain of the redundancy of soap opera, I would suggest that the radical discontinuities of the text require extensive, albeit interrupted, engagement on the part of the audience, before it becomes pleasurable. This is not to designate *Crossroads* 'progressive' but to suggest that the skills and discourses mobilised by its despised popularity have partly been overlooked because of their legitimation as natural (feminine).

Chapter 2

Writing about soap opera[†]

Soap operas, such as *Crossroads, Coronation Street* and *Brookside*, do not just exist in the hour or so of broadcast television a week that each is allotted. The central fiction of the genre, that the communities represented exist outside the box, as well as on it – the idea that the Grants, or Ken and Deidre, or Jill and Adam could watch the news, just like us – is supported and sustained across a range of media material. Newspaper articles, novels, souvenir programmes, *TV Times* promotions, even cookery books, function to support the simultaneous co-existence of them and us.[1] It is possible to wear the same clothes, use the same decor, follow the same recipes and even pore over the same holiday snaps as the people in the Street, the Close and the Motel. It is even possible to buy *Ambridge, An English Village through the Ages*, the book that Jennifer Aldridge and John Tregorran researched and wrote together while listeners nationwide followed their growing pleasure in each other's company.

The promotional material produced by the television companies and associated bodies and the spin-off material produced under licence from the television company all work to sustain the reality of the fiction. Much of this material strives quite specifically to implicate the viewer or reader in this suspension of disbelief.[2] The *TV Times*, for example, at moments of soapy ritual like weddings, produces 'snaps' of past weddings and vanished characters. The fan is exhorted to test memory, to remember the televisual past in the same way as we remember our own pasts. That same moment of recognition, 'Oh, look, there's X' 'Do you remember . . .?' followed by the assertion of the naturalness of 'now' – 'Look at that dress/hat/hairdo'. The soap opera world and our world are brought together in this blurring of private and public repertoires.

These are, however, not the only discourses which construct and comment on the soap opera world. 'True stories', usually by cast and ex-cast, and usually in the popular Sundays or weeklies, promise to take the lid off the fiction. Autobiographies by people like Pat Phoenix and Noele Gordon offer

†First published in *Television Mythologies*, edited by Len Masterman (London, Comedia: 1984).

1 *Crossroads Monthly* 1 (1976) (ATV Licensing)

glimpses of the relation between personality and character. You can go and see the Archers at agricultural shows. Noele Gordon writes about cancer as *Woman* of the week, 'Dammit, I haven't got time to die' (26 May 1984). Some of this material can be thought of as 'soap opera as news'. Exposés are certainly national news. But so are illness, death, legal prosecution, accidents, marriage and divorce of the actors and actresses. Often, these stories of 'real life' run as a kind of sub-text, or parallel soap to the one we watch on television. This sub-text is not kept separate when watching. The knowledge you have about particular characters 'in real life' feeds into and inflects the pleasure of soap watching.

It has been argued that soap operas make their viewers carry on watching because they want to know what will happen next. For the soap fan, one of the moments of pleasure is when you can say 'Oh, I *knew* that was going to happen.' But this is not quite the same feeling as the attendant fascination of *how* it is going to happen. At the moment, I don't really think that Sheila Grant is going to have the baby that she is pregnant with. My reasons are partly generic – I know that a very high proportion of soap opera pregnancies come to little more than a few months' story. They are partly what I experience as 'intuitive' – she is in her forties, she has already got three children, the house isn't big enough. Partly cynical – she's the only character of child-bearing age on the Close who wouldn't have an abortion (Heather, Karen, Michelle (?)) or hasn't already got young children (Marie), so she's the only one that pregnancy will be a big issue for. If I'm right, what I don't know is how she is not going to have it. So my pleasure (rather unpleasantly, in this case) is in how my prediction comes true.[3]

Brilliantly, at this point, *Brookside* has combined Edna Cross's pre-disposition to a bet with Marie's second sight to allow the viewer to have her predictions explicitly debated on screen. Edna and Marie had a bet about whether Alan and Samantha would finally get married. We all wondered. But as soap opera is news, in the doings of both characters and actors or actresses, and it was 'known' that Dicken Ashworth, who plays Alan, was leaving, the viewer had to juggle another sort of knowledge in the attempt to get the prediction right. Will it be easier for him to be written out if he does or doesn't get married?

So soap opera as news can increase the pleasure of the hermaneutic speculation, as it increases the constraints in play. The viewer has to juggle all the different sorts of knowledge to get it right. With this much practice from television entertainment – and entertainment that is widely regarded as requiring little effort on the part of its addicted viewers – small wonder that we reproduce some of the dominant ideological paradigms in our own lives. Of course, extra-textual determination can become excessive, as has happened in the last eighteen months with *Coronation Street*, where possibility has no dynamism, and the programme keeps having to come up with solutions to one loss after another.

It is not only as news or plot speculation that soap opera features in newspapers. All newspapers have some form of television criticism, and soap opera makes episodic appearances in these columns.

Television criticism in newspapers does not generally directly address soap operas. The regular exception here is Nancy Banks-Smith of *The Guardian*, who not only watches soaps but has a very sharp eye for the use of the soap register in 'life', i.e., other programmes such as The News. The metaphorical value of J. R. Ewing and Alexis Carrington has extended beyond the entertainments page of most newspapers for some time. However, in the main, soap opera functions, within writing about other programmes, as a symbol of the truly awful. Thus, in a discussion of American television, Rod Allen, writing in *The Listener* (8 July 1976), observes that these programmes 'would make *Crossroads* look like Oscar Wilde by comparison'. Reference to *Crossroads* in particular functions as an abbreviated way of invoking bad scripts, bad acting, cheap sets, poor timing – and *stupid* fans. Thus Sue Arnold, in *The Observer* (8 May 1983), discussing the travails of finding a nanny, can say:

> I have had 16-year-olds straight from school with basic common sense whom I would trust implicitly to cross the King's Road with a pram and three ancillary children, and girls with 10 years of experience who would still be watching *Crossroads* when the house burned down.

As all soaps attract large audiences, and *Crossroads*, for example, in its heyday, was usually watched by about thirteen million people, there is a lurking problem about the nature of television criticism here. There is an uneasy relationship between institutionalised television criticism and popular taste and audience. What is the role of television criticism which can neither explain the popularity of a programme like *Crossroads* nor, indeed, even take this popularity seriously? The repressed question of television criticism can be traced: 'Who is this critic speaking for and to?' Occasionally critics directly address this issue:

> To criticize *Crossroads* (ATV) is to criticize sliced white bread, or football or keg beer – you are made to feel it's a class snobbism, you're trying to show yourself superior to what the ordinary people enjoy. Unfortunately, the ordinary people are wrong, and the critic is right and *Crossroads is* bad, slack, inept and untruthful, even within its own miserable limits.
>
> (No author credit, *Sunday Telegraph*, 6 April 1975)

This explicitly 'classed' notion of the critic as specialist judge and arbiter of taste is the opposite to the position argued in one of the more substantial defences of soap opera, Dorothy Hobson's 1982 book on *Crossroads*. Hobson upbraids television critics for employing critical criteria derived from high art in the evaluation of a popular form such as soap opera, and appears to argue that popularity itself should be a central evaluative criterion. Most usefully, she shows that the audience for *Crossroads* is mainly female and often elderly. Here we begin to see that it is issues not only of class but also gender and age status of the audience which may inflect critical judgement.

Most critics, however, choose to avoid the question of 'tendency', explicit or otherwise, in critical judgement. There are two main strategies used here, to bridge that gap between critic and audience. The first, which has a long history in relation to popular art forms, and was, for example, used in relation to the novel, is what we could now call the addiction strategy.

The critic and the reader can together perceive the soap opera fan as acting without desire:

> These were the ones with the worst symptoms of withdrawal pains. For them this four times a week shot of soap opera had become as habit forming as a drug.
> (written of *Crossroads* fans during the 1979 ITV strike, Hilary Kingsley, *Sunday People*, 28 October 1979)

> People who become addicted to a serial as bad as *Crossroads* are people who would not fight for a seat on the bus.
> (Peter McKay, *Evening Standard*, 6 August 1980)

The advantage of the addiction metaphor is that even if the reader is the viewer, because addiction is constructed as involuntary, the reader can concur with the condemnation of his or her habit. This model is used by both left and right, although the feminist press would not express quite this contempt:

> Perhaps its success is partly due to its timing – 4.30 being a particularly boring time for bored housewives who've got nothing to do but wait for their husbands to ring and tell them they'll be late at the office again!
> (Virginia Ironside, *Daily Mail*, 13 November 1970)

Soap opera is seen as the opium of the masses, particularly the female masses – soothing, deluding, product and producer of false consciousness. The other strategy – it's so bad it's good – could be called the kitsch strategy. The same features are commented on, but become cause for pleasure:

> I am addicted to *Crossroads* (ATV) not for its virtues, which escape me at the moment, but for its faults. I love it because of its warts, as it were. An infatuation based on faults is difficult to cure . . .
> (Nancy Banks-Smith, *The Guardian*, 8 August 1972)

Crucially, what both strategies do is avoid confronting the fact that millions of people do enjoy, and take seriously, *Crossroads* and other soap operas. It is unarguable that the production values of *Crossroads* in particular are low. Hobson makes a clear argument about why they are unlikely to improve. But to millions of fans production values are clearly not the point – or at least

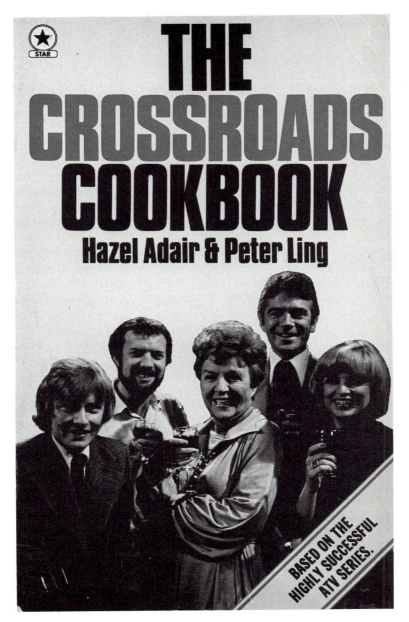

2 *The Crossroads Cookbook* (ATV Licensing)

not the main point. I can spot shaky scenery, a muffed line, an odd shadow, as well as the next fan. But what I watch for is different. It is partly a ritual pleasure, which offers reassurance in its familiarity and regularity. The credit sequence and theme tune are quite important here. Unlike the 'hook' of the crime series – often up to three minutes of action before the familiar break into the theme – the credits of *Brookside, Coronation Street* and *Crossroads* all work primarily to establish a sense of place. It is not character, in the sense of heroes and heroines, or the promise of action, and enigmas resolved, that is central, but the establishing of the 'where' – the place that we know, where life is going on. And it is surely the predictable familiarity of the life represented which pulls us in. Because all British soap operas have some relation to realist conventions, the problems and worries of characters are recognisable. We, too, live in the world of family squabbles, demands for television licence fees and rising unemployment. It is not so much that 'life is like that' – it doesn't need content analysis to establish that the more dramatic things happen more often to more characters in soaps than 'in life' – but that the generic lack of closure, in combination with the realist premise, offers a homology between soap life and viewer life. Like us, soap opera characters have to live with the consequences. It is usually only when an actor or actress takes the option we haven't got and leaves the programme that there is any chance of a happy ending. Elsie may have gone off to a golden sunset – but what comfort or hope is there for Rita? Or Hilda? Or Mavis, Emily, Bet or Betty? And what has Deidre settled for – the possibility that Ken will have an affair? Soap opera characters are doomed to live out the truth of the old adage that 'No news is good news' – and no news is no soap.

Of course this 'generic unhappiness' has its own counter-balances. *Coronation Street* has increasingly dealt in comedy and *Crossroads* has always had strong affiliations with the overdrive of melodrama. *Brookside* relies mainly on the youth of many of its characters, in combination with fairly regular celebrations and location work. These emphases allow us to be entertained, to laugh and look, as well as think about life. I am not arguing that soap operas are tragic. Nor would I dispute that the way in which hope, happiness, a future, etc., are constructed within the programmes is very much within the ideological norms of Happiness = white middle-class heterosexual family unit (house owning). So, yes, sure, soaps must, at one level, work to reproduce the dominance of these norms – but this is only, in a way, to the extent that they provide a site for viewers to become involved in problems, issues and narratives that do touch on our own lives. You don't get involved with, or like, all of the characters – and quite often stories are not interesting or sympathetic. But that is part of the point.

Chapter 3

Feminism and soap opera[†]

Liking soap opera has always been a risky business. Wooed by the television companies with an endless stream of character-centred publicity – for the soap watcher is that most desirable statistic, the regular and committed viewer – the fan is frequently abused by both the quality and the popular press.[1] Even those involved in the production of soap operas, from actors to producers, are frequently apologetic about their occupation and their product.[2]

The advent of the new 1980s soaps, *Brookside* and *EastEnders,* with higher budgets and determined appeals to a wider and younger audience of both sexes, has to some extent improved the public profile of soaps. Similarly the recession chic of the American prime-time serials, *Dallas* and *Dynasty*, which have exported padded shoulder fantasy worldwide, has to some extent allowed the particular pleasures of serial viewing to be more publicly acknowledged, as Ang (1985) demonstrates. Still trash, soaps have, in some circles, been elevated to good trash. As a recent article by Elizabeth Walton in *The Times* rather exquisitely put it: 'It was Sir John Betjeman who made it respectable to admit to an addiction to *Coronation Street*' (25 November 1985: 12).

It is in this context, one in which fans are frequently ashamed of their pleasures, that we have to place the contradictory feminist response to soap opera. Initially predominantly one of fierce rejection, feminist response was partly determined by the way in which soaps were seen as women's programmes. Feminists in the 1970s were particularly aggressive towards 'women's genres' – the feminine ghetto of soap operas, fashion, romances and women's magazines.[3] I have been ticked off more than once at feminist conferences for even watching the programmes. (I say this not to draw attention to my daringly *outré* tastes but as evidence of the way in which many feminists *assumed* that soaps were such a bad thing that erring sisters should be pointed back to the right road.)

Soaps were criticised for offering stereotypical and unrealistic images of women which confirm us in our subordination. To a certain extent there is a

†First published in *Out of Focus*, edited by Kath Davies, Julienne Dickey and Teresa Stratford (London: The Women's Press, 1987).

truth in this argument – what I want to do here is tease out some of the complexities and problems that this simple political criticism ignores.

Like much political criticism, the argument was a realist one. It was assumed that there were (readily available) more realistic representations of women which would better serve a feminist argument. There are at least two kinds of realism in a soap – an 'external realism' created through reference to the outside world, through set, modes of dress, discussion of contemporary events, etc., and an 'internal realism', whereby characters conform to our knowledge and expectation of them, which is derived from having watched the serial. To call for more realistic female characters involves a rather complicated negotiation of these realisms. As soaps grow old, instead of wrinkles, they get a lack of fit between these two types of realism. Thus although *Coronation Street* has conformed to the demands of 'internal realism' over the years, its 'external realism' has become much more obviously constructed in comparison with the fresher conventions and representations of *EastEnders* and *Brookside*. The 'lack of fit' between these realisms means that, paradoxically, it can be argued, as for instance in Geraghty (1983), that the female characters in *Coronation Street* are much 'stronger', more independent figures than those in the more (externally) realistic recent soaps.

Thus firstly we have a feminist rejection of soaps, which, although couched in different terms, is, in effect, almost homologous with the traditional high cultural contempt for soaps. This was followed by a certain revaluation which coincides, across the women's movement, with the revaluation of conventionally feminine skills such as embroidery and the admission of enjoyment in some of the pleasures of traditional femininity, like dressing up. More positive attitudes – and I don't want to claim that these necessarily apply to all feminists – have been based partly on a recognition of the strength of female characters such as Meg Mortimer in *Crossroads*, Bet Lynch in *Coronation Street* and Sheila Grant in *Brookside*, and partly on the revaluation of women's genres as such. Perhaps soap opera has such low cultural status not because it is any more trashy than war movies or westerns but because the people who watch it have less cultural power?

The argument about realism is a tricky one. Soaps have very strong *generic* features – rules and conventions which all soaps share – like the idea that these people carry on living even when we're not watching them. It is partly conformity to these generic rules which produces the 'internal' realism of the serial. The 'external' realism is not so much a matter of direct comparison with the Real World (i.e. 'I live in Liverpool, and it's not like *Brookside*') but of the way in which the soap opera partakes of, and contributes to, all the different ways in which we make sense of the Real World. Soaps are dependent on already existing discourses – in the papers, on the news, about law and order, about young people – to represent the Real World to us. But the representations they produce also contribute to our understanding of what that world is./Feminists have argued that dominant discourses in this culture are ones which both devalue women and repeatedly insist on the social power of sexual difference. It is these dominant definitions which are most powerful in constructing our image of what the Real World is. Thus for feminists to call for more realistic images of women is to engage in the struggle to define what is meant by 'realistic', rather than to offer easily available 'alternative' images./Feminists are quarrelling not just with soap opera, but, fundamentally, with the Real World there represented. Arguing for more realistic images is always an argument for the representation of 'your' version of reality. 'Realistic' to a feminist will often seem propagandist and thin to a political opponent. The image will precisely lack the sedimented 'concreteness' of a dominant image. This problem – of the lack of credibility of alternative and oppositional representations – is particularly pronounced in a form like soap opera which is mainly pleasurable in its predictable, conservative, repetitive elements, and its necessary generic commitment to realism. It is extremely difficult to construct plausible, but challenging and different, characters and situations.

A good example of this is the women's screen-printing co-operative which appeared on *Brookside*. Unlike the years of television living rooms, and mums getting the tea, this location and these characters have almost no television history at all. Although it may, in one sense, be more realistic, in that it shows representations of women doing things other than servicing men – what one might call 'feminist realism' – it is also deeply implausible.

Chapter 4

The role of soap opera in the development of feminist television criticism†

In recent years I have more than once set an examination question for third-year undergraduates along the lines of 'Why have feminist critics been so interested in soap opera?'. To my recurring disappointment, no student has yet attempted this question, which I think is probably a tribute to their much underrated ability to identify their teachers' research agendas, and the way in which these tend to frame unanswerable questions. There is also a way in which the answer can seem very obvious – because soap operas are women's programmes – which may make it very unattractive in the competitive context of an examination. This essay is my attempt at an answer to this question, but I should make clear that I think this bald and simple answer, in the West, in the key period of feminist interest, is fundamentally correct, and that all that I shall do is to make things a little more complicated. This I shall do in two main ways. Initially, by sketching a rather broader semi-historical context for feminist analyses of soap opera – a 'when' of this interest – and then by tracing the different modalities of this interest – a 'how'. In this process I hope to provide an account of the role of soap opera in feminist television scholarship. Before I start, though, I want to spend a moment on establishing why I think the question is itself interesting.

Firstly, despite what I am going to say later in the essay, I think there is still a piquancy in the juxtaposition of 'feminists' and 'soap opera'. Each noun connotes a different engagement with femininity. The commonsense understanding of 'feminist', a much more problematic term within common sense than 'soap opera', is partly constructed through the negation of more familiar modes of femininity. In the popular imaginary, feminists are still women who don't shave their legs, don't approve of page three girls, and don't like soap opera. Given the extent of feminist scholarship on soap opera in the 1980s, this residual piquancy is intriguing. What is at stake in the relationship between feminists and soap opera?

Secondly, the very extent of recent scholarship on soap opera, much of it

---

†First published in *To Be Continued . . . Soap Operas Around the World*, edited by Robert C. Allen (London: Routledge, 1995).

within, or influenced by, feminist paradigms, provokes reflection. Ann Kaplan, in her 1987 review of feminist television criticism, points to the centrality of feminist work on soap opera to the increased attention to the genre from the mid-1970s. Robert Allen traces the contours of research on soap opera in his 1985 book, *Speaking of Soap Operas*, outlining the growth in social science research on the genre between 1972 and 1982. It is towards the middle of this period that the feminist work starts being published, as I outline below. The status of soap opera, as an object of academic study, has changed radically in the last twenty years. At its simplest, this is to say that soap opera is at present studied within the academy in a wide range of disciplines – something that would have been quite inconceivable in 1970. Allen's collection, for which this chapter was first written, in its very commissionability and existence, testifies to this point. Soap opera has been peculiarly significant for the development of feminist television criticism, and I think it is arguable that it is for the study of soap opera that this criticism is most visible in the wider arena.

So underlying my question about why feminists have been interested in soap opera is the paradox that, on the one hand, there is a perceived incompatibility between feminism and soap opera, but, on the other, it is arguably feminist interest that has transformed soap opera into a very fashionable field for academic inquiry.

THE GENERAL CONTEXT OF FEMINIST TELEVISION SCHOLARSHIP

Many commentators have pointed out the significance of what are usually called 'the media' to post-1960s feminism. Key texts of second-wave western feminism such as Betty Friedan's 1963 *The Feminine Mystique*, Germaine Greer's 1971 *The Female Eunuch* or Sheila Rowbotham's 1973 *Woman's Consciousness, Man's World* all have central concerns with the available repertoire of images of femininity, with the way in which women are represented. This feminist movement was, from its inception, a believer in the reality and importance of images. The twenty years or so since these founding texts were written have seen enormous changes in the analysis of images of women. For our purposes, perhaps the most significant is that this type of analysis has shifted from being primarily a political, extra-academic project to having a substantial academic existence. Many courses, in subjects such as English, history of art, communications and media studies, offer units on 'the representation of women' or 'images of women'. With the percolation of feminist ideas into the academy, which has happened differentially across disciplines, there have been several key debates which have taken place in rather different forms across different disciplines. At a general level one of the most significant of these can be seen as the debate about realist paradigms.

Early feminist approaches to the media, for instance King and Stott (1977), were usually within a realist paradigm, comparing real women, or the reality of women's lives, with the available images thereof. Real women were found to be imperfectly formed, hard-working, multi-ethnic and extremely various in contrast to the dominant ways in which they were represented. This important strand of criticism, which still has relevance today, was challenged theoretically by feminists who wanted to break with the realist paradigm, and what they saw as the false distinction between 'real women' and 'images of women'. These feminists wanted to argue that what we understand as real women, indeed, how we experience ourselves as such, is inextricably bound up with these images of femininity. That is, they argued that it is not clear what 'a woman' is, except through representation. (See Cowie *et al.* (1981) for an early formulation.)

These theoretical arguments, and the related debate about 'essentialism', structure feminist academic endeavour in a range of fields. Indeed, Michèle Barrett and Anne Phillips (1992) have recently argued that we can make a periodising distinction between 'modernist' 1970s feminism, with its optimism about discovering the cause of women's oppression, and postmodern 1990s feminism, with its sense of the fragmentation of the category 'woman', and its stress on the significance of difference. In relation to the study of the media we can mark a move away from the study of images of women to the study of the construction of femininity, or the inscription of sexual difference. So if the general theoretical terrain involves the move from the affirmation of the presence of 'woman' in the 1970s to doubt about the validity of this category in the 1980s, there are also marked changes in attitudes to conventional/traditional femininities. The recognition that women were perhaps rather more engaged with, and constituted by, available discourses of femininity than second wave feminism had first insisted, fundamentally shifts the objects and purposes of feminist media analysis. This we can see most clearly in the changing attitudes to the mass-produced genres of femininity: romance fiction, film melodrama and 'weepies', women's magazines and television soap opera. Key feminist books of the early 1980s, such as Rosalind Coward's 1984 *Female Desire* and Janice Radway's 1984 *Reading the Romance*, articulate a much more sympathetic engagement with mass media femininities, even as writers such as bell hooks challenge the racism of these femininities and feminisms.[1] It is these changes which are most relevant to the construction of soap opera as an object of study central to feminist television scholarship, and which are most interesting in the answer to my question, why were feminists so interested in soap opera? Before proceeding to this issue it is necessary to outline some distinctions in the expanding field of feminist television research.

FEMINIST RESEARCH ON TELEVISION

Feminist scholarship on television can be found in a series of academic disciplines: film studies, communication studies, mass communications,

cultural studies, sociology, English, women's studies. These different disciplinary contexts govern the construction of the object of study and the
methodologies employed. What researchers are interested in, and how they
proceed to explore it, has to be understood partly within each disciplinary
context. Thus, for example, work within sociology is more likely to be
concerned with the pattern of women's work within the television industries
than work within English, which may be more concerned with narrative
structure of particular programmes. However, many of the disciplines that
have proved most permeable to feminist concerns, such as cultural or media
studies, are themselves only semi-institutionalised – only intermittently
recognised as proper subjects. This fact, in combination with the relative
youth of feminist scholarship on television, and the common political origins
of much of the research, means that there is also a high degree of interdisciplinarity, and a determined tendency to breach disciplinary boundaries.
Widely cited work like that of Ien Ang (1985), Ann Kaplan (1983b), Tania
Modleski (1982), or Michele Wallace (1990), which is to varying degrees
directly concerned with television, cannot be contained by just one discipline.

So, within a framework in which we initially understand feminist research
on television to be both interdisciplinary and dispersed across academic
disciplines, we can distinguish four main categories of scholarship.

The real world of women working in television

Scholarship in this area investigates patterns of employment, promotion and
power of women in television. There are two main issues here. Firstly, the
exploration and documentation of the manifest and continuing discrimination
against women at nearly every level of programme-making apart from
secretarial work. This was a particular focus for feminist work in the 1970s,
for example Gallagher (1981) and Beasley and Silver (1977); in some countries
coinciding with the period before discrimination on grounds of sex became
illegal. Unless otherwise specified, 'women' here is usually a unitary category,
as is characteristic of early second-wave feminism. Margaret Gallagher has
continued to produce extensive data for UNESCO (Gallagher 1987), and
Abrahamsson and Kleberg's 'Gender and Mass Media' newsletter consistently
reports on new work in the area. It is, however, surprisingly difficult to obtain
recent information for some professions and countries, which might be seen
as symptomatic of what Margaret Gallagher (1992) identifies as an overall
retreat from the public political arena in feminist media research.

Secondly, more theoretically, there is the issue of the extent to which the
gender of the producers does determine media output. The notion of the 'male-
dominated' media was a popular explanatory factor in the early days, but has
become noticeably less prominent. There is an almost total lack of what might
be termed feminist political economy, which perhaps points to the difficulties
of using gender alone as an explanatory category. There has not been much

theoretical discussion of this issue either, although Liesbet van Zoonen reviews what literature there is in her 1994 book *Feminist Media Studies*.

Instead, although relatively undocumented in the academic literature, there are the accounts by individual women and groups of women of their attempts to break into the industry and make programmes. These accounts have many different forms and emphases, depending partly on their addressees. For example, Annette Kuhn (1984b) uses a letter form in a feminist journal for her reflections on working in the Pictures of Women collective, while Karen Alexander is interviewed on her video work in the same publication (Nava 1984). Helen Baehr and Angela Spindler-Brown (1987) discuss their involvement in Broadside (a feminist company producing news and current affairs programmes for early Channel 4) in an article in an academic collection, while there are now several survey articles, such as those by Marilyn Crafton Smith (1989) and Linda Steiner (1992), which include television work by women in accounts of (mainly US) women's work in a range of media.

For our purposes, it should be noted that soap opera is not a positive term in work in this category. With some exceptions, like the lesbian soap *Two in Twenty*, feminists have not been drawn to making alternative or feminist soaps, nor has it been in relation to this genre that inequality of opportunity or employment discrimination has been felt most acutely. It has been in relation to news and current affairs that the aspiration, and the exclusions, have been felt.

Content analysis of the presence of women on the screen

Although early feminist critique had generally involved some notion of counting – how many women appeared on screen to read the news? what sort of roles did women generally have? which women? – it has been mainly within the discipline of mass communications that questions about gender have been added to the array of quantifying projects. Gaye Tuchman's 1978 formulation of 'the symbolic annihilation of women' provided a vivid hypothesis about the absence of women on television, as well as specifying their generic presence: 'with the exception of soap opera, where men make up a "mere majority" of the fictional population, television has shown, and continues to show, two men for every woman' (Tuchman 1978: 10). There have been a series of studies which have focused on soap opera in the investigation of the type of roles available for women, and the type of women likely to fill them since Tuchman's article, and the early piece on the heroine of the daytime serial by Downing (1974), such as Cassata and Skill's (1983) *Life on Daytime Television* or Matelski's (1988) *Soap Opera Evolution*. The extensive collecting of statistics about gender is not, of course, necessarily informed by a feminist project.

Alongside this type of analysis, which remains very much within the paradigms of mass communications, there has been a strong critical current which mobilises feminist argument to support a methodological and sometimes epistemological attack on the practices of mass communications research. Key texts here would be Noreene Janus's 1977 attack on the assumptions of quantitative methodology, published, indicatively, in the *Insurgent Sociologist*, Lana Rakow's work (1986), and a series of journal special issues, such as the 1986 issue of *Communication* edited by Paula Treichler and Ellen Wartella.[2] This feminist attack on dominant disciplinary paradigms has been frequently associated with a more general ferment in the field, and the increased influence of critical or cultural studies methodologies. So within this category of research soap opera is a significant, but methodologically contested site.[3]

Textual or programme studies: 'heroine television'

The detailed analysis of television programmes as 'texts' is a relatively new practice, and has generally been conducted by scholars whose first training is in a text-based discipline such as English literature or film studies. Feminist textual analysis has in the main been directed at two types of fictional programmes: those addressed *to* women and those centrally *about* women characters. It is perhaps thus not surprising that soap opera is such a presence in this category of research. The two other main genres that have attracted feminist interest are sitcoms with distinguished comediennes, such as the 'Lucy' and Mary Tyler Moore shows, and, interestingly, one of the main sites for 'positive images', the crime series, most significantly *Cagney and Lacey*.[4] Both these genres, given the type of feminist interest that has been manifested, could be subsumed into a larger category of 'heroine television' which includes all the later fictional programmes which have been attractive to feminists such as *Kate and Allie, The Golden Girls, Designing Women* and *Murphy Brown*.[5] 'Heroine television' is centrally about female characters living their lives, usually working both inside and outside the home, usually not in permanent relationships with men, sometimes with children, and trying to cope. It is the 'trying to cope' which is critical. These shows are all, in some fundamental way, addressing feminism, or addressing the agenda that feminism has made public about the contradictory demands on women. Sitcoms seem to be the dominant form – the irresistible comedy of being a modern woman – but certainly in Britain there has been considerable exploration of the crime series, most notably through *Prime Suspect* and the work of Lynda La Plante.[6]

Soap opera isn't quite 'heroine television', but it was mainly attractive to feminists as an object of analysis because it was perceived to be both for and about women. I discuss this at more length below, as I do the multi-referentiality of the portmanteau 'soap opera'. Here it is important to note that the early work on soaps tended to come out of work concerned at a more general level with media directed at female audiences. Thus Carole Lopate wrote about US daytime television in general in 1976. Dorothy Hobson (1980) started off her research with an investigation of women's daytime radio listening. Tania Modleski (1982) looked at soaps along with other mass-produced fiction aimed at women. It is also historically significant that 1978 saw the launch and subsequent international success of *Dallas*. So the interest displayed by feminist critics in television programmes directed at women or housewives coincides with popular serial melodrama as a worldwide phenomenon. Feminist work on soap opera develops alongside studies of the international reception of *Dallas* (Liebes and Katz 1990).

Audience studies

As is clear from the section above, the feminist interest in television programmes was from the beginning formulated through ideas about the audience. Several early analyses of soap opera make hypotheses about how women respond to soap opera, and many later studies attempt to test these ideas.[7] Thus the Tübingen/Volkswagen (Seiter *et al.* 1989) study explicitly tests some of Modleski's formulations, and Andrea Press (1991) asks questions drawn from a variety of cultural studies work. Ien Ang (1985 and 1990) offers both an extensive reading of *Dallas* and an audience study. This work, too, needs to be seen in the broader context. Thus while feminist researchers were particularly concerned with the way in which women 'read' or enjoyed television programmes, there was a new attention to audience 'decoding' in general, as any review account of media research in the 1980s indicates (see Corner 1991b: 267–84).

We can quickly note two tendencies in recent studies, in both of which feminist research is prominent. Firstly, there has been an increased emphasis on the domestic environment and familial relationships therein. Ann Gray's 1992 work about the use of the video recorder offers one example of this, while Lynn Spigel's 1992 research on 'making room for the television' is another. Secondly, there is a growing literature on audiences-as-fans and fan identity as such, which would include Constance Penley's 1992 work on *Star Trek* fans, and that of Lisa Lewis (1990) on music videos.

As with the textual analysis of programmes, I think we can observe a pattern in which feminist work is initially clustered round soap opera but then begins to move away from the mid-1980s onwards.

Within the context of this brief mapping, I can now offer a time-line of feminist work on soap. This is not meant to be exhaustive – a task which would, given the interdisciplinarity of the research indicated above, be very difficult – but it is meant to signal when key articles and books were written in relation to each other.

Feminist research on soap opera: time-line

1974
* Helen Butcher, Ros Coward, Marcella Evaristi, Jenny Garber, Rae Harrison and Janice Winship, *Images of Women in the Media* (University of Birmingham, CCCS Stencilled Occasional Paper no. 31).

1976
Carol Lopate, 'Daytime television: you'll never want to leave home', *Feminist Studies* 3, 3–4 (spring/summer): 69–82.
† Horace Newcomb (ed.), *Television: The Critical View*, 1st ed. (Oxford: Oxford University Press). Includes: Renata Adler, 'Afternoon television: unhappiness enough and time', *New Yorker*, 12 February 1972.

1977
Richard Dyer, Terry Lovell and Jean McCrindle, 'Soap opera and women', *Edinburgh International Television Festival Official Programme*: 24–8.

1978
Lesley Stern, 'Oedipal opera: *The Restless Years*', *Australian Journal of Screen Theory* 4: 39–48.
* Gaye Tuchman, A.K. Daniels and J. Benét (eds), *Hearth and Home: Images of Women in the Mass Media* (New York: Oxford University Press).

1979
Tania Modleski, 'The search for tomorrow in today's soap operas', *Film Quarterly*, 33, 1: 12–21.

1981
Richard Dyer, Christine Geraghty, Marion Jordan, Terry Lovell, Richard Paterson and John Stewart, *Coronation Street* (London: BFI Television Monograph no. 13).
Charlotte Brunsdon, '*Crossroads*: notes on soap opera', *Screen*, 22, 4: 52–7.
Michèle Mattelart, 'Women and the cultural industries', *Media, Culture and Society* 4, 4: 133–51.
Gillian Swanson, '*Dallas*', *Framework* 14: 32–5.

1982
Dorothy Hobson, *Crossroads: The Drama of a Soap Opera* (London: Methuen).
Ellen Seiter, 'The role of the woman reader: Eco's narrative theory and soap opera,' *Tabloid* 6: 35–43.
Ellen Seiter, 'Promise and contradiction: the daytime television serials', *Film Reader* 5 (Evanston, Ill.: Northwestern University).
Ien Ang, *Het Geval Dallas* (Amsterdam: Uitgeverij SUA).
Tania Modleski, *Loving With a Vengeance* (Hamden, Conn.: Shoe String Press).

1983
E. Ann Kaplan (ed.), *Regarding Television* (essays by Allen, Flitterman, Modleski) (Los Angeles, Calif.: American Film Institute).
Muriel Cantor and Suzanne Pingree, *The Soap Opera* (Beverly Hills: Sage).

1984
Jane Feuer, 'Melodrama, serial form and television today', *Screen*, 25, 1: 4–16.
Annette Kuhn, 'Women's genres', *Screen*, 25, 1: 18–28. Later reprinted in Christine Gledhill (ed.), *Home Is Where the Heart Is* (London: British Film Institute, 1987).

1985
Ien Ang, *Watching Dallas*, trans. and rewritten (London: Methuen).
Robert C. Allen, *Speaking of Soap Operas* (Chapel Hill, NC: University of North Carolina Press).
† Elihu Katz and Tamar Liebes, 'Mutual aid in the decoding of *Dallas*', in Philip Drummond and Richard Paterson (eds), *Television in Transition* (London: British Film Institute).

1986
Mary Ellen Brown, 'The politics of soaps', *Australian Journal of Cultural Studies* 42: 1–25.
Jane Root, *Open the Box* (London: Comedia), chapter on soaps.
† John Tulloch and Albert Moran, *A Country Practice: Quality Soap* (Sydney: Currency).

1987
* Helen Baehr and Gillian Dyer (eds), *Boxed In: Women and Television* (London: Pandora).
† David Buckingham, *Public Secrets: EastEnders and its Audience* (London: British Film Institute).
E. Ann Kaplan, 'Feminist criticism and television', in Robert C. Allen (ed.), *Channels of Discourse* (Chapel Hill: University of North Carolina Press).

1988
Sandy Flitterman-Lewis 'All's well that doesn't end', *Camera Obscura* 16: 119–29.

1989
† Sonia Livingstone, *Making Sense of Television: The Psychology of Audience Interpretation* (Oxford: Pergamon).
Ellen Seiter, Hans Borchers, Gabriele Kreutzner and Eva-Maria Warth (eds), *Remote Control* (London: Routledge).

1990
Mary Ellen Brown (ed.), *Television and Women's Culture* (London and Newbury Park: Sage).
Prabha Krishnan and Anita Dighe, *Affirmation and Denial: The Construction of Femininity on Indian Television* (New Delhi: Sage).
Tamar Liebes and Elihu Katz, *The Export of Meaning: Dallas* (Oxford: Oxford University Press).

1991
Andrea Press, *Women Watching Television* (Philadelphia, Pa.: University of Pennsylvania Press).
Christine Geraghty, *Women and Soap Opera* (Cambridge: Polity Press).
* Ien Ang and Joke Hermes, 'Gender and/in media consumption', in James Curran and Michael Gurevitch (eds), *Mass Media and Society* (Sevenoaks: Edward Arnold).
* Liesbet van Zoonen, 'Feminist perspectives on the media', in ibid.

1992
* Margaret Gallagher, 'Women and men in the media', *Communication Research Trends* 12, 1: 1–15.
Christine Geraghty, 'British soaps in the 1980s', in D. Strinati and S. Wagg (eds), *Popular Media Culture in Post-War Britain* (London: Routledge).
Christine Gledhill, 'Speculations on the relationship between soap opera and melodrama', *Quarterly Review of Film and Video* 14, 1–2: 103–24.
† Richard Kilborn, *Television Soaps* (London: Batsford).

* denotes that the work is important in feminist approaches to the media, but only deals tangentially with soaps.
† denotes that the work is about soaps, but is not strongly (or at all) informed by feminist approaches.

WHY AND HOW WERE FEMINISTS INTERESTED IN SOAP OPERA?

Having established some sense of the distribution of feminist research on soap opera – that feminists have indeed been interested in the genre – and that some of the best-known feminist television criticism, such as that of Ang, Hobson and Modleski is on this topic, I want finally to move towards an answer to my motivating question. So – why were feminists interested in soap opera?

Because soap opera is a woman's genre

From their origins in the US radio serials directly sponsored by detergent manufacturers, soap operas have been specifically aimed at female audiences. This is less true now than at any earlier point, but the connotational femininity of the genre remains overwhelming. The early research on radio soap opera conducted by Herta Herzog (1944), Rudolf Arnheim (1944), and Helen Kauffman (1944) under the aegis of the Radio Research bureau investigated only female audiences. Thelma McCormack (1983) has analysed the assumptions about the female audience in other US research literature on the genre.[8] Ellen Seiter (1989) has revealed the commitment of Irna Phillips, prime mover behind many US radio soaps, to educating women, as well as exhorting them to buy. Christine Gledhill (1992) has examined the gendering of soap opera in the context of a discussion of the melodramatic mode in general. In short, women have been targeted by the makers of soap opera, women have been investigated as the viewers of soap opera, and the genre is widely and popularly believed to be feminine, despite stubborn evidence that it is not only women who watch.[9]

Early feminist writing on the media, which was strongly dependent on the idea of 'stereotyping', characterised the representation of women as dominated by two figures, the sex-object and the housewife. If the former was found in beauty competitions and ads for cars, the latter lived in soap operas and ads for washing powder. So one of the early feminist responses to soap opera was simply hostile. The programmes were one instance of the brainwashing project of the mass media, the project to keep women thinking that all they could do was be housewives. The women who watched soap opera, in this type of analysis, needed consciousness-raising, while the women portrayed were without interest. Feminists were interested in soap opera only to the extent that they purveyed ideologies of femininity and family against which feminism was defining itself. It was a combative interest, a commitment to knowing thine enemy.

But it was also more complicated than that.

Because 'the personal is political'

'The personal is political' is the most resonant and evocative claim of 1970s western feminism. This slogan reminds us of the particular flavour of the anglophone feminist movement that emerged from the political and social upheavals of the 1960s with its fierce belief in the significance of individual experience, but its absolute determination to understand this experience socially. This slogan, while evoking a specific political movement, also has a certain familiarity which is not specific, and which indicates to us something of the influence of this movement. The radical redefinition of the personal and the political associated with 1970s feminism affected a wide range of fields, among them, media research. I want to suggest here that it is partly the direct political challenge of 'the personal is political' which contributes to the changing emphasis of media research in the 1970s and 1980s away from hard news and current affairs to softer programmes. Further, I want to suggest that soap opera, and the feminist-influenced analysis of soap opera, is pivotal to an understanding of this structural shift in the field. Thus we cannot understand the impact of a book such as John Fiske's 1987 *Television Culture*, with its radical shift away from 'hard' programming, without noting the attention paid therein to a feminist agenda. For it is feminist criticism significant and not some mystified 'effect' of an economic determination elsewhere.

In arguing for the historical significance of the assertion that 'the personal is political' for an understanding of certain patterns in media research I don't dispute the deconstruction of the personal/political opposition as specific to white middle-class women that has been offered by scholars such as Aida Hurtado (1989). Jacqueline Bobo and Ellen Seiter (1991) map out some of the implications of this argument for media research, and particularly for domestic ethnographies, in their article on *The Women of Brewster Place*. The point here though, is that it was precisely those women not subject to state surveillance and harassment in their homes and personal lives who not only argued that the personal was political, but who also turned their attention to the media representation of women's lives. It is the same moment, the same movement, which declared that the personal was political, and which saw that this might change the significance of soap opera to radical analysts of the media.

If the personal is political, if it is in the home, in relationships, in families, that women's intimate oppression – or the oppression of women as women – is most consensually secured, then the media construction and representation of personal life becomes fascinating and an urgent object of study. If the traditional leftist critique of the media, with its structuring sense of class conflict, was drawn to the reporting of the public world – to industrial disputes, to the interactions of state and broadcasting institutions, to international patterns of ownership and control – emerging feminist scholarship had quite another focus. The theoretical impulse of feminism pushed scholars not to the exceptional but to the everyday. There was, as discussed above, research into patterns of employment for women in the media, but textually the concern to look at the representation of women of necessity led away from hard news and current affairs. So the theoretical conviction that there was a politics to everyday life and that women's hidden labour in the home was essential to capitalism coincides with the actual generic distribution of (white) women on television. If the project was to analyse the representation of women on television, there was of necessity a focus on genres other than the traditional objects of critical analysis because, in the main, women neither read nor featured in hard news and current affairs.

Because 'soap opera' has a metaphoric meaning

It is evident that in the late 1970s and the 1980s the term 'soap opera' was used about programmes that are in fact rather distinct: South American telenovelas, US daytime serials, British social realist serials, US prime-time shows. What do they have in common that attracts feminist scholars to all of them?[10] Here the answer is again the perceived femininity of the programmes, but here in a rather more metaphorical sense – the feminine as contemptible, as banal, as beneath serious critical attention. Thus the unity of these different programmes – the reason why, in a certain sense, it was correct to call them all 'soap' in a particular period – lies in their shared place at the bottom of the aesthetic hierarchy. It was to this gendering of aesthetic judgement that feminist critics were partly addressing themselves, as we see in this comment from 1981 by Terry Lovell: 'Yet *within this almost universal denigration*, soap opera does provide the pleasures of validation, and of self-assertion, which must surely go some way to accounting for its lasting popularity with women' (Lovell 1981: 51, emphasis added).

Because they shouldn't be: feminist ambivalence

Early feminist work on soap opera is marked by a profound ambivalence. On the one hand, there is the repudiation of the genre that I have discussed. On the other, this sense that these programmes are something that 'other women' – non-feminists – watch, offers a political rationale for an engagement with the genre. The drive here is to make a political analysis of pleasure – pleasure that is seen to be politically regressive. However, sometimes, underneath this explicitly feminist repudiation/re-engagement structure, there is a more elusive presence, a ghost of past femininities. For many feminists, writing about soap opera – and, I would argue, comparable genres and media such as romance fiction and women's magazines – entailed an investigation of femininities from which they felt, or were made to feel, a very contradictory distance.

Ien Ang discussed this directly in her *Dallas* project where she inscribed a sense of generally condemnatory attitudes towards soap watching in her original advertisement: 'I like watching the tv serial *Dallas* but I often get odd reactions to it' (Ang 1985: 10). She is, in the first instance, concerned to investigate what she names the 'ideology of mass culture', but later in the book explicitly criticises a tendency towards 'the overpoliticizing of pleasure' present in much feminist work on popular fiction. Janice Winship has written about this vividly in the introduction to her book on a related genre, women's magazines, published in 1987:

> Admitting within feminist circles that I was doing research on – of all things – women's magazines used to make me feel just as comfortable as when I hastily muttered an explanation of my 'study' to politely inquiring friends of my parents. . . . Whether feminist friends voiced it or not I felt they were thinking that if I really had to do research. . . . I should do it on something more important politically. . . .
>
> Yet I continued to believe that it was as important to understand what women's magazines were about at it was, say, to understand how sex discrimination operated in the workplace. I felt that to simply dismiss women's magazines was also to dismiss the lives of millions of women who read and enjoyed them each week. More than that, *I* still enjoyed them, found them useful and escaped with them. And I knew that I couldn't be the only feminist who was a 'closet' reader.
>
> (Winship 1987: xiii)

The self-conscious use of 'closet' here points to the way in which the first feminists doing academic studies of these popular forms really did face opposition not just from the academy, but also from within feminism. Some parts of 1970s feminism were very keen to construct a distance between feminist identity and more conventional forms of femininity. We see this tension again when, writing five years earlier, Terry Lovell defends both the watching and the study of the British soap opera *Coronation Street* in these terms:

> *Coronation Street* offers its women viewers certain 'structures of feeling' which are prevalent in our society, and which are only partially recognised in the normative patriarchal order. It offers women a validation and celebration of those interests and concerns which are seen as properly theirs within the social world they inhabit. Soap opera may be the opium of masses of women, but, like religion, it may also be, if not 'the sign of the oppressed', yet a context in which women can ambiguously express *both* good humoured acceptance of their oppression *and* recognition of that oppression, and some equally good humoured protest against it.
>
> (Lovell 1981: 51)

This mild defence of soap opera comes after nine pages of closely argued theoretical writing about why the genre is worthy of notice.

It is this final reason 'why' that brings me back to my starting-point, that of the perceived piquancy in the relationship between feminism and soap opera. Because of the sedimented gendering of the genre, there was no way in which a political movement which was challenging gender definition could ignore soap opera. But neither could it, finally, repudiate these pleasures and identification, nor simply celebrate them. Feminists were interested in soap operas because they were women's programmes, but each of these terms proves unstable on closer inspection. What was referred to as 'soap opera' often had little more than seriality and lack of prestige in common. 'Women', as I have repeatedly found while tracing this history, has proved a very tricky category for feminism, both necessary and impossible, often excluding more people than it includes. And finally, feminist interest in these programmes has had rather different forms and motivations at different moments. And in this intricate dance of attitudes and categories a little sub-field of academic study has been created.

CONCLUSION

Through tracing a set of interwoven histories I have tried to suggest what was most significant about the feminist encounter with soap opera. The tense is important, for I think we can date the key period of this encounter between 1976 and 1984, and it is in these years that we see both feminism and soap opera first becoming established in their much disputed and often ridiculed academic identities. In crisis in the political arena, feminism began to establish some toe-holds in the academy, sometimes in 'its own' discipline, women's studies, sometimes in the newer disciplines such as cultural or media studies, and occasionally in more established fields. The study of television, too, changed, and the interest in popular genres, perhaps partly focused by the international success of *Dallas*, was enriched and explicitly feminised through the attention to soap opera.

Secondly, the study of soap opera provided a particular generic site in a new medium for the investigation of the female viewer. The question of the female reader/viewer/spectator/audience has been a recurring topic to occupy feminist scholars in a range of disciplines at both a theoretical and an empirical level. Soap opera, perceived as so evidently gendered, while also very popular internationally, provided an excellent site for the analysis of this figure, whether she was theorised as a textual construct or investigated as a sociological fact.

Finally, I think we could say that feminist media scholarship explores and defines itself a little in this encounter. Taking soap opera seriously – and perhaps, most significantly, taking soap opera fans seriously – as this early feminist work began to do, also involved taking the skills, competencies and pleasures of conventional femininities rather more seriously.

Doing research with 'real people' raises complex and difficult ethical issues. It has been partly through the exploration of this 'woman's genre' and its audiences that some of the simplicities and blindnesses of second-wave feminism have been challenged. So if feminism has been important in producing a context in which soap opera can be taken seriously, soap opera has been significant as a site in which feminism can learn to address its others with respect.

Part II

Career girls

V. GOOD   GOOD   ENTERTAINING   FAIR   BORING

Introduction

This part of the book addresses the take-up and presentation of feminist ideas in mainstream film and television. It is about popular versions of feminism since the 1970s, and the emergence of particular characters or personae who can, in some sense or aspect, be seen to represent either 'the feminist' or 'the liberated woman'. The particular figures I am concerned with here are: '*Cosmo* girl'/ 'the independent woman'; 'the strong woman/the boss' and 'the post-feminist girly'. These are not the only figures produced in this period with a relation to feminism – nor indeed, is feminism their only origin. Chris Holmlund (1991; 1993) has pointed to the significant production of films featuring either 'the deadly doll' – women who kill – and 'the mainstream femme' – the lesbian lead who is not stereotyped as butch or unambiguously lesbian, found in films such as *Lianna* (directed by John Sayles, USA, 1983), *Entre Nous* (Diane Kurys, France, 1983) and *Desert Hearts* (Donna Deitch, USA, 1986). Wahneema Lubiano (1993), in an analysis of the Anita Hill/Clarence Thomas hearings (in which Clarence Thomas's nomination to the supreme court of the USA was challenged by Anita Hill's accusation of sexual harassment) argues for the tenacity of two figures in the representation of African American women, the 'black lady (over-achiever)' and the 'welfare queen'. These two are figures that have some relation to feminism in their positing of a certain autonomy in the figure of the feminine – although, as Lubiano argues, each has a founding history in the pathologising of the African American family – but it is significant that the 'black lady' has hardly made it to the screen, although the welfare queen does figure, particularly in US crime fiction. In US cinema the lead characters in *Waiting to Exhale* (Forrest Whitaker, USA, 1995) offer the most notable instances of the independent woman or black lady figure, a character always poised on the edge of culpable over-achievement. In British film and television even this image does not seem available – a point exemplified by the career of Cathy Tyson, whose two highest profile roles have been as a prostitute in *Mona Lisa* (Neil Jordan, 1986) and, a decade later, as a prostitute in *Band of Gold* (Granada, 1995 and 1996, written by Kay Mellor), the successful female-authored television series set among a group of working women in Bradford.

Each of the three essays in this section is concerned with fictional texts which centre on female characters. The Hollywood films discussed in Chapters 5 and 7 centre on individual women, played respectively by Jill Clayburgh, Melanie Griffith and Julia Roberts, while the British television crime series analysed in Chapter 6 focuses on a group of four women, although the Ann Mitchell character is clearly privileged. The essays are presented chronologically, addressing the 1970s cycle of 'independent women' films, mid-1980s 'women-in-TV crime' and the late 1980s to early l990s post-feminist Hollywood. Thus the film and television here discussed span the period from 'women's liberation' to what is now sometimes called 'post-feminism', offering a series of addresses to, and representations of, women in this period.

In each case we find a negotiation of what it is to be a heroine in contemporary fiction, a negotiation which I think is best understood in relation to the increasing prominence of discussion about appropriate feminine destinies in this period. This gendering of particular destinies, a gendering always conducted through a 'classing' and 'ethnicising', has always been subject to negotiation, as the work of feminist historians has repeatedly shown us. I am not suggesting that these debates started with the 1970s – and indeed, the work of Pam Cook (1996), Sue Harper (1994), Lola Young (1995) and Christine Geraghty (1997) reveals to us the particularities of these negotiations in, for example, postwar British cinema – but I do think that certain challenges to conventional femininities originating in the 1970s women's movement have left traces in these texts. Specifically, I think there are three ideas circulating, which, while by no means new, gather a much greater prominence in this period. These – which are all to do with appropriate (western) feminine destinies – can be summarised as follows. Firstly, the notion of the woman's *right* to fulfilment, a fulfilment which can be located outside the domestic sphere of home and family. Secondly, the notion of financial independence and the idea of the woman worker who earns more than pin-money: the self-supporting woman. Thirdly, the separation of ideas of female sexuality from the necessary consequences of maternity and domesticity. Each of these ideas points to a more autonomous, self-defined idea of feminine destiny, which, although it may have very class-specific and ethnically specific origins – many women have had to work for more than pin-money for a long time – did gain a wider currency in this period. In narrative terms, what was posed was the existence of female characters who were more like a hero than a heroine. Perhaps female characters could go out and have adventures?

As a vocabulary of critique, the language of 1970s feminism expressed these ideas through notions of 'sex-object' and 'stereotype', calling instead for 'positive images', and displaying a repeated interest in role-reversal scenarios. These terms reverberate through the texts here discussed. *Widows* is in some ways a role-reversal story, with the female protagonists dressing up as men, learning to walk appropriately, learning to lower the register of their voices and physically training themselves to carry out the robbery. *An Unmarried Woman* attempts rather laboriously to give its blondish heroine interiority, a non-maternal sexuality and a dream of her own. The film traces the journey of an initially married woman away from the stereotype of 'wife' to a rather more uncertain future. In this, as Robin Wood (1985) has pointed out, the film shares a structure with *Alice Doesn't Live Here Anymore* (directed by Martin Scorsese, 1974), a structure which he suggests is characteristic of 1970s Hollywood feminism and its emphasis on the individual. Wood's abstraction of the narrative structure of 1970s Hollywood feminism is useful in enabling us to see the constraints and negotiations in the presentation of these female characters who flirt with occupying the position 'hero' – or at least chivy at the stasis of the position 'heroine'. However, there are also aspects of the presentation of the lead characters in these 1970s films which are significant in thinking about how 1970s feminism appears on Hollywood screens. The self-presentation of the heroines is dominated by a repertoire of naturalness which has origins in 1960s counter-cultures as well as feminist repudiation of stereotypical femininity. The most significant film to get Hollywood distribution from this point of view was Claudia Weill's independently produced *Girlfriends* (1977), in which Melanie Mayron was both the lead and overweight. However, generally, 1970s heroines were groomed to suggest that their hair-styles were natural and that they were not wearing make-up. The apogee of this presentation was the way in which crying was shown to make the face swollen and puffy, rather than be a matter of beautiful glistening tears sliding down a still beautiful profile. These were, as the rhetoric of the time suggested, presented as real women. At least real Hollywood women. This claim to the real is not made in the later 1980s films, where indeed the self-conscious occupying of stereotypically feminine roles such as secretary and hooker is part of the skill of the heroine. The adventure has reduced in scope – these heroines are definitely heroines, determined to marry the prince, even if they do have 'a head for business' or fully appreciate the mechanical qualities of luxury cars.

Chapter 7, which was written for this book, discusses what has happened to the Hollywood independent woman fifteen years on, suggesting that one process has been a splitting between 'the girly' and 'the bitch from hell' (see Jermyn 1996). Rather against the tenor of much feminist enthusiasm for strong women like Thelma and Louise, and even Alex in *Fatal Attraction*, I suggest that there is something to be learnt from the girly figure, who represents one version of what Hilary Radner has called the new 'public femininities' (1993: 58) (see also White 1989). And that is another way of conceptualising the concerns of these three essays, a repeated engagement with the continuing negotiation of the mapping of gender identity across the spheres of public and private life. Chapter 6 reveals this through the examination of an instance in which female characters move genres, into central roles in the crime genre.

Widows is interesting in relation to several different histories. Firstly, it offered a set of unfamiliar roles for women in a genre in which women are generally prostitutes, victims or shoplifters. The series had a simple, effective conceit which was initially condensed into the opening credits in which we saw a carefully planned robbery of a security van go badly wrong, with the apparent death of all participants. The widows of the title are the three women left alone by this catastrophe which has befallen Harry's gang. They decide, under the leadership of Harry's widow, Dolly (Ann Mitchell), to follow through the already laid plans for the next robbery – which they will conduct themselves after recruiting another recently widowed woman, Bella (Eva Mottley). This simple variation on a traditional crime story formula – the gang of robbers planning and carrying out a raid under the surveillance of the police – offered a series of pleasures for both male and female viewers in what is traditionally a men's genre. The production company, Euston Films, had a strong track record with the crime genre, and characteristics of the Euston series included London location shooting in a 'fast' realist style, working-class and often semi-criminal milieux and sharp scripts (Alvarado and Stewart 1985). *Widows* offered these familiar pleasures, but also engaged with changing ideas of appropriate feminine behaviour by audaciously presenting the widows of the title tutoring themselves in criminality so they could be agents not victims. In this sense the series, as well as being clearly a Euston product, must also be understood in relation to earlier shows which had tried to insert women into the crime genre – such as *Cagney and Lacey*, *The Gentle Touch* and *Juliet Bravo* (see D'Acci 1994 for the best discussion of women in a crime series). The difference with *Widows* was that the women were on the wrong side of the law.

Following the success of the first series – which had six episodes and a continuous narrative – a second series was commissioned and the two were broadcast together in 1985 (a less successful third series, *She's Out*, was broadcast in 1995). Again, the narrative was continuous over the two series, and at the end of *Widows II* the central character, Dolly Rawlins (Ann Mitchell), was imprisoned. It was two aspects of this second series which prompted Chapter 6. Firstly, my sense of disappointment in the second series. Secondly, the change of cast from Eva Mottley to Debby Bishop as Bella. *Widows* was initially unusual in casting a black actress in one of the four leading roles. Mottley's death meant there had to be a substitute, and I was intrigued by the choice to cast Bishop. On the one hand, the first series had no explicit recognition of ethnicity as either identity or problem. So Eva Mottley could just have been playing 'a (non-ethnicised) character' rather than 'a black character'. On the other hand, choosing to replace Mottley with another black British actress reinscribed the unspoken difference of this character, a difference that was repeatedly articulated through sexuality for the Eva Mottley Bella. This history pointed to one of the repeated difficulties for black actors in which it is assumed that black actors can only act 'black'.

There are differing views on the desirability of what is usually called 'integrated casting', but it is surely a travestied understanding of what acting actually is – making believe that the actor is someone else – if black actors cannot, at least theoretically, act without being ethnicised as black. The issue is enormously complicated by the fact that Euro-American culture does indeed ethnicise blackness. This is the marked term, leaving 'whiteness' as transparent, unethnic, the norm. Therefore it would seem possible to argue that black actors can only be 'black' because audiences are likely to read them as such. In this context, it is perhaps no coincidence that some of the most interesting work of Josette Simon, the actress who in Britain has successfully played the greatest range of roles traditionally cast in a taken for granted way as 'white', has been in theatrical, rather than television productions. Simon herself is on record as having been told at drama school that she would find it virtually impossible to do classical work (quoted by Michael Billington in 'The Colour of Saying' *The Guardian* 1 November 1990: 22).

It is also the case that there are different histories in relation to different genres and media. Meera Syall, the British Asian writer and performer, has recently pointed out that none of the cast of the comedy show *The Real McCoy* (BBC first series 1991, fifth series 1996), which features a distinguished cast of black British, British Asian, Asian and African Caribbean actors and has run successfully on British television for five years, has been offered parts in 'non-ethnic' shows, an outcome she argued would be inconceivable for the cast of a successful comedy show written and played by a Cambridge group (interview, *Medium Wave* BBC Radio 4, 2 July 1996). And comedy is, historically, relatively porous, if also, arguably, one of the historically most conservative sites on British television in the area of racial representation. A genre like the crime series offers different problems, problems which have led Jim Pines (1989) to raise the question of whether the genre itself is racist. Pines concludes that this is not the case, but points to the very limited range of black characters and suggests that this genre among others is saturated with what he calls 'race relations' conventions which govern the representational possibilities. I would agree that the crime genre is not *necessarily* racist, although it has often been so *historically*. Pines suggests that British television crime fiction – the genre which has dominated the 1980s and 1990s has particular features which make the genre of special interest:

> The sense of immediacy is obviously an important element in the 'success' of the TV crime fiction – the (racial) topicality of many of its themes and imagery are clearly drawn from what can best be described as 'tabloid reality', which gives the stories their particular energy. TV crime drama often evokes a kind of vulgarity which seems to go straight to the heart of British social anxieties, which other kinds of TV programmes (including race relations documentaries) rarely if ever manage to achieve.
>
> (Pines, 1989: 69)

3 *Widows I*: Bella (Eva Mottley)

Widows had perhaps more elements of 'tabloid fantasy', but the narrative was firmly embedded in the realist conventions of the crime genre, and certainly the first series had precisely the energy Pines describes here. Although there are a great many reasons not to isolate particular characters for approval or disapproval, I would now argue that the Eva Mottley performance of Bella really did allow the character to transcend her relatively stereotypical confines, a transcendence lost in *Widows II*.

The final history to consider in relation to *Widows* is that of the role of women in television production. The series had unusually strong female involvement, written by Lynda La Plante, with Verity Lambert as executive producer and Linda Agran as producer. The series marked Lynda La Plante's first successful foray into a territory she has made peculiarly her own, the hard world of women in the television crime genre. Her subsequent projects, which include the internationally successful *Prime Suspect*, where Helen Mirren plays a chief inspector on a murder case, and *The Governor*, where Janet McTeer plays an inexperienced governor given a prison to run, have tended to place their central female characters within a male hierarchy and visual repertoire. Here they must both confront the prejudice of their colleagues and successfully inhabit and wield power in the context of law enforcement and criminal justice. In contrast, *Widows* the first of La Plante's 'women in a man's world' dramas, was set explicitly within a criminal milieu with the women attempting to support themselves through robbery, rather than learning how to occupy masculine positions of power. Because they have to learn to perform as men, femininity is made strange, and becomes a way of behaviour that the women consciously turn on when they need to escape detection. They are career girls with a difference.

Chapter 5

A subject for the seventies †

An Unmarried Woman is one of a number of 1970s Hollywood films which could be read to address and construct, however obliquely, changing conceptions of the appropriate modes of femininity in contemporary western culture. Films such as *Alice Doesn't Live Here Anymore* (Martin Scorsese, 1974), *Three Women* (Robert Altman, 1977), *Looking for Mr Goodbar* (Richard Brooks, 1977), *The Turning Point* (Herbert Ross, 1978), *Julia* (Fred Zinneman, 1978), *Girlfriends* (Claudia Weill, 1978), *Old Boyfriends* (Joan Tewkesbury, 1979) can be loosely grouped together through their use of central female protagonists.[1] In the main, they can be seen as aimed at a specifically female audience, in a period where there has been increasing differentiation of target audiences.[2]

The existence, and construction, of this 'new' female audience can be properly understood only in relation to a whole range of extra cinematic social, political and economic factors (for example, changing patterns of women's employment and education; increasingly effective and available contraception; the fall in the birth rate, with changing patterns of marriage and divorce; the impact of the women's liberation movement itself) whose interplay is too complex to be investigated here.[3] The cinematic history of these films lies partly with the 'woman's pictures' of the 1930s, 1940s and 1950s, and, later, with television soap opera. Crucially, all these texts can be read to be concerned with the conflicting demands on, and contradictory and fragmented nature of, femininities constructed within masculine hegemony (which is not to suggest that these texts are all reducible to the same concerns, or can be compared with 'non-patriarchal' femininities). These 1970s films have received a fairly mixed reception from feminists and film critics concerned with sexual political issues, ranging from angry rejection ('incorporation') to qualified welcome. I would argue that they are of interest to those concerned with sexual politics because they represent an address to, and the attempted construction of, a new audience – 'Cosmo girl'. White, youngish, heterosexual and an aspirant professional (Alice may wait tables,

†First published in *Screen* 23, 3–4 (1982).

but she really wants to be a singer), *Cosmo* girl aspires to the sexual satisfaction that was connotatively denied to the 'career girl' of the 1960s. Moving into the 1980s, *Cosmo* girl has options and makes choices. However her new subject position is potentially contradictory, retaining femininity, while moving into traditionally masculine modes (alert, aggressive, ambitious). There is thus a constant tension in the way she must always already be desirable (feminine), as well as desiring.

This type of contradiction is particularly noticeable in 'post-feminist' advertising for products aimed at women: Virginia Slims cigarettes, Pretty Polly tights, Lovable underwear (Coward 1981) or the advertisements for tea recently run in British women's magazines (Fig. 4). The slogan 'Meet the new tea lady' addresses the change by making explicit reference to old feminine stereotypes and recognising the new woman. The new tea lady almost dresses like a man – dark suit, white shirt and tie. But hers is a knickerbocker suit, and the lounging cross-legged posture, shot from a high angle, functions to foreground the signifiers of classically sexy femininity – black stockings and red nail varnish. The woman is nearly pouting, and looking out of the photograph at an angle. She has neither the downcast eyes of the passively waiting female nor the directly challenging stare and open mouth of the come-on. Aggressively ignoring the spectator, the new tea lady breaks with tradition. But the camera angle, and her positioning within both the chair and the foreground of the image, produces her – despite her crossed legs – as open to our penetrative gaze. This penetration is supported by the depth of field and the strongly patterned floor, which, colour matching her chair, takes our gaze both further into the image and back again to her.

The new tea lady of 1982 is more assured and aggressive than the heroines of the 1970s films. Iconographically she is post-punk, and thus the way she looks is not naturalistic. She is more clearly constructed, more put-together, than the 1970s heroines. As Sue Clayton (1982) has observed, 1970s Hollywood heroines were, at some level, offered as representations of 'real' – natural as opposed to Hollywood – women. However I think some of the same sexual contradictions can be seen at work in these films, exemplified in this discussion by *An Unmarried Woman*.[4]

Two major criticisms were made of *An Unmarried Woman* when it appeared in 1978. Firstly that the film, with its upper-middle-class setting, trafficked in a type of feminist chic, which made visible some of the concerns of the women's movement, but trivialised or caricatured them, thus deflecting their political force. Secondly, that with the appearance of Alan Bates the film degenerated into romanticism. (See, for example, Polly Toynbee (1978), David Ehrenstein (1978) and Gitlin and Wolman (1978).) Obviously, the two criticisms are related, the appearance of Alan Bates usually functioning as the last straw. On both counts, the film stands accused of failing to represent 'real women'.

4 The New Tea Lady (The Tea Council). Post-feminist advertising aimed at women

This chapter engages only marginally with the class position of the first criticism. (The attendant element of this argument, concerning the 'unrealistic' attractiveness of Jill Clayburgh, is addressed in section 2 below.) I would argue that the upper-class milieu of the fiction does not of itself necessarily lead to a trivialising of feminist concerns,[5] although it does contravene conventions of 'social extensiveness'[6] associated historically with realism. However, perhaps more significantly, it does point to the way in which *Cosmo* girl originates within the concerns of the women's movement, the extent to which much feminism is not explicitly anti-capitalist. As Elizabeth Cagan (1978) has argued, there is a place for 'the new woman' within capitalist social relations, even if this place is contradictory for patriarchal discourses. It *is* significant that *An Unmarried Woman*, like most of these films, seeks to address the problem of how to live 'new' femininity in isolation from questions of class and ethnicity through its choice of an 'unmarked' – white, middle-class – protagonist.[7] More generally, however, it is clear that the film is not a sexual political manifesto, nor is it made within a documentary realist tradition. It also fails to analyse the power at stake in male/female relationships. But as a successful film, it seems of interest precisely because of the way in which it constructs femininity, sex, romance and marriage as narratively meaningful.[8]

The question of the 'descent' into romanticism is considered in detail in section 3. Many of the critics concerned point to the heritage of the woman's picture and the melodrama. The film itself rather coyly makes this connection in the 'Where are all the wonderful women?' (Joan Crawford, Bette Davis) scene. However, instead of functioning dismissively, the reference to romantic fictions should surely be inflected to ask how, historically, romantic fictions can be understood to relate to women's subordination, and what readings it is possible to make of the particular romantic element of this film. I would argue that *An Unmarried Woman* attempts to 'make sense' of contemporary heterosexual relationships by separating out marriage (Martin), sexual practice (Charlie) and romance (Saul); that the move to the closure of romance is made explicitly fictional; that this closure cannot be completed because of the critique of marriage; and that the ambiguity of the film's ending is necessitated by the failure to interrogate the power relations of heterosexuality which subtend marriage, sexual practice and romance.

1 AN 'UNMARRIED' WOMAN

An Unmarried Woman offers, as its title, the description of a woman in relation to the central heterosexual institution of marriage. This, we might assume, is a film about a woman who is not married. The derogatory cultural term, with its connotations of 'not-having-been-able-to-get-married', is spinster – or even old maid. So the more neutral 'unmarried' seems immediately to suggest either that this is a position of choice, or that there is still 'hope'.

5 *An Unmarried Woman*: the happy family. Erica (Jill Clayburgh), Martin (Michael Murphy) and Patti (Lisa Lucas) (© Twentieth Century Fox)

The film opens, however, with the representation of a marriage and, I would argue, a marriage that is represented as 'good'. This much is signified by finding time for 'a quickie' after jogging (and an argument), and before work. Similarly, the daughter is shown to be at ease with her parents' sexual pleasure – 'Did the earth move?' she asks casually as she comes in to find her mother looking sexually satisfied on the bed (in a series of shots in which her naked thighs are always in frame), as her father dresses. A later scene, set in the evening of the same day, again shows the wife, Erica (Jill Clayburgh), as desirable to her husband, although at this point, when she has come in from seeing her 'club', she initially resists sex. Thus we have the primary establishment of the Jill Clayburgh figure as a woman who is desired, and, furthermore, as a woman who can be sexually satisfied by her husband. This initiates the central mode of differentiation of this character from all the other female characters in the film.

So this movie, as becomes clear when Martin (Michael Murphy) tells Erica that he has fallen in love with someone else, is about reluctantly becoming unmarried. Its heroine, unlike that of say, *Girlfriends* or *Looking for Mr Goodbar*, is not someone who *is* unmarried, who might be unwanted. The unhappiness of being unmarried is thus initially contrasted with the happiness, the normality, of being married. Furthermore, as it is Martin who rejects Erica, the disruption that initiates the narrative – Erica's voyage of self-

6 *An Unmarried Women*: good sex. Erica (Jill Clayburgh) (© Twentieth Century Fox)

discovery – is produced through masculine activity. Thus, although in the central part of the film, Erica has to consider initiating sexual activity, this independence has been thrust upon her. She is presented initially as both desirable, satisfiable *and* passive – a victim.

I want later to argue that the film is partly interesting because its representation of heterosexual relations does involve a shift, a marginalisation of marriage, but here want to stress that the construction of this 'independent woman' heroine as both 'desirable' and 'OK', as opposed to 'desirable but dangerous',[9] or 'desirable but a mess', which is the condition of the credibility of this later shift, is achieved primarily through the introduction of the character as a *dependent* woman. So although the film does, to some extent, offer us representations of the oppression for a woman of being single (both available to all men and socially illegitimate) in a couple-dominated world (the doctor's pass; the blind date; going to a bar by herself) the poignancy of the representation is founded on these experiences being exceptional for Erica. She has been constructed as both normal cinematically (she is an object of desire, and she does not initiate action) and normal ideologically – happily married.

It is within the play of these two forms of normality that we can most usefully situate *An Unmarried Woman*. For if, as I have argued, the introduction of Erica as married (possessed) is necessary to a representation of her as 'normal' (sexual, but not dangerous, threatening or neurotic), at the same time, by the same movement, Erica's unmarrying narratively legitimates the cynical tone of the film's discourses on marriage. Before the break-up this is represented by the Club, and Patti's taxing question to her mother: 'Name three (happily married couples)'. Following the break-up, Erica too can criticise her marriage – for it was a condition of ignorance, she did not *know* she was about to 'join the crowd'. She tells Martin that she was his hooker, displays anger about her sex life with her therapist (never expanded on), and discusses with Saul the problem of always having been 'Erica and Martin'. When Jean, an artist (not normal), expresses surprise at Erica's separation: 'You seemed so normal', Erica responds 'It's only the normal people who get divorced nowadays. No one else bothers to get married.' So the 'problem' of the film is marriage, not heterosexual relations. We have a shift in the institutional configuration of the ideological field or problematic of heterosexuality. Marriage is no longer central, although femininity remains a condition which is 'neurotic' if uncoupled. And it is this concern with a 'contemporary' heterosexuality which I wish to consider, firstly in the

7 *An Unmarried Woman*: Erica's *Swan Lake* solo (© Twentieth Century Fox)

construction of the heroine, and then in the appearance of the hero, late in the narrative.

2 THE CONSTRUCTION OF THE HEROINE

The difficulty for the 'independent woman' film lies partly in constructing female characters who can plausibly do, as well as be done to and looked at. A difficulty because this is not the traditional mode for the representation of femininity, and so a femininity with the attribute of competence outside certain limited spheres is perceived as deviant or abnormal.[10] I have already stressed the importance of Erica's marriage – the normal femininity of being possessed – within the narrative. I now want to go on to argue that it is the construction of this character as cinematically 'feminine' to be looked at, a legitimate site of visual pleasure for the audience[11] – which produces her within the narrative as successful in her search, a suitable mate for Saul.

Erica's 'Swan Lake solo' is exemplary, and, appearing very early in the film, functions importantly in the construction of this character. Minimally, the scene has two functions. Firstly, to present Erica to us as 'subject' – active, desiring agent – and secondly, as spectacle, as object of our gaze. The sequence opens with a close-up on Erica's face as she leans back on bed pillows, the camera to her left, in a position which has shown both Patti and Martin bend down to kiss her. The camera has in fact moved into close-up on Martin kissing Erica goodbye, remaining on her face as he leaves the frame, and holds on her, with closed eyes and a dreamy smile. This moment of transition, from Erica with husband to Erica by herself, offers punctuation before our first privileged glimpse of 'Erica for herself', but a punctuation which consists of a meditation on Erica's contented face. As music starts, Erica begins a semi-ironic fantasy commentary on her own successful debut dancing the lead in Swan Lake. The substance of this privileged view into the central character's privacy is her fantasy of being appreciatively watched. In a change to long-shot, Erica rises, and, in the diegetic imagination of being watched, quickly and neatly adjusts her bikini knickers to fully cover her buttocks as she begins to dance. Narratively, this is a scene which functions to give 'more depth' to the central female character – fantasising about being a ballerina, taking pleasure in her body. However, the sequence also functions quite clearly within the tradition of 'woman displayed as erotic spectacle'. And this is how we as audience are invited to watch, as the camera nudges round corners, or she emerges from behind a potted plant, silhouetted against the long low windows in her knickers and T-shirt,[12] legitimated in our gaze by Erica's own fantasy. A truly intimate voyeurism.

The visual pleasure of this daytime 'married' scene, which uses only three long mobile shots when Erica is dancing, can be contrasted with the later night-time 'unmarrying scene', when Erica piles her husband's possessions together on to a sort of funeral pyre. This 'unmarrying ritual', culminating in the removal of her wedding ring, is accompanied by the saxophone-dominated 'mood' music (as opposed to the 'external' ballet music of the earlier scene) which forms the sound track for all Erica's 'alone' moments. After the opening shot, the camera is mainly static, and there are frequent shot changes, with many close-ups on parts of Erica's body (face and hands), or the objects she is collecting. 'Unmarrying' produces a literal fragmentation of visual pleasure. The longer meandering shots return in the later part of the film when she is with Saul, although after meeting him, we see her undressed only very briefly.

The *Swan Lake* solo, the spectacle of a satisfied woman, is also opposed to the subsequent introduction of the 'Club', setting up the primary differentiation of Erica from her friends. Apart from her dominance of screen time, there are many other minor differences: Erica arrives later, and leaves earlier, in two of their meetings – thus constituting the other three as a group, and also allowing admiring male gazes at Erica to be shown as she arrives. She is frequently isolated in close-up – for example in the ice-skating scene, which opens on her exhilarated face. But, crucially, these scenes establish a normal/abnormal axis – Jeanette is sleeping with a nineteen-year-old, Elaine drinks too much and Sue tolerates her husband's infidelities to keep the marriage together – in which only Erica is normal. Kept un-neurotic by a happy marriage, displayed to the audience as an object of desire, 'the heroine' is distinguished from 'the women'.

3   THE APPEARANCE OF THE HERO

The introduction of the Alan Bates character two-thirds of the way through the film seems to have caused most difficulty for contemporary reviewers. Without exception, this was recognised as a 'magical' resolution in the tradition of feminine romance. One group of critics clearly despise romance (or romantic melodrama) as a genre,

> one can only cringe with amused horror and recall Warner Brothers' romantic tosh of the '40s.
> (Geoff Brown, *Financial Times*, 11 August 1976)

> fatally soft-centred, as becomes all too evident on the descent into romance
> (Patrick Gibbs, *Daily Telegraph*, 25 May 1978)

a genre for women at that:

> what finally is women's magazine romance.
> (David Robinson, *The Times*, 11 August 1978)

While another group (including most of the women reviewers), attack the film (and sometimes the genre) for its lack of realism:

not fair to women who want films to deal with their real problems for a change, and not their fairy tales.

(Gavin Millar, *The Listener*, 17 August 1978)

it's easy to choose to be independent for just so long as the choice is yours . . . and Mr Bates will be delighted to greet you in Vermont tomorrow. . .

(Toynbee 1978)

it might be argued that not every deserted wife can expect the chance to turn down an Alan Bates.

(Ted Whitehead, *The Spectator*, 19 July 1978)

The first group of critics display a sense of betrayal in the plausibility of the narrative as it moves towards its close. This is perhaps partly informed by what I have termed the generic instability of this whole group of 'independent women' films, and is thus a difficulty which would not have occurred in the viewing of a 1940s 'weepie', generically marked by fatal coincidence and dramatic plot reversal. The 'realist' critics would presumably have raised similar criticisms of earlier Hollywood woman's pictures. However in relation to the perceived 'failure' of the film at this point to both groups of critics, it seems relevant to consider the introduction of Saul Kaplan in relation to some of the work that has been done on 'happy endings' in melodrama, such as Halliday (1971), Elsaesser (1972) and Mulvey (1977). Crudely, does the happy ending (qualified in this case) 'make the aporia more apparent'?[13]

An Unmarried Woman is structurally similar to *Alice Doesn't Live Here Anymore* in the delayed introduction of a big-name male star. In both cases the delay allows the heroine the experience of romance-free sex and thus offers a definition of independence as the occupying of what is usually a masculine position. As Erica says: 'I'm a short-term guy.' 'Plausibility' is not a problem in each of these encounters. However, the melodramatic coincidence of the meetings with the male star – Saul *is* an artist, and Erica *does* work in an art gallery, just as Kris Kristofferson ate in the café where Alice waited tables – is partly dependent on extra-textual knowledge of Alan Bates and Kris Kristofferson as stars. We know that Kris Kristofferson is not just going to drink his coffee and leave, nor Alan Bates just drop into the gallery to hang his paintings. And this knowledge, even if limited to reading the credits at the beginning of each film, can affect an understanding of the nature (and permanency) of Erica's distress. She may be unhappy (manless) now, but . . . .

There is a certain amount of play in the introduction of Saul, with a long-shot which starts very close to a painted canvas, pulls backward some distance, and then seems to be located as the point of view of an as yet unfamiliar male character who appears in frame on the right, walking backwards at about the same pace as the camera. It is only after 'looking with his eyes' that the back-view figure is shown, as the camera pans round, to be Alan Bates. So the shot ends with Alan Bates, Erica and another man in frame, all standing looking at the canvas on which the shot started, the diegetic space having been established. The next shot, a mid-shot of Saul against a completely plain white background, immediately seems to remove him from diegetic space. As Elaine, who also makes the most cynical comments about men throughout the film, later observes to Erica: 'You know how rare a man like Saul is . . .'. The film 'embodies' this rarity – acceptable masculinity – rather literally through the choice of a 'quality' British star, who, to the extent that he is playing a famous British painter within the fiction, is made doubly exceptional.

This is accentuated in this second shot – the 'portrait-like' framing of Alan Bates, isolated, immediately after his introduction into the narrative, as if marking the 'non-realism' of his arrival, swapping star-image for narrative involvement. Thus it seems possible to argue that the late introduction of the romantic hero, the way in which he is introduced, and the type of character he is playing, all work together to emphasise the 'fictiveness' of the narrative – and to accentuate the device of this potentially happy ending – rendering its romance transparent, and hence, to some degree, recognising its 'impossibility'.

After the introduction of Saul, however, the self-consciousness of the film's concern with romance seems to fade until the ending, where it reappears narratively as Erica's dilemma. By the end of the film – and to an extent by the time she meets Saul – Erica has become modern as well as being normal. She has had sexual relationships outside marriage, but has not degenerated to the level of her women friends, nor become lesbian like her therapist. She too is exceptional, and thus she and Saul make a perfect couple. The contradictions of *Cosmo* girl seem almost resolved. But of course, and this is what initially interested me about the film, Erica chooses not to go to Vermont with Saul. This refusal seems again to flirt with the analysis of the impossibility of romance which is played with in the introduction of Saul. The film does seem to recognise the contradiction between its story, Erica's odyssey of self-discovery and what is implicit in its potential ending of a return to coupledom. However, as none of the terms in play have been shifted – masculinity and femininity have been ultimately constructed in 'old' modes in new situations – the film can't do anything with this recognition.

The final image of *An Unmarried Woman* is ambiguous – or perhaps more accurately a double-bind: Erica half-teetering, half-blown down a New York street, out of control because of Saul's surprise goodbye gift of a huge painting. She doesn't go to Vermont for the summer with him – she doesn't give in, but on the other hand she is practically immobilised.

It is possible to read this image in other ways (as a metaphor for painful steps to independence, etc.) but I want to conclude by stressing the semi-

8 *An Unmarried Woman*: Erica with the farewell gift (© Twentieth Century Fox)

paralysis of the end of this fiction. For although the film has produced a marginalisation of marriage which makes it impossible for Erica to go with Saul, to be his, the construction of Erica makes it difficult for her to *do* anything else. In the same way that the film is supremely ambiguous in its sexual politics – criticising the institution of marriage and taking the 'impossibility' of romance seriously, yet constructing an unmarried woman who signally fails to do anything but find another man – so the image seems to represent Erica choosing independence, but at the same time shows her made impotent by a male gift.

CREDITS

An Unmarried Woman

USA, 1978, production and distribution: Twentieth Century Fox. *Director*: Paul Mazursky. *Producers*: Paul Mazursky and Tony Ray. *Screenplay*: Paul Mazursky. *Leading players*: Jill Clayburgh (*Erica Benton*), Alan Bates (*Saul Kaplan*), Michael Murphy (*Martin Benton*), Cliff Gorman (*Charlie*), Pat Quinn (*Sue*), Kelly Bishop (*Elaine*), Lisa Lucas (*Patti Benton*), Linda Miller (*Jeannette*).

Chapter 6

Men's genres for women[†]

Rough stuff, this female macho.

(headline, 'Last night's view', *Daily Express*, 17 March 1983, p 21)

The Euston Films series *Widows* was first shown on British television in spring 1983. Following the success of this first series (six episodes), in which four women successfully carry out a robbery which was planned by their husbands, three of whom died in a similar raid, a follow-up series was made. The two series were then broadcast in the spring of 1985, at 9 p.m. on a Wednesday evening. The first series had been successful and cultish. The second series had more problems, which I discuss below, but still the June 1985 issue of *Spare Rib* enthused:

What is it about *Widows* that had us abandoning half-made cups of coffee in the kitchen at the sound of the ... theme music? Not just a female version of *The Sweeney* – *Widows* was brilliantly scripted, dazzlingly performed and had a great plot.

(Alison Whyte, *Spare Rib*, June 1985, p. 41)

Feminist enthusiasm for television crime series is uncommon, and indeed the genre is generally thought of as one which appeals to a male audience. Gillian Skirrow (1985) opens up some questions of the appeal of *Widows* in her analysis of the first series in which she is particularly concerned with the way in which masculinity and femininity are shown to be constructed by the text.

Early feminist criticism was concerned to document available images *of* women. Argument that the proper object of study should instead be the system(s) of representation in which women are produced as a meaningful and different category shifted the emphasis from a comparison between images and real women to the construction of gender within a given text or set of texts.[1] *Widows*, a man's genre with women, offers a rich text for either

†Written for the conference, 'Women and the Electronic Mass Media', Copenhagen University, April 1986. First published in *Boxed In*, edited be Helen Baehr and Gillian Dyer (London, Pandora: 1987).

or both of these approaches. A traditionally masculine genre which attracted a strong female following, the series also provokes questions about whether we can speak of masculinity and femininity in relation to practices of television viewing.[2] The series is, I would argue, not only a man's genre with women but also a man's genre for women. It is thus also an exemplary site for thinking through some of the connections of gender and genre.[3]

Skirrow (1985) argues for the progressive potential of the series being located not so much in the representations of women but in a plot which necessarily brings performance to the foreground and the commentary this new plot makes on both existing genre and gender conventions. There is certainly a level of generic self-consciousness and play within the first series, which potentially opens up questions of appropriate gender behaviour, in a way that is quite different to the self-congratulatory generic reference – and rather trying archness of, for example, the American *Moonlighting* (in which a woman owns a private investigation agency).

In the hard world of the crime series Skirrow looks on the bright side. I agree with the substance of her analysis, but want to take a bleaker perspective, to look for the troubles of the text. My main motivation is the disappointment I felt during the second series of *Widows*. The comparative failure of the second series is linked to some of the difficulties and uncertainties of the first. As a critical operation, I am not trying to provide another reading, or to challenge Skirrow's, but to use different emphases to point to some of the major problems which arise in the attempt to produce different, popular, pleasurable and recognisable representations of women.

THE FIRST AND SECOND SERIES

> And speaking of mysteries, the new series of *Widows* (ITV) is a major disappointment, having *somehow* failed to capture *something*.
> (Danny Kelly, 'On the box', *New Musical Express*, 20 April 1985, p. 21)

All sequels and follow-up series face the problems of building up new, but familiar, excitement after the denouement of the first, as well as attracting new audiences while satisfying the old. This demand for 'the same but different', which has been argued to be one of the characteristics of television programming, is more difficult to satisfy when the original is, as *Widows* was, premised on a 'novelty' story line. If *Widows I* offered some different pleasure to the sameness of the crime series, what could *Widows II* offer? I want to suggest that the second series, in its differentiation from the first, inexorably returns to some of the traditional patterns of the genre, particularly in relation to the representation of gender.

Sympathising with criminals on a weekly basis is a complicated project, and British television series based on the wrong side of the law have either had a humorous edge, like *Minder, Budgie* and *Porridge*, or else have had a limited and completable narrative structure, like Euston's *Out*, or the BBC's *Law and Order*. There was comment in the press reviews on the fact that the widows got away with the money at the end of the first series, and I think it would have been too much to expect that they would be living happily ever after in the second.[4] It is significant, though, that the retribution of the second series comes not from the classical opponent to the criminal (the law) but from the mastermind of the original plan (Dolly's husband Harry). Arguably, this retribution in fact comes at the end of the first series, which I discuss below. The point here is that, having 'got' the money in the first series, the women have to spend their time and energy in keeping it in the second. I want now to concentrate on some of the particular strains that the original dramatic premises for the first series put on the continuation in the second.

As a television genre, the crime series is seen to have a privileged relation to reality (Alvarado and Stewart 1985; Hurd 1981). A range of newspaper critics made reference to the realism of *Widows* – thus Bronwen Balmforth in the *Sun* wrote, 'The six part series is so tough and realistic it could give real criminals a few ideas. . . . The three actresses . . . are all relatively new faces to television and this adds to the realism' ('Big job for the girls', 16 March 1983). Peter Ackroyd in *The Times* commented, 'The series . . . is really the feminist answer to *The Professionals* and as a result is couched in a more realistic and less sentimental manner' ('Ladies in liberation', 17 March 1983). Ackroyd also compared *Widows* with *Minder*, 'the same mordant realism in its depiction of "cops and robbers"'. The titles and vocabulary of these reviews point to an opposition between that form of femininity known as being a lady, and realism, which is made explicit in this comment from the *Daily Star* (6 April 1983): 'There is nothing very ladylike about the four stars of Widows (ITV 9 p.m.). They are rough, tough and very believable.'

The realism of a television programme is constructed through a range of devices and conventions which derive their significance primarily from generic and textual histories, rather than from any direct relation to the real. *Widows* has an oblique relation to these conventions, which means that the series teeters on the edge of implausibility in its most ambitious moments. 'I've heard chaps quibbling about its authenticity. They can't believe that women would turn to crime like that. Indeed they would' (Nina Myskow, 'Crime queens steal the show,' *Sunday People*, 20 March 1983). The central protagonists are precisely not the usual male protagonists – but related to them, of the same subculture in terms of class and milieu, but with different attributes (femininity) – a production company's dream for adding zest to an audience-pulling genre which needs new angles. However, the plot availability in a realist genre of these new, different protagonists is premised on their sudden, tragic widowing, and plot interest, in the first series, is partly founded on their unfamiliarity with their generic role as male criminals. The pre-credit sequence of the first series shows the fatal raid in which the men die, and the episode opens with an introduction to the women at three different funerals.

There are thus two disruptions which set the narrative of the first series going, neither of which can be re-used in the second series. Firstly, the widowing. This, and divorce, have been relatively common narrative devices to produce central female protagonists to whom things can happen (they can meet men) but who are thus also affirmed as being properly feminine (men have wanted them).[5] This first disruption constructs and makes available the heroines of the series. The second disruption is not so much a narrative event, although it exists as that, but a breach in the normal order of the crime series – the widows' world – brought about by their audacious decision to carry out the next robbery. It is this decision which moves the widows into the narrative space of heroes. It is also this decision which delightfully makes them, in the first series, undetectable, because they are, within the terms of the genre, inconceivable. Detective Inspector Resnick approaches closest to the truth, not because he has any intimation of it but because of his obsession with Harry Rawlins.

The neatness of the storyline is that it does not try to make its audience believe in four fully fledged mistress criminals. After the double disruption sets the story going, the plot is largely pre-ordained, literally planned and written by Harry Rawlins. As Skirrow has observed, the pleasure of the series lies partly in the way in which the familiar visual imagery of the genre is 'made strange' as we watch women mastering the skills and physical postures of the crime series. This pleasure is in the first series articulated through and with the iconographic familiarity of the triangle of police, criminals and rival gang. The elegance of the deployment of these familiar narrative elements is that all are in pursuit of something that they cannot find, for it is the women (in that narrative other space of the crime series, the domestic) who are the perpetrators of crime.

These structural relations, inevitably, are changed in the second series. The second series has none of the goal-oriented simplicity of the first. The double structure of suspense in the first – 'Will the women pull off the raid, as men?' and 'Will they get away with it, from men?' is reduced to only the second question. The first series had Harry's plan, a known structure, and the women's performance, the unknown realisation. The second series has 'living with the consequences'. These consequences necessarily involve more conventional organisation of the relation of gender and genre.

HEROES AND HEROINES

It is safe to say that beside the Widows, *Minder* looks effeminate.
                    (Daniel Farson, guest critic, *Mail on Sunday*, 17 April 1983)

Linda is not the sort of girl you would like to meet in a dark alley.
                    (Peter Ackroyd, 'Ladies in liberation', *The Times*, 17 March 1983)

9 *Widows I*: woman as male robber (courtesy of Thames Television)

Much of the interest of the first series came from the way in which the widows were called upon to occupy two roles, those of heroes and those of heroines. The narrative placing of these women is as heroes, those who do, rather than those who are done to. This different placing of the women, in a broadly or associatively realist genre, produces certain problems. Centrally these are to do with the conflicts between the demands of generic realism and the plausibility of the different placing of the women. The problem can be taken two ways. Either the women are not perceived as plausible in their new roles as criminals, or, using the femininity and competence contradiction (mutually exclusive terms outside certain limited spheres), if successful as criminals, the women have their femininity thrown into doubt. The question is one of plausibility in both cases, once in relation to genre and once in relation to gender.

This coalescence of gender and genre into issues of plausibility can be seen in a range of critical response to both series. In the first series, a realism of effect was usually granted, despite a recognition of the 'difficulty' of the original widowing device. Thus Herbert Kretzmer wrote in the *Daily Mail*: 'The whole premise of *Widows* strikes one as most unlikely, but it's carried off with confidence and looks good for a run' ('An equal right to do wrong', 17 March 1983). Stanley Reynolds wrote in the *Guardian* (21 April 1983): 'If anything, it got better as it went along. I suppose one dropped the original barrier of disbelief at the preposterous plot.' This device is crucial, as I have already argued, in establishing the women in the genre milieu – but also in establishing them *as women*. However, as the comments at the head of this section indicate, women as heroes are often perceived as threatening or unpleasant – or not women. There are a range of additional narrative devices in the first series which function to guarantee the femininity of all the women, although in different ways. As Gillian Skirrow (1985) has observed, particularly the beauty competition and the strip show, to the extent that they involve the performance of femininity, can in this context be read as investigations of the signifiers of gender. There are ironies too in Linda's choice of lover, in that he is also shown to be having an affair with Arnie Fisher, from the rival Fisher Brothers gang. However, if read like this, it is important that femininity is also guaranteed for each of the four women, in ways which are generically consistent with the iconography of the crime show and, indeed, we have with Euston's particular, rather seedy world. Thus we have Shirley appearing in a beauty contest, and Bella in a strip show (see below). Linda is shown to be heterosexually active through her affair with Carlos. Dolly's case is slightly different, and I shall discuss it in more detail in the context of the ending of the first series. However, the paradox of the programme's necessary 'double guarantee' is rather neatly pointed by this letter to the *TV Times* during the transmission of the first series:

> I didn't believe that bank robbery on ITV's *Widows*. I'm not being sexist, but I think a group of women like those in the programme, would have chosen a far more straightforward crime with less bravado and one which involved no other people. The action packed heist on the security van may have been suitably dramatic but it was hardly credible.
>
> P. Wilson
> Luton, Bedfordshire (*TV Times* 28 May 1983)

This writer accepts the femininity of the widows, and thus finds the 'physical and complicated' crime implausible. The plausibility cover provided by the narrative – Harry planned the crime – is ignored, and there is an invocation of femininity as necessarily leading to a less spectacular, and more humane ('no other people') choice of crime. The double placing of the women (as heroes and heroines), with the plausibility problems this entails in the first series, are shifted by the second series when the narrative come-uppances of the first series 'get' the women, and push them back to much more traditional feminine narrative roles. Possessors of the profits from the raid, the women become the object of pursuit. It is this (necessarily) changed narrative structure, when the women are returned to the sort of roles which are more familiar in crime series, which partly accounts for the disappointment of the second series. One of the people interviewed by David Morley in a series of interviews about family viewing commented on the second series as follows:

It's [*Widows*] gotten silly – they should have left it. When it was first on it was really good. You didn't know whether he was dead – it wasn't until the end that you found out he was alive. Now it's gotten silly because, I don't know, when you bring women into it, I mean I'm not a feminist and I should really be, but *when you start bringing women into it, it gets silly because they don't write good enough parts for them.*

(Morley, 1986;[6] my italics)

This speaker, a woman, becomes almost incoherent in her attempt to say *something* about the problem of the second series. She is engaging directly with the mismatch, the sense of disappointment produced by the tension of the innovation in a generic form. I don't wish to over-read this comment, to sweep the woman in Morley's survey into my own world view, but I think she is talking about the same disappointment that I felt in *Widows II*, the inadequacy of dramatic role in relation to the perceived and remembered strength and performance of the actresses. What is important is the change in direction in her argument. She starts off almost as if she's going to say it gets silly because it's got women in it, but this causes a crisis in the sentence which leads her to make external, apologetic, framing reference to her own politics, and the problem becomes one of scripting, some perceived mismatch between the women and the parts.

There are other factors leading to the difference between the first and second series, one of which, a cast change for the character Bella O'Reilly, I discuss in more detail in the next section. There were also a number of changes in the production team, the most significant probably being the direction, from Ian Toynton (first series) to Paul Annett. The script for both series was written by Lynda La Plante.

BELLA

She claimed sexual and racial prejudice with the production crew of the series, but she was more emotional and upset about that than depressed.
(Mr Anthony Earlham, stepfather of Eva Mottley, quoted by *The Times* in its report on the post-mortem of Ms Mottley, 21 March 1985)

Although all publicity for *Widows* showed four women, three white, one black, in the first episode we are introduced only to the three white women, widows of the men who died in the underpass raid. Of course, we later learn that Dolly Rawlins, one of these women, was not in fact widowed in the raid, the third widow was in fact Jimmy Nunn's wife, Trudie. The fourth widow of the credits, Bella O'Reilly, is recruited by her friend, Linda Perelli, in the second episode. The original three have discovered that they will need a fourth, and Bella's suitability occurs to Linda when her co-worker, Charlie, comments of Bella that 'she looks too much like a fella', to be attractive. It has earlier been established that Bella too is now a widow ('My old man did the final load three months ago') and is working as a prostitute and in strip clubs. It is for this work that Dolly abuses her ('tart', 'slag') when first introduced, but there is no racial abuse for Bella in the first series as there is for the 'rhymed' Afro-Caribbean male character Harvey in the second. He cannot comment that a uniform is a bit small without being called 'ape man', and is shown to be recruited to Harry's gang only as a last resort. In the first series, it is only when Bella is taken for a man that she is referred to as black, by a security guard and the police, trying to identify 'the black bloke' after the widows' raid.

There is no verbal discourse on race in the first series, although racial difference is marked in a range of ways (see below). The second series introduces two new Afro-Caribbean characters, Harvey Rintle and a girl friend of Bella's, Carla, as well as a stereotypical Jewish antique-dealer/ 'fence' (pawnbroker figure), Sonny Chizzel. It also returns to a more conventional 'realist racism'. Harvey becomes the site for the display of the normal and casual racism (realism) of the Rawlins world, threatened because he has a relationship with a white woman and subjected to *Black and White Minstrel Show* jokes when he joins the gang. Carla is mistaken for Bella, and brutally beaten up in the second episode of the second series. When Bella tells the others of this, she loses her temper with Linda for failing to grasp the racist element in the attack: 'Of course he did [think it was Bella] – I'm black, she's black, we all look alike in the dark, stupid bitch!' This comment works very curiously with the most noticeable feature of the Bella character, which is that she is played by two different actresses: Eva Mottley and then in the second series Debby Bishop. This substitution, itself uncommon in British television drama, stands in relation to the national, unsympathetic and uninformative coverage of Eva Mottley's death in February 1985, shortly before *Widows I* was repeated, and several months after she left the set at the beginning of shooting *Widows II*.[7]

The crime series offers particular problems for the representation of race it the production company wishes to move away from the stereotypical presentation of black villains. The problem lies in the way in which the effect of realism is created in a genre. If we take what we might call the internal realism of the genre – its intertextuality, its construction of the 'reality effect' through particular codes and conventions – the way in which realism as an effect has more to do with the reality constructed in other crime series than with reality as such (out there), we can only conclude that sympathetic characters are white. There are exceptions, like *The Chinese Detective*, but the very title of the series indicates the exceptional juxtaposition of 'Chinese' and 'Detective'. *Wolcott*, with an Afro-Caribbean policeman in the title role, was not extended after the pilot.[8] Sympathetic black characters aren't in this genre at all, except in the USA – they are (or were) over in *Ebony, Eastern Eye* and *Black on Black*, or, since *Widows* was first transmitted, in Albert Square. The realist codes and conventions of the genre are homologous with those of television as an institution, in which 'ethnicity' applies only to the non-white.

I am thus suggesting that there is little generic support for Bella as a sympathetic, realist character, which increased the demands made, in the first series, on Eva Mottley as an actress. The strength of her acting was arguably undercut, during the first transmission of *Widows I*, by the repeated blurring of character and actress in press features.[9] By implication it wasn't acting, it was just natural, as Eva Mottley had served a prison sentence for a drug offence and had started acting while in prison. Bella, in the first series, is characterised as particularly tough. Shirley and Linda are both, in different ways, *girls*. They are quite frequently shown as weak, hysterical, frightened and vulnerable. Dolly, a *woman*, does not reveal the same weaknesses but does have vulnerability in relation to Harry. Dolly is shown to be stern and brusque (one reviewer commented on wishing to cross the road to get out of her way), and even slaps the hysterical Linda at a meeting during the second episode. Later in the same episode, in a rhyming gesture, Bella too slaps Linda (who is at that point drunk). It is this gesture which is shown to cause Dolly to reconsider her original rejection of Bella. Bella, in the first series, is never shown to be out of control. The repeated guarantees of 'femininity through vulnerability' which are used in relation to the other widows are not employed in relation to Bella. It is perhaps this uncompromising representation of a strong, cool, tough woman which led to many critics referring to her as 'threatening' and 'androgynous'. It is this latter appellation that is the more revealing, hinting at the proposition that a woman without vulnerability might not be one.

Bella's difference – apart from her later narrative arrival – is most noticeably marked in the opening pre-credit sequence, which partly reflects her different route in. Each week, viewers are brought up to date by a male voice over a series of images, some from previous episodes. After Bella's appearance, for episodes three and four the audience is introduced to the widows with an image which offers the simulcrum of a page from a family photographic album. In individual snaps Linda, Shirley and Dolly appear not 'now' (alone, or with each other), but with their husbands, happy and relaxed in their socially legitimate past. Bella, on the other hand, appears alone. There are, to an extent, narrative reasons for this – Bella's husband, unlike the others, has no plot significance. To have given Bella the same socially legitimate past, coupleness, could well have been confusing to viewers. But the effect is to mark her difference, to offer her without the visual guarantee of a heterosexual past.

Although all the women were married to criminals, and Linda's job in the amusement arcade is fairly rough, Bella is clearly perceived as less respectable than the others. There seems to be a division between good clean family crime and drugs and sex, with Bella on the dirty side, and this despite the fact that Audrey's first explanation of her daughter Shirley's sudden wealth

10 *Widows*: poster, *Widows I.* Left to right: Linda Perelli (Maureen O'Farrell), Shirley Miller (Fiona Hendley), Bella O'Reilly (Eva Mottley) and Dolly Rawlins (Ann Mitchell) (courtesy of Thames Television)

is that she is 'doing tricks'. Linda asks Bella about her drug use on greeting her, and while Shirley enters for the rather affectionately ridiculed Miss Paddington competition, Bella wears a dog collar, black leather and brandishes a whip to earn money from that favourite post-colonial strip show theme, black woman as dominatrice.

Debby Bishop, who had worked with Eva Mottley in *Scrubbers* and apparently had Mottley's full support, played a very different Bella. Mottley's Bella had real hauteur and style – she was completely believable at the end of the first series when asked about their celebratory meal: 'Book a table? Did I book a table – we are taking over the joint!' In the first episode of the second series, Bella is shown to have become engaged to an evidently rich Brazilian aristocrat who knows nothing of her past. He treats her like a princess, and looks very much like a Mills and Boon hero. Bella – and it is slightly difficult to imagine Mottley in this role, given the strength of the Bella she played – is quite correctly very anxious that her past might catch up with her and ruin her happy ending. This it does, and for the rest of the series Bella is portrayed as one who has loved and lost. In episode four she confides to Dolly, 'I reckon I lost my chance'.[10] Bishop's Bella, although still

11 *Widows*: cast, *Widows II*. Left to right: Linda (Maureen O'Farrell), Shirley (Fiona Hendley), Bella (Debby Bishop), Dolly (Ann Mitchell) (courtesy of Thames Television)

tough and at points rather unpleasantly bossy, is vulnerable in ways which make her seem much more like Linda and Shirley. This is partly a quality of performance, but is also a result of the very different narrative structure and positions of power in the second series, in which the women really are more vulnerable.

THE END OF THE FIRST SERIES

I like *Widows*, now that's a thing we both sit and watch together.

(Morley transcripts)

Crime series are traditionally programming for men. *Widows* was innovatory not only in its cast and storyline but in its appeal to women as audience. An identifiable product of an industry which has noticed feminism not so much for its politics but for its constitutive power in relation to a new, attractive-to-advertisers audience, *Widows* makes a bid for *Guardian* readers, as well as offering more pleasure for women in a genre which they probably have very little choice about watching in the first place.[11] As recent television research has alerted us to the power struggles in the home over programme choice,

Widows can be seen as a text which tries to negotiate this dynamic context of viewing. It tries to maximise its audience by offering gendered pleasure for both men and women. Its traditionally generic elements offer conventionally 'masculine' pleasures, while some of its innovatory elements – with some difficulty – offer more feminine pleasures. The tension of this double gender appeal, together with many of the other elements already discussed, can be seen clearly in the ending of the first series.

The last scene of the first series takes place in a suite in the Hilton Hotel in Rio de Janeiro. All the women have managed to escape from England. The scene opens on classic, indeed clichéd, images of criminal success: champagne and piles of money. This is the moment of the pay-off, not only for the women but also for the programme-makers and audience, in that the new element – women as criminals – permits the (re)use of these images which would otherwise signify 'caper movie', or comedy. Also, because conventional femininity is, historically, partly constructed and signified through conspicuous consumption, women as successful criminals are a much more glorious sight than men. The banter among the women is all about their clothes, and their spectacular outfits and make-up are a counterpoint to the unmade-up, black clothed 'heroes' of earlier episodes. The

12 *Widows*: cast relaxing, *Widows I* (courtesy of Thames Television)

moment of celebration, indeed the mode of celebration, is a return to femininity.

This return – and the irony of their route – is articulated by Shirley in a moment which condenses the strengths of the series, and would have provided a triumphal end. The three younger women are toasting their success, and Shirley, champagne glass in one hand, cigarette between her lips, parodies her own entry, desperate for money, in the Miss Paddington competition in the first episode, 'And now, for the next contestant, Miss Shirley Miller'. Shirley continues, now acting herself in a very little girl voice, 'I like reading, writing and robbing banks.' This moment, which offers parody of both femininity and genre, and concludes a narrative in which the women functioned as both heroes and heroines, is followed by Dolly's entrance and a scene in which success is turned to bitterness. Dolly reveals that she knows that Harry is still alive, and that despite his humiliation of her she still wants him. The series finishes with the rising of Dolly's loss theme, the lament from *Orfeo and Eurydice*, as the camera pans slowly across the young women's faces, to finish on Dolly – also restored to femininity, but with the knowledge of loss and grief that this position properly entails. This final, conclusive feminisation of Dolly, the 'strong man' of the series, also shifts the final register of the series from heist to romance. In order to conclude this rather unfamiliar story, the unfamiliar element – women as heroes – must be transformed. The move is from man's genre to women's genre, the women's genre at its most masochistic.[12]

It is this restoration, this clarifying of the gender of the genre, which marks the starting point of the second series. In the second series, the women are demoted to accessories, and hindrances, to Harry's quest. The grammar of one of the voice-overs which introduce and up-date each episode reveals this clearly, 'the Widows know they cannot be safe until they get Harry Rawlins off their trail' (voice-over opening titles, episode four, second series). Although the widows are the subject of the sentence, that is their only active moment. The active agent is Harry Rawlins, the widows' desires are all to do with stopping being the object of his agency. The narrative structure of the second series allows the widows to have no goal of their own. Their relation to the money becomes completely displaced, as Ann Mitchell observed in an interview, 'in the second series, the money becomes quite incidental. We are forever dropping it, flicking through it – no-one wants to hold onto it' (Ann Mitchell – Dolly – interviewed by Nicola Roberts, 'Not so merry widows', *New Musical Express*, 11 May 1985). The only plausible goals that can appear are completely conventional – Shirley wants to be a model, and Dolly might, just might, get something going with Vic. However, these women would clearly make unlikely housewives and by the end of the second series two of them are dead, one is in prison and Bella has left the country.

CREDITS

Widows I

Executive producer: Verity Lambert. *Executive in charge of production*: Johnny Goodman. *Producer*: Linda Agran. *Director*: Ian Toynton. *Script*. Lynda La Plante. *Production manager*: Stephen Pushkin. *Location manager*: Ray Freeborn. *Director of photography*: Ray Parslow. *Camera operator*: Mike Proudfoot. *Supervising editor*: Roger Wilson. *Assistant editor*: Colin Chapman. *Art director*: Christopher Burke. *Sound mixer*: Derek Rye. *Boom operator*: David Pearson. *1st assistant director*: Ted Morley. *Casting director*: Marilyn Johnson.
Cast: Ann Mitchell (*Dolly Rawlins*), Maureen O'Farrell (*Linda Perelli*), Fiona Hendley (*Shirley Miller*), Eva Mottley (*Bella O'Reilly*), David Calder (*Det. Insp. George Resnick*), Paul Jesson (*Det. Sgt Alec Fuller*), Maurice O'Connell (*Harry Rawlins*), Stanley Meadows (*Eddie Rawlins*).

Widows II

Executive producers: Linda Agran, Johnny Goodman. *Producer*: Irving Teitelbaum. *Associate producer*: Ron Purdie. *Director*: Paul Annett. *Script* Lynda La Plante. *Production manager*: Ron Holtzer. *Location managers*: Micky Moynihan, Nick Page. *Director of photography*: Dusty Miller. *Camera operator*: John Boulter. *Editor*: Roger Wilson. *Art director*: Christopher Burke. *Music*: Stanley Myers. *Sound mixer*: Bill Burgess. *Boom operator*: Simon Hayter. *1st assistant director*: Simon Channing Williams. *Casting director*: Ann Fielden.
Cast: Ann Mitchell (*Dolly Rawlins*), Maureen O'Farrell (*Linda Perelli*), Fiona Hendley (*Shirley Miller*), Debby Bishop (*Bella O'Reilly*), Maurice O'Connell (*Harry Rawlins*), Stephen Yardley (*Vic Morgan*), David Calder (*Det. Insp. George Resnick*).

Chapter 7

Post-feminism and shopping films

Working Girl (directed by Mike Nichols, 1987) and *Pretty Woman* (Garry Marshall, 1990) were immensely successful and popular films. *Pretty Woman* transformed Julia Roberts to a major star, doomed for ever to strive to repeat the success of the 'shopping sequence'.[1] *Working Girl* was seen as a return to form for director Mike Nichols,[2] while Melanie Griffith's performance was widely regarded as one of her best although there was some complaint about her 'squeaky voice'.[3] Responses to Sigourney Weaver's Katherine in the same film were a little more muted, as most critics recognised that this character somehow bore the brunt of the film, most explicitly in the repeated reference to her 'bony ass' at the end.[4] Both films were aimed at, and enjoyed by, a female audience. A clear signifier of this was the concern within each with dress and the performance of femininity. They were girls' films. However, this address, as I will discuss below, was more complex than that of, for example, the 'independent woman' group of 1970s films I discussed in Chapter 5. There is here a different kind of bodily display, a different kind of catering to reluctant husbands and boyfriends who might be in the audience. Nevertheless, both films were clearly recognised as feminine in their concerns and newspaper reviewers were quick to point out the re-telling of *Cinderella* in these women's pictures for the late twentieth century.[5]

Both films have proved troubling to feminist critics in ways that are reminiscent of the mixed feminist response to the 'independent woman' cycle of the 1970s (*Alice Doesn't Live Here Anymore* (directed by Martin Scorsese, 1974), *Unmarried Woman* (directed by Paul Mazursky, 1978), *Julia* (directed by Fred Zinneman, 1977). Then the trouble lay in the way in which these films were some kind of response to – even, in some cases, dramatisations of – feminist demands, but they were not movement-originated and they were also, unavoidably, Hollywood films. So although they might have core narratives about women finding themselves, there was constant feminist criticism of the type of women involved (white, middle-class), the focus on the individual and the relative ease of their quests for meaning, and, most problematic of all, a man. Those films were criticised both for their lack of realism and for their generic origins in melodrama, romance and the woman's picture. In short, for what we could call their Hollywoodness. Concepts frequently invoked in discussion of this cycle were 'recuperation' and 'inoculation', both of which imply a model in which feminist ideology and demands exist outside dominant structures such as Hollywood and are rendered innocuous when mobilised by Hollywood in its constant search for novelty and new audiences.[6]

With *Working Girl* and *Pretty Woman* the trouble is articulated slightly differently, for each film has been seen as symptomatic of a 'backlash' against feminism, or in some ways representative of a 'post-feminist' era. So while to a large extent the realist feminist critique would still apply – these are still white girls' stories focused on an individual's search for what turns out to be a man – these have not been the terms of critique. These films have not been criticised for distorting or rendering safe feminist critique, but rather for bypassing, ignoring or attacking feminism.[7] Thus US feminist comment on *Pretty Woman*:

> The immensely popular film *Pretty Woman* is emblematic of the post feminist genre. A glitzy reworking of the classic Cinderella tale, *Pretty Woman* offers yet another backlash dystopia: a world where women are whores with warm hearts of gold and men are rich corporate raiders with organs in need of thawing by those self-same hearts.
>
> (Walters 1995: 126)

and *Working Girl*:

> Suave technique cannot mask this film's hateful and divisive representation of women in the business world as bimbo or bitch cut throats who compete for career advancement and male bed-partners. And, let me tell you, that's not my idea of a pro-career woman movie . . . . I hear tell that some of those male critics who liked *Working Girl* saw it as a throwback to the career-women comedies of the '40s. Which comedies are those: *Working Girl* is nothing like any of the classics I remember. Try to picture Katherine Hepburn or Rosalind Russell playing one of their career parts as this kind of bimbo. Maybe you can. I can't. They had more respect for themselves and the women they played.
>
> (Kathy Maio 1991: 87)

Even the British critic for the *Financial Times* could see the periodisation:

> *Working Girl* is not so much screwball, more screwtop. Each time the comic contents are opened and poured, they seem flatter than the last time. And when you look at the story's sell-by date, it says 'Early 1980s, before feminism lost its fizz'.
>
> That in the late 1980s an audience still willingly consumes the movie is a tribute to the extraordinary Melanie Griffith. Her role is supposed to be pre-feminist and post-feminist simultaneously.
>
> (Nigel Andrews, 'From bimbo into boss', *Financial Times*,
> 30 March 1989: 25)

Emma Soames, writing in the *London Evening Standard*, offered a particularly lucid account of what many commentators found to be at stake:

> I have been struck by how many people, particularly women, have totally succumbed to the charms of the film *Pretty Woman*. It is the only movie I can get any of my friends to sit through, even though most have seen it at least once. I feel positively ashamed as I revel in the music, the settings and the sex-on-a-piano scene in a film which, in principle, I despise . . . .
>
> One of my American friends has a transatlantic idea that it represents some form of post-feminist escapism. Ten years ago she and her friends would have been picketing a movie like *Pretty Woman*. Her theory is now that we have all grown up, we can accept the film's moral limitations and just enjoy its fairy-tale redemptive quality.
>
> ('The charms of a tart tale,' *London Evening Standard*, 15 August 1990: 9)

Certainly, each film has a very different relationship to feminist discourse than that we find in what now, retrospectively, seem the rather innocent and optimistic films of the 1970s cycle, and Soames here points to the contradictions at stake. What I want to do here is to attempt to analyse this new relation. In some ways, my project here is a sequel to my project in Chapter 5. There I was examining the production and address to what I argued to be a new character for the 1970s, the independent woman. Here I ask, what happened to this character in the 1980s?

Feminist discourse, I would suggest, is profoundly structuring of each of these films, as it is of a range of 1980s and 1990s media representations. However, while these films could not have been imagined without the particular history of 1970s western feminism, it is the disavowal of this formation which is most evident. I want here to look at each film in detail to show how it is formed by, but also disavows, feminism. This project demands an engagement with the notion of 'post-feminism', a greatly contested term within feminist critical work. I want to suggest that 'post-feminism' has considerable purchase in any approach to this type of material, not least because of the way in which it attributes an historical specificity to the women's movement of the late 1960s and 1970s. It is a useful term historically because it does allow us to point to certain representational and discursive changes in the period since the 1970s. At the same time, I will argue a more orthodox feminist position – although I will only touch on this latter point as it is more readily available – and suggest that 'post-feminism' is a profoundly ahistorical concept, and in that sense misleading and not useful to the feminist political project.

Underlying both arguments and the choice of films is a desire to juxtapose two terms, 'post-feminism' and 'shopping'. My hypothesis here – of course not mine alone – is that something happens in the 1980s in the conjunction (in the West) of the new social movements, with their stress on the claiming and reclaiming of identities, and the expansion of leisure shopping and consumption. To trace this conjunction just in relation to feminism – and I should stress that I don't think it happens only in relation to women and feminism[8] – we can initially refer to a useful periodisation of feminism made by Michèle Barrett and Anne Phillips in the introduction to their collection *Destabilizing Theory* (1992).

Barrett and Phillips suggest that a distinction can be made, in western feminism, between what they call '1970s' modernist feminism and 1990s post-modern feminism. The labels of 1970s and 1990s are offered in their account as convenient shorthand with some temporal reference, and I will follow their example. They suggest that the well-known differences within 1970s feminism in understanding women's subordination concealed considerable agreement that it was possible to specify a cause of women's oppression. Although there was great disagreement about what it was, there was consensus that this cause could be found at the level of social structure, be that characterised as patriarchy or capitalism. The term for women's subordination was un-questionably that of 'oppression', and, analytically, the sex/gender distinction was talismanic. In this context, it is conventional femininity that is seen as particularly problematic (Barrett and Phillips 1992: 2–3).

Postmodern 1990s feminism, in contrast, in their argument, is a humbler, less universalistic and much less unified current. Challenged both internally and externally on the differences between women, and most particularly on issues of sexuality, racism and ethnocentrism, 1970s feminism was forced to recognise its particularity and the inadequacy of the concentration on class and gender alone. A range of positions and practices contested the axiomatic quality of the sex/gender distinction, which became much trickier to maintain. Postmodernism and post-structuralism offered theoretical challenges of a different order. That is, 1970s feminism was, in the 1980s and 1990s, challenged on both political and theoretical grounds. Or, to put it another way, 1990s feminism itself is post-1970s feminism in ways that are not simply chronological. 1970s feminism produced a particular inflection of the category 'woman' through which identity political mobilization could take place. 1990s feminism deconstructs this category, while still arguing for its salience.

Barrett and Phillips are mainly concerned to highlight differences between 1970s and 1990s feminism in relation to theory, politics and feminist intellectual work, while being insistent that they are not offering a simple progress model. I want to address their periodisation in relation to feminist ideas about consumption and identity. With all the necessary caveats about broad generalisation, it seems possible to make some clear distinctions. 1970s feminism, which in both Britain and the USA arose partly out of the New Left and the Civil Rights and anti-war movement, and generally involved women with access to higher education (although of quite mixed class origin) was anti-consumption, often in a quite puritanical manner, across the range of goods (houses, clothes, make-up and high art such as opera). Ideas of identity, which often draw on 'anti-repression' theories, were marked by notions of sincerity, expression, truth-telling. 1990s feminism, in contrast, partly through the 1980s feminist defence of 'women's genres' such as fashion, soap opera and women's magazines, is permissive and even enthusiastic about consumption. Wearing lipstick is no longer wicked, and notions of identity have moved away from a rational/moral axis and are much more profoundly informed by ideas of performance, style and desire.[9]

Barrett and Phillips carefully avoid 'post-feminism'. Their project is to think changes in feminism in relation to other posts, such as postmodernism and post-structuralism, and indeed their periodisation is, essentially, a distinction between a modernist 1970s feminism and a postmodern 1990s feminism. The changing concerns round consumption and identity that I have sketched can be satisfactorily mapped across this distinction. However, the rediscovery of the pleasures of feminine consumption associated with postmodern feminism are also congruent with what is popularly formulated as post-feminism. By this I intend to designate a journalistic or popular periodisation in which 'women's lib' is somehow over in the mid-1980s (Walters 1995 offers one account but she understands post-feminism simply as backlash). The reference is usually to a series of popular cultural representations which are both dependent on but transcendent or dismissive of the impulses and images of 1970s feminism. Women's and girls' magazines themselves are an interesting site here, as suggested by both McRobbie (1996) and Winship (1985), while cable networks like *Lifetime* (see Feuer 1994), or British television shows like *Absolutely Fabulous* and *The Girlie Show*, all offer post-feminist versions of femininity. That is, I would propose the necessity of marking and recognising a qualitative shift in the repertoire of anglophone popular femininities from (approximately) the early 1980s. The reasons for these changes are extremely complex, and include punk as much as women's liberation, changing patterns of employment as well as AIDS, but the point here is that they are labelled and recognised within the popular media in which they appear as being 'post-feminist'.[10] The privileged site for academic discussion of this type of image has been, repeatedly, Madonna (see Schwitchenberg 1993, hooks 1992 and Ang 1995b) but I would suggest that both *Working Girl* and, in a different way, *Pretty Woman* offer exemplary instances of post-feminist women characters.

The key point in this popular story is that the post-feminist woman has a different relation to femininity than either the pre-feminist or the feminist woman. As a persona in the public sphere, the post-feminist woman is also not necessarily 'white', which I think is the case, historically, with the persona '1970s feminist' – which of course is not to say that only white women were or are feminists. Precisely because this postmodern girl is a figure partly constructed through a relation to consumption, the positionality is more available. She is in this sense much more like the postmodern feminist, for she is neither trapped in femininity (pre-feminist), nor rejecting of it (feminist). She can use it. However, although this may mean apparently inhabiting a very similar terrain to the pre-feminist woman, who manipulates her appearance to get her man, the post-feminist woman also has ideas about her life and being in control which clearly come from feminism. She may manipulate her appearance, but she doesn't just do it to get a man on the old terms. She wants it all. The Melanie Griffith character in *Working Girl* wants a career *and* Harrison Ford. The Julia Roberts character in *Pretty Woman* won't settle for being kept as Edward's (Richard Gere) 'beck and call girl'. She demands a proper rescue by her prince and 'the whole fairytale'. When she has this promise (implicitly, marriage), 'she'll rescue him right back'. Exactly to the extent that this persona is constituted through a desire to make it individually, it is a persona that can be accommodated within familiar (if historically masculine) western narratives of individual success. The key narrative trope for this figure in 1980s Hollywood cinema – the site of both the inscription and the remaking of femininity – is shopping and trying on clothes. Post-feminist woman can try on identities and adopt them, as we have seen in a range of films, from *Desperately Seeking Susan* (directed by Susan Seidelman, 1985) to *Clueless* (Amy Heckerling, 1995). Now I am not suggesting that in the authentic 'outside' of politics in the 1980s there was a considerable transformation in radical thinking about identity which wicked Hollywood recuperates as shopping and identity swapping. For I would want to argue against this separation of an authentic outside and realm of representation. Instead, I am suggesting that, despite 1970s feminism, Jane Gaines's observation that 'it is the woman's story that is told in dress' (1990b: 181) is still true. However, the woman's relation to costume in the 1980s and 1990s is slightly different, as is the understanding of femininity. What in current critical theory is called the performativity of gender, always an element in the common sense of women's magazines, is currently much more widely available in the popular media. *Working Girl* and *Pretty Woman* are two films in which the performance of femininity was much foregrounded – to the evident enjoyment of huge audiences, but considerable ambivalence from feminist critics.

Working Girl is the story of Tess McGill (Melanie Griffith), who works as a secretary but wants to move into the stock market. Tess has put herself through night school but is repeatedly turned down for the 'entry program'. For this both class and gender are explicitly blamed in the film. Tess's first boss points out that she is competing with candidates who have been to Ivy League schools such as Harvard, while she herself recognises that her position makes her good ideas inaudible. As she observes to her boss early in the film: 'He doesn't want to hear it from a secretary.' The film has very clear generic antecedents in the sex comedies and proletarian women's films of the 1930s and 1940s while also offering that popular American tale, the triumph of the common 'man'.[11] However, it can also be grouped synchronically, as suggested by both Judith Williamson (1991) and Elizabeth Traube (1992), with other Hollywood 'business films' of the 1980s, of which *Wall Street* is the best known. Williamson argues persuasively that the most popular and satisfying of these 1980s Hollywood business films draw on both populist and puritan US traditions to reveal the perfect dovetailing of success and moral righteousness (Williamson 1991: 152). My concern here will be with the way in which this narrative of individual, righteous success is gendered. The film explicitly engages with feminist ideas and fantasies about feminism. Indeed I would argue that the film is inconceivable without second-wave feminism, although its repeated move, as is also the case with *Pretty Woman*, is one of disavowal.

The first and most obvious feminist inheritance in the narrative is 'girl as hero'. Tess is the common man, the ordinary American who wants to make it to the top, and it is a significant historical variant in that, although she does pick up a romantic partner on the way, the film finishes with Tess's joy at her career elevation. It is to her former female colleagues in the typing pool that Tess announces her triumph, and it is the cut from their cheers to the Carly Simon soundtrack with the zoom out from Tess's office building which finishes the film on the high of Tess's achievement.[12] This ordinary American has made it – her quality, despite humble beginnings and a vicious adversary in her quest, has been recognised by all the senior players. So if Tess, unlike the independent women of the 1970s movies, has a specific career aim, like them, she is made special, worthy of her narrative prominence, through constant explicit and implicit comparison with other female characters.

Bonding between women, 'sisterhood', is evoked in the contrasted pairs of Tess and her best friend, Cyn (Joan Cusack) and Tess and her new boss, Katherine (Sigourney Weaver), 'We're almost twins'. A collectivity of women – women who will never make it, and indeed, don't have this aspiration – are offered by the typing pool. These other secretaries, with their vivid make-up and big hair, silently watch the arrival of Katherine Parker and then Jack Trainer, organise a collection for Tess when she is sacked, applaud her public kiss with Jack Trainer and cheer her final triumph. They function as a chorus, enacting for us, the audience, the appropriate attitudes to each event in Tess's story: anticipation, excitement, pity, pleasure and triumph. But they also function as a backdrop for Tess. They repeatedly remind the viewer where Tess has come from – and in that simplest of Hollywood methods of characterisation, in their ill-assorted physical appearance, they show us, over and over again, that she is too good-looking to remain the same as they.

Tess is also contrasted with Doreen (Elizabeth Whitcraft), the woman who gets Tess's man, Mick. Doreen, unlike the women in the typing pool, is conventionally pretty, and, unlike Tess, quite petite. Doreen, who has sex with Mick (Alec Baldwin) while Tess is at night class and goes on to run his boat hire business, before, we assume, marrying him, is the woman that Tess does not become. Doreen appears to have no ambitions of her own other than getting Mick. Indeed, the character never appears in frame without Mick except when she is disconsolate when Tess returns to the neighbourhood for Cyn's engagement party. Doreen is an old-fashioned girl. She would be happy with the endless birthday gifts of lacy black underwear that give such pleasure to the giver, while Tess comments that 'you know, Mick, just once I could go for like a sweater or earrings – you know – a present I could actually wear outside of this apartment'. Doreen does not compete with Mick, but supports him, 'helping out with working the lines'. In fact cinematically she very precisely fits into the same frame as Mick, while Tess, after a while, literally, takes up too much room.

So Tess is constructed as different from the other girls of her class origins, both domestically and at work. She has ambitions of her own, and is not satisfied with occupying a traditionally feminine position in either sphere. These ambitions mean that she doesn't fit in either the neighbourhood or the typing pool. The question of the film is whether she can find anywhere she does fit, or whether she is literally stuck on the Staten Island ferry on which she travels at the key moments of the narrative. It is this spatialisation of aspiration, carried partly through soundtrack and skimming water shots of the harbour, which makes satisfying Tess's achievement of a room of her own at the end of the film, and makes poignant the moments before she recognises the room as her own.

Tess's quest evidently owes something to feminism, but this debt is the debt the film tries to erase. If Tess abandons the class-specific conventional femininity of her origins, we are repeatedly shown the dangers of this journey in the range of monstrous career women who people her destination. These are the women who, in Jack Trainer's much-quoted words, 'dress like a woman thinks a man might dress if he was a woman'. The women who ape masculinity: 'Trainer, we've got him by the balls, we must go in for the kill.' The women who are particularly snobbish to Tess, exemplified by Ginny, 'You! read *W*?' Katherine Parker is the main site of the elaboration of attitudes to this career feminism, a feminism that has gone monstrous. In the first instance she provides an embodiment of one of the popular personae of feminism in the 1980s, the lady boss (the bossy woman). This figure is a particularly significant one in the popular imaginary of feminism, for it offers, rather literally, a fantasy of a (white) woman with executive power. If one of the iconographic sources for this figure is Mrs Thatcher, her embodiment as a tough senior executive, such as, for example, Diane Keaton's 'Tiger Lady' in *Baby Boom*, (directed by Charles Shyer, 1987), is the Hollywood version. However, in *Working Girl* this figure is immediately 'othered' as we see her striding confidently and expensively past the watching floor of suddenly silenced secretaries. As neither audience nor Tess know at this point that her new boss is female, the film immediately poses the question of what it would be like to work for a woman. Thus when Tess first meets her she says 'I've

never worked for somebody who is younger than me before, or a woman.'
Katherine, with the practised ease of one who has fielded these questions
before, responds, 'It's not going to be a problem, is it Tess?' This is a modern
woman, aware of archaic discriminations, but in control and unperturbed by
her own power. We know Tess's male bosses have treated her badly. Are
women different?

Yes, initially thinks innocent Tess. And she tries out this idea on Mick as
they walk home from collecting take-away pizzas. She recounts with enthusiasm that working under her new boss is so different, and then tentatively
formulates an explanation, 'and I think, and I know you hate it when I say
things like this, I think, it's because she's a woman'. It is Katherine's betrayal
of this tentative belief of Tess's which legitimates all subsequent deception,
impersonation and man-stealing. Katherine's femininity, as the film shows
repeatedly, is merely a mask to conceal her calculating self-absorption and
killer instincts. While seeming to suggest that Tess is wrong – that women
bosses are *not* different – I think the film proposes the opposite. Women in
power are different: they are much worse. Indeed Katherine's ruthlessness
shows how benign are the senior, honourable patriarchs who own and govern
their empires with such integrity.

13 *Working Girl*: Tess (Melanie Griffith) before and after, (© 1988 Twentieth
Century Fox Film Corporation)

The complexity of what is at stake in the Katherine Parker figure, though, is shown by the way in which it is Katherine on whom Tess models herself. Indeed, after Katherine's skiing accident, signalled clearly as 'what we deserve', Tess starts living Katherine's life. She copies her voice, wears her clothes, accepts her invitations, lives in her parents' house and sleeps with her lover. As with *Pretty Woman*, our heroine is required to masquerade a different class of femininity. 'We have a uniform: simple, elegant, impeccable'. Indeed, the class freight and ethnic specificity of certain kinds of feminism is rendered obvious in both films. Being equal means being more middle-class, less local and more WASPy. Crucially in both these films, being successful means passing as naturally classy, correctly understanding the deployment of the appropriate accoutrements, be they 'serious hair', vowels or knives and forks. This foregrounded performance of femininity is a familiar trope in the American cinema, and one which has been of considerable interest to feminist commentators. I will return to the feminist readings of Bette Davis's transformation in *Now Voyager* in the context of *Pretty Woman*. Here, Tess's speedy absorption of Katherine's advice on self-presentation, 'You might want to re-think the jewellery', provides the visual proof in the film that Tess is both bright and deserving of elevation. If the narrative proves Tess's worth through the successful brokering of the deal based on Tess's original idea, it is the visual transformation of the class-meaning of Tess's appearance which guarantees her ability. Tess really is meant to leave Staten Island because she, unlike her best friend Cyn, recognises that the plain black $6,000 dress ('not even leather') she is proposing to borrow from Katherine does not need 'some bows or something'. But if Tess becomes classier as the narrative progresses, Katherine becomes more grotesque.

This monstrosity is first apparent on the day of Katherine's birthday when her office – very much against the simply chic dress codes she has been expounding – is festooned with flowers and balloons in a suddenly busy *mise-en-scène*. Most noticeable is the very large pot of yellow orchids, not a plant which has ever signified moral probity. Katherine – and we already know she smokes – is rotten rich. She is not, in the metaphor repeatedly applied to Tess at the beginning of the film, sufficiently 'hungry' to be a deserving populist heroine. This is a drama driven by class played out in lingerie and bracelets. As Tess begins to look more comfortable in monochrome outfits and discreet make-up, Katherine is demobilised her broken leg, strung up in hospital sling, decked out in lacy and flowery nighties and given a giant gorilla to carry. The gorilla, a knowing reference to Sigourney Weaver's role as Diane Fosse (in *Gorillas in the Mist*), points to a key element in the casting of Weaver as Parker – the actress's history as a cult feminist heroine, most trilogy. This history ensures that it is not just an upper-class bitch who is getting her deserts in the humiliation of Katherine. This character is also

14 *Working Girl*: monstrous Katherine (Sigourney Weaver) (© 1988 Twentieth Century Fox Film Corporation)

carrying a set of meanings about feminism and the independent woman heroine. Although Katherine, like, most obviously, Alex (Glenn Close) in *Fatal Attraction*, is made monstrous and vanquished in a particular narrative context, she also functions more generally as character given life and cultural resonance through fear and hatred of what Judith Williamson has called the SWW (single working woman).[13] Thus Katherine is a complex figure partly because of how she is required to function in the narrative and partly because of the relation between these demands and broader cultural shifts in attitudes to feminism. These factors, in turn, produce quite complex readings, what one might call post-feminist readings against the grain, when feminist critics refuse to see Katherine as monstrous and instead see her as set up. Thus Suzanne Moore observed:

> My sympathies were with Katherine. She is so completely set up as a male fantasy of a ball-breaking career bitch – her viciousness in the boardroom matched only by her voraciousness in the bedroom – that it's hard not to fall in love with her.
>
> (Suzanne Moore, 'The real McCoy', *New Statesman and Society*, 7 April 1989: 49–50)

While Cindy Fuchs argued:

> Tess's catty disparagement of Katherine's 'bony ass' (later reprised by Daddy Trask) underlines the film's retrograde insistence on a woman's silent place in that corporate world. Given her one-note characterisation, Katherine's demise is an especially annoying cheat. If there's anything she does know, it's how to perform for an audience, particularly in a boardroom setting . . . Katherine is too sophisticated a cobra to be brought down so clumsily. That the most forceful invective against her has to do with her unfeminine body only adds sexist insult to moralistic injury.
>
> (Cindy Fuchs, 'Working Girl', Cineaste 27, 2(1989): 50–1)

In one sense, what each of these critics is doing is making a clear oppositional reading of the text. However, each does this with some sophistication, recognising that the Katherine Parker figure carries more than just a film-specific narrative destiny. It is precisely the wider cultural resonances, meanings and aspirations of the single working woman that are here being overloaded with monstrousness. Fuchs declares herself annoyed by the gross change in characterisation, but Moore plays a wittier game, producing a speaking position which is a perfect example of post-feminism in the sense that I am using it. She declares that it is hard not to fall in love with Katherine.

Katherine and Tess in *Working Girl* offer one example of the splitting or dispersal of 'independent woman' characteristics over two characters. If Katherine is the power-mad boss from hell, Tess is ambition made cute. The constrasted body types of Sigourney Weaver and Melanie Griffith literally embody this distinction. There is a feminist inheritance here, but it is one which is iconographically rejected after Tess has taken on many of Katherine's attributes and Katherine is expelled from the deal. Elizabeth Traube, who uses models drawn primarily from the study of folklore in her analysis of 1980s Hollywood cinema, suggests that Katherine is an example of one of the traditional trickster figures, the shape changer (Traube 1992: 106–14). She points out that, in contrast, Tess, despite her continual efforts to 'shape-change', is repeatedly arrested in identities she is attempting to transcend. Thus her meeting with Bob in Arbitrage turns out to be another seduction attempt (she is pinioned in femininity when she is trying to be accepted as a dealer), while her choice of (Katherine's) dress for the party at which she meets Trainer for the first time precisely betrays that she is not familiar with the world in which she is trying to pass. This comparison of Traube's is illuminating, but she does not pursue the way in which character is constructed through these different relations to shape-changing. For if it is Katherine's facility which labels her as morally duplicitous, it is precisely Tess's failures which guarantee her moral integrity. It is because she can't shape change that she is lovable and deserving. This integrity is displayed in her costume after her downfall when she has returned to the office to pick up her possessions. Like Vivian (Julia Roberts) near the end of *Pretty Woman* when it appears she has lost Edward, Tess is coded at this point as natural and without pretence: both wear jeans. It is impossible to imagine Katherine in jeans. She is a character without this inner core of jeans-wearing natural integrity. This display of authenticity at this late point in the film is particularly significant, for the next scenes show that Tess has indeed successfully changed shape. Looking 'serious' in taupe, (a discreetly checked jacket – very close to the colour Katherine wore on her first appearance) she is breakfasting in Trainer's grey apartment before leaving for her new job. The jeans scene authenticates the class mobility. Tess has shape-changed, but not with facility. She has persevered through hard work and humiliation: she deserves what she has got. She has left the jewellery and bright colours of her origins for the monochrome of the fast lane. Traube argues that it is unlikely that Tess will ever rise above a low managerial rank. This may be a correct projection, but I think it is driven by Traube's own interest in pursuing her analysis of these 1980s business films in a fairly direct relation to the analysis of changing US class structures associated with the work of Barbara Ehrenreich

15 *Working Girl*: Tess wearing jeans (© 1988 Twentieth Century Fox Film Corporation)

and Fred Pfeil (Traube 1992: 110–14). The point surely is that Tess is confirmed as a natural woman. She is a natural, as opposed to a calculating, shape-changer.

This naturalness of the heroine is of key significance in the other film for discussion, *Pretty Woman*. Here there is no bitch career woman to be evicted, but there is again an upwardly mobile transformation of a post-feminist woman who is shown to deserve this elevation innately.

The explicitness of the reference to *Cinderella* in this very successful romance has tempted some critics to see this film as a reversion to a pre-feminist narrative. But just as the reference to *Cinderella* is contemporary and self-conscious, so is the invocation of the romance genre and the construction of the heroine. Kit (Laura San Giacomo), Vivian's best friend, tries to answer the question, 'But who does it work for?' and, after searching through their mutual acquaintance, comes up with the only answer, 'Cinder-fuckingrella'. Similarly, the film is framed with a street voice from Hollywood Boulevard, opening with 'Welcome to Hollywood, everybody comes to Hollywood's got a dream, what's your dream?' and closing with 'This is Hollywood, land of dreams, some dreams come true, some don't, but keep on dreaming'. This is a film that is at pains to point out that its fantasy is a similar one. Its heroine, too, seems familiar. She is part whore with the heart of gold, part Eliza Doolittle. But she is also post-feminist in the sense I am suggesting the term is useful. For Vivian has a vocabulary of self and attitude towards her profession which are historically specific. Hilary Radner (1993) has very usefully shown the way in which Vivian belongs both in the post-1960s history of the single girl – a story in which Helen Gurley Brown figures prominently – and in the even longer history of the heroine's role in the marriage plot. In my analysis of *An Unmarried Woman* I suggested that the 1970s figure of the independent woman was formed in the contradiction of the demand to be both desirable and desiring (see Chapter 5). Radner, discussing Vivian, suggests that the single girl is subject to a double injunction:

> the single girl must represent desire for the masculine subject while simultaneously acting as the agent of her own desire – must re-enact the specular image of consumer desire and yet assume agency and autonomy in the context of her own wishes.
>
> (Radner 1993: 66)

I think the particular configuration of desirable/desiring that we find in these 1980s films is a key element in the popular perception of them as post-feminist. In this popular image 'feminist' would thus signify only 'desiring' and, by implication, the repudiation of the necessity for the feminine subject to also be desirable. And it is shopping and dressing up which makes one desirable.

Pretty Woman is very knowing about its retrenchments, simultaneously informed by feminism and disavowing this formation. Thus the narrative scenario, although deeply indebted to the screen history of the whore with the heart of gold, would be unimaginable without second-wave feminist perspectives on sex-work. *Klute* (directed by Allan J. Pakula, 1971) and *McCabe and Mrs Miller* (directed by Robert Altman, 1971), with Bree Daniels (Jane Fonda) and Constance Miller (Julie Christie), introduced that generation of independent women for whom prostitution is a job like any other, and the best paid one to which they have access. For Kit and Vivian working on the street is a dull necessity, a way of paying the rent. The film uses these post-feminist attitudes – notably explored in films like Jan Worth's *Taking a Part* (1979) or Lizzie Borden's *Working Girls* (1986) – to disavow any voyeurism associated with this particular way of paying the rent, indeed to legitimate a scrutiny of Vivian's preparation for work, and to show both Vivian and Kit displaying themselves for trade. Thus in an ego-boosting session on Hollywood Boulevard Kit and Vivian chant what is clearly a feminist derived mantra: 'We say who, we say where, we say how much', affirming both their own control and their independence from a pimp.

One of the concerns of this film, as with *Working Girl*, is the performance and masquerade of a class-specific femininity. In each film the heroine has to labour to carry off the performance of the right sort of femininity. Tess has to go to speech class, Vivian to learn about the tines of forks. However,

16 *Pretty Woman*: Kit (Laura San Giacomo) and Vivian (Julia Roberts)

while the narrative of the film would suggest that it is in Vivian's act as Edward's hired companion that we would find the primary locus of pretence and disguise, in fact the reverse is true. So although Vivian's masquerade as Edward's classy latest is threatened with exposure by Edward's lawyer, through performance and *mise-en-scène* we learn that Vivian's real masquerade is as a hooker. That is, although Vivian is working as a prostitute for most of the film, the dominant presentation of her is as naturally not-a-hooker. It is the blonde wig and the cheap tarty dress which turn out to be the real disguise. This is achieved through a variety of devices and narrative contrasts, the most significant of which are Vivian's attitude to money and the contrast between her and her friend Kit.

Pretty Woman offers itself as being up front about the importance of money in contemporary US society. One of the few distinguishable comments in the early part of the pre-credit sequence, a party for Edward (Richard Gere) thrown by his lawyer, is 'It's all about money', knowingly offered to the audience when the screen is still dark. This film, the strategy suggests, is a film which is all about money which knows it's all about money. The promise, of course, is that this type of self-consciousness about money and Hollywood might be prompted by other values, but in fact the film *is* all about money and the appreciation of its value. Thus the first moment of rapport between Edward and Vivian is when she proves herself a tough bargainer, saying 'I never joke about money'.

Similarly, Vivian is initially differentiated from her friend Kit through their attitudes to money. Despite working as a hooker on Sunset Boulevard, Vivian is shown to be a nice girl with housewife potential because she saves the rent. That she has to keep it in the lavatory cistern is what she later calls 'just geography'. It is Kit who is essentially of the street, foolishly blowing the secret rent stash on drugs. The essential straightness of the Julia Roberts character, one of the key elements of the characterisation, is first established as she wails at Kit: 'You spent the rent money on drugs . . .'

Edward, at the other end of the money spectrum, is shown to have no real sense of what money means, particularly to those who have less than himself. He doesn't understand the value in which he deals. At the beginning of the film he commandeers his host's new car with no recognition of its value to Philip – a well-documented fictional characteristic of the very rich – and then cannot drive it. It is Vivian who recognises its value as a car, not just for the money it means but for its mechanical properties. She can drive it with the skill and appreciation it demands. That is, although on the streets Vivian is shown to have an instinctive or natural appreciation of the accoutrements of great riches which bypasses their financial cost, and goes straight to their heart, be it a fifth gear or an aria. So we have here the basic division of qualities through which the romance will work: she has no money but a sense of value, whereas he has lots of money but doesn't always understand what things mean. The image offered for this is his penthouse suite (the best) with a balcony that he can't use because he's afraid of heights. She appreciates what he's got – and she will eventually rescue him, show him how to appreciate it too.

To be able to do this plausibly – even in a film which self-consciously nominates itself as a fairy tale – Vivian's quality has to shine through her street apparel. This is managed in a range of ways in the film: the Roberts performance, responses of other characters and a series of texts and tests. It is the mutually confirming affirmation of Vivian's great value through each of these which contributes to the righteous outcome. Vivian gets her prince because she deserves him, as we learn throughout the film. Hilary Radner points to Vivian's character-revealing encounters with texts such as *The Lucy Show* and *La Traviata*. Liking *Lucy* reveals an ordinary American down-home innocence, while being moved by *La Traviata*, as the film labours to point out, reveals that Vivian has a 'soul'. Similarly, both the really rich (James Morse/Ralph Bellamy), and those who cater to them (Bernard the hotel manager/Hector Elizondo) recognise her quality. Morse leads her into eating hors d'oeuvres with her fingers when she is confused about cutlery, while Bernard makes possible her first dress purchase as well as helping her with her table manners. The Roberts performance is complicated by the widely disseminated knowledge that a body double was used for key scenes, particularly the opening sequence of getting dressed. Radner offers an excellent discussion of the use of the body double within her general argument that Vivian's progress in the film is from object of voyeuristic gaze to object of a fetishistic gaze. Here I would merely point to the way in which it is the body double scenes, particularly the use of sub-pornographic codes in the opening, which point to the ambitions of the film's address. I observed earlier that the address of these post-feminist films was more complex than that of the 1970s independent woman films. There is an attempt to offer pleasures within what are generically women's films, to viewers occupying a conventionally masculine position. In *Working Girl* this was almost put in quotation marks in the gift scene: Melanie Griffith tries on black lacy underwear in front of a mirror (so we have front and back views), while Mick watches from bed while reading *Motor Tread* magazine. In *Pretty Woman* Vivian's profession is used to legitimate close-ups on body and underwear in the early part of the film. The fact that it is the body double in these scenes offers a rather literal rendition of the difficulty of this double address to a lusting and an identifying audience. One actress alone, even Julia Roberts, cannot or will not meet the contradictory demands of femininity. More generally we are cued to read the performance – the mixture of bravado, vulnerability, street smarts and innocence – through the extract from *Breakfast at Tiffany's* which is shown on television in the hotel room. Roberts manages to project sincerity through a certain unpredictability in her timing. Edward says he finds her surprising, and he also tells her repeatedly to stop fidgeting. Her performance emphasises these two elements: a certain nervi-

17 *Pretty Woman*: Vivian natural (© Touchstone Pictures, all rights reserved)

ness which is repeatedly transformed by a smile or a tableau of her beauty. Roberts never leads a scene with her wide, dazzling smile, instead only offering it as a revelation as she tosses the hair from her face or slowly turns round. Similarly, there is an occasional awkwardness in her deployment of her limbs, as if her long legs are sometimes a little outside her control. These are signifiers of a non-manipulative sexuality, a guarantee that, even though Vivian works as a prostitute, she is unconscious of the power of her beauty. She just naturally sits down for breakfast the first morning, firstly on the edge of one of the dishes and then on a chair with her knee peeking through her white towelling dressing-gown while she hungrily and unselfconsciously tears into a croissant. She might be a hooker outside, but she's clean inside.

Vivian, as she tells Edward while offering him a selection of condoms, is 'a safety girl'. She works the street, but, as the film is at pains to point out, she flosses her teeth. Vivian's profession makes it narratively impossible for there to be a withholding of sex – as she puts it herself, 'I'm a sure thing'. However, romantic narrative demands a withholding, and this is achieved through the displacement of the customary narrative importance of inter-course to 'kissing on the mouth'. This device allows Vivian to remain pure while working as a prostitute, and also allows a proper romantic courtship working up to the night when they really 'do it'. Here she is crucially contrasted with Kit, whose destiny, we know, is like that of Skinny Marie. Kit will never leave the street – her fate sealed in her readiness to party, her incontinence with drugs. Kit spends the rent money – she betrays her room-mate. She is not really a bourgeois housewife in waiting – she would not 'clean up good'. And she doesn't seem to have the 'non-street' normal clothes that Vivian is revealed to possess in the last scene. It is Kit's destiny which gives the poignancy to their farewell.

However it is the prerequisites of the clean-up, the clothes purchased in the shopping trip on Rodeo Drive, which have provided a central focus for fans and critics. Radner argues that Vivian becomes 'pretty' only when she starts shopping. Certainly this is when the title song first appears. However, I have tried to suggest that Vivian is shown to be already 'pretty' *before* she gets the accoutrements of expensive femininity. It is only because, as I have discussed at length, Vivian is *already*, naturally, underneath 'not-a-hooker' that she *can* clean up good. In this the film can be usefully contrasted with *Now Voyager*, which also has a transformation of a central female character. Charlotte (Bette Davis) too cleans up good, but in her case she moves not from street-femininity to penthouse-femininity but from non-sexual spinster aunt to desirable sexual and maternal woman. The plucking of eyebrows, the weight loss and the hair cut are the essentials here – in conjunction with psychiatric help and an originally loaned new wardrobe and identity. As several critics have commented, *Now Voyager* reveals the labour of feminin-ity, the difficulty of successfully inhabiting this contradictory position (see for example, Maria LaPlace, 1987). In that sense *Now Voyager* has been read

18 *Pretty Woman*: Vivian dressed up (© Touchstone Pictures, all rights reserved)

to reveal the constructedness of femininity. In contrast *Pretty Woman* while showing the transformation achieved through the series of expensive outfits and offering what can only be described as a triumphant shopping binge, implicitly uses a natural model of femininity. In the shopping trip Edward's credit card buys for Vivian what she already deserves. She naturally deserves it, for the reasons discussed, but, just to make sure, she narratively deserves it as well because of her humiliation the previous day when the snooty shop assistants refused to serve her. Just like Tess, Vivian proves a successful shape-changer, a righteous inheritor of one of the new 1980s 'public' femininities, to use Radner's term.

Jennifer Wicke, in an acerbic recent article, argues for the significance of 'the celebrity zone' as 'the public sphere where feminism is negotiated, where it is now in most active cultural play' (Wicke 1994: 757). She proposes the category 'celebrity feminism' as a significant media category, arguing that a woman with a profile in the public sphere will be assimilated to this category. Wicke argues that the familiar binary division of feminism into 'movement' and 'academic' is near-useless, and that the domain of celebrity feminism demands engagement, for this is the most significant contemporary site for the generation of meanings round feminism. She argues that a range of US figures are best understood within the celebrity feminist zone – Camille Paglia, Oprah Winfrey, Whoopi Goldberg, Catherine McKinnon, Naomi

Wolf and Judith Butler – and engages with the different politics associated with each. But what she is most insistent about is that celebrity feminism cannot be dismissed in the name of some real authentic feminism which is 'elsewhere'. I want to use a comment she makes about Naomi Wolf to approach my conclusion to this essay. Wicke writes, 'However problematic, some form of feminist discourse is occurring within Wolfian celebrity space' (1994: 765). I think the same could be said of these two films. However problematic, some form of feminist discourse is occurring within these women's films for the 1990s. Julia Hallam has shown how *Working Girl* was widely recognised as engaging with feminism, generating a whole series of articles that were not film-specific about women in the workplace, the glass ceiling, etc. (Hallam 1994). Hilary Radner has argued that *Pretty Woman* marks a specifically 1990s reconfiguration of the marriage plot and that the film attempts to 'imagine a fantasy in which a woman always receives a just return for her investment without relinquishing her right to the pursuit of happiness' (Radner 1993: 75). That is, both these writers can be understood to argue that something to do with feminism is happening in these films. I have suggested that the term 'post-feminist', routinely rejected by feminist critics, *is* useful in an approach to these films as it marks the considerable distance that we find here, in popular representation, from popular representation of 1970s feminism. If the 'independent woman' of the 1970s cycle marked a response to the women's movement – and the new female audience – of that period, this figure has all but disappeared by the mid-1980s. Instead, we have a new kind of girly heroine who, while formed in the wake of 1970s feminism, disavows this formation. But the post-feminist girly is only one of the Hollywood cast of post-feminist characters. As we have seen in *Working Girl*, we also have monster-career woman, and, in another genre, as Carol Clover (1992) suggests, we also find what she calls 'the final girl'. Feminist critics have tended to be more attracted by less girly characters such as Thelma and Louise (see, for example, Sharon Willis 1993), but I have argued that something to do with feminism is going on in this girly space. For the disavowal of 1970s feminist formation does not, in some ways, seem important. Why should 1970s feminism have a copyright on feminism? As Angela McRobbie (1996) has argued in another context, the old vocabularies of 1970s feminism are not adequate to the experience of young women growing up today. That is, I would argue that the very currency of the term *post-feminism* needs addressing, and that it is quite useful if used in an historically specific sense to mark changes in popularly available understandings of femininity and a woman's place that are generally recognised as occurring in the 1980s. These changes may also have a very particular generational resonance. The story of 1970s feminism can be seen in some ways as the story of the baby boomer generation, growing up between the pill and AIDS.[14] However, in its very historical specificity, 'post-feminism', it is also not useful at all in two different ways. Firstly, it is not useful if it

Part III

Questions of quality

Introduction

Each of these essays was written in the late 1980s, and each bears the mark of its time of writing: particular arguments were being made in particular disciplinary circumstances. Two factors are most significant in shaping the contexts to which these polemics were addressed. The first of these was the increased institutionalisation of television studies in the anglophone academy and the second the dismantling of European public service broadcasting, which in Britain was closely tied to the radical free-market deregulatory regime of the Conservative government of Mrs Thatcher. I will address each of these contexts briefly as a way of locating the key concerns of this group of essays, which are with issues of taste and judgement in relation to television. If the essays in Parts I and II address issues of taste through the film and television there discussed – generic, feminine material traditionally perceived as off the taste map – the essays in Part III begin to address the consequences of refusing to take seriously only serious programmes. In some ways the essays in this section reflect on the strategic paradoxes of the success of the formative popular culture/relativist current in film and television studies – which had its origins in a different historical moment – in the broader context of an anti-mandarin right-wing populist government.

In the brief histories of the new disciplines of film, television and cultural studies the later 1980s marked a period of intellectual settling down and institutional consolidation. Degrees and courses in television, media and cultural studies had proved attractive to students, and this gave an unfamiliar institutional (semi)security to teachers in these areas while expanding enrolment continued. While this had specific material consequences in terms of the massive expansion of books published in this field – a comparison of the Routledge catalogues from 1986 through to the present would be particularly revealing – this expansion both marked and concealed a change of intellectual tone. As the study of television within the academy became more acceptable, less energy and argument had to be expended on legitimating this study. Instead of arguments about whether and why classroom time might be devoted to television – as in Chapter 1 of this book – the demand is for textbooks, standard accounts and introductions to the study of television. The inaugural books of television studies published in the 1970s concentrate on establishing television as a specific object of study which exceeds the paradigms of, on the one hand, political economy or sociology of mass communication and, on the other, literary or dramatic criticism. While drawing on work from these different disciplines, television studies in particular will address the particularity of the television text, its representations and address. Here we can place Williams's *Television: Technology and Cultural Form* (1974), Newcomb's *TV: The Most Popular Art* (1974) and Stuart Hall's early writing on television (Hall 1973, 1998). The first tranche of work includes Fiske and Hartley's *Reading Television* (1978), the BFI Television Monographs (1973–82), Len Masterman's *Teaching About Television* (1980), Stuart Hood's *On Television* (1980), the Open University/BFI collection *Popular Television and Film* (Bennett *et al.* 1981) and, perhaps concluding this period, John Ellis's *Visible Fictions* (1982) and Ann Kaplan's *Regarding Television*, the 1983 book from her 1981 conference.

We can usefully distinguish this first phase of 'television studies' books – and it is significant that many of them are British in origin, pointing to the relative weakness of the 'mass communications' tradition in Britain, as well as, arguably, a different, less entertainment-orientated television tradition – from a more established second phase of textbooks in the mid to late 1980s. These come, in the main, from the USA. John Fiske's influential 1987 book *Television Culture* became a standard text and was seen to represent a cultural studies approach to television. Horace Newcomb's 1976 anthology *Television: The Critical View*, which had a clearly legitimatory project in its first incarnation, was, by the fourth edition in 1987, able to draw substantially on the accumulating scholarship in the field. The 1994 fifth edition is clearly a 'television studies' book, secure in its assumption that such a field of study exists. Robert C. Allen's *Channels of Discourse*, also first published in 1987, is quite explicitly a textbook, addressing its reader as someone new to the study of television and providing further reading after each chapter's exposition of a different approach or field of study. Television studies – and the study of television – has developed, by this stage, a certain autonomy from its rather diverse disciplinary origins.

Chapter 8 belongs to this second phase and is able to draw on the expanding field of television scholarship. My concern was partly to trace the development of this field, and partly to argue that the particular contours of this development made it peculiarly difficult to integrate discussion of value and judgement into the study of television. This was because, culturally, television was often the bad object against which other discriminations could be made, and therefore television studies was partially formed in the validation of television and popular taste. This essay was written when much of the new and interesting research in television studies was concentrating on the audience, often revealing how very little attention television audiences paid to watching television. There seemed a possibility that the television text, as an object of study, was going to disappear into its often inattentive audience. I argued that it was analytically necessary to retain the category of 'the text', in face of the erosion of this category through a range of different routes, if any distinctions were to be made about television.

This discipline-specific argument was given a wider resonance in the context of public debate in Britain in relation to the Conservative government's plans for the future of British broadcasting. The later 1980s in Britain marked the close of the first decade of Conservative government under Mrs Thatcher following her 1979 victory. As many commentators have pointed out, the characteristics of this government were in many ways far from conservative, and the radical and tenacious commitment to the free market had particular consequences both for television and, rather paradoxically, also for the study of television. For television, and broadcasting generally, the commitment to deregulation and consumer choice hit directly at the assumptions and practices of public service broadcasting which had historically dominated both the BBC and independent television. Specifically this meant a shift from an address to the citizen to an address to the consumer, which carries with it an assumption that programme provision will be governed by the market rather than any notion of what is good for the nation. There were two publications in the late 1980s which offer expositions of these shifts: the 1986 Peacock report and the 1988 White Paper, *Broadcasting in the '90s: Competition, Choice and Quality*. The Peacock report advocated a move towards a market system based on 'consumer sovereignty', although it did not recommend advertising for the BBC. The White Paper, which finally became law, somewhat modified, in 1990, specifically addressed changes in the regulation of commercial broadcasting which resulted in the institution of a 'sealed bids' system of franchise allocation which operated alongside a notion of a 'quality threshold'. These documents have to be seen alongside a series of key personnel changes in the 1980s, of which perhaps the most obvious is the removal of Alistair Milne from the BBC in early 1987, shortly after the appointment, with Mrs Thatcher's support, of Marmaduke Hussey as Chairman of the Governors.

In this context the issue of quality in television suddenly acted as a focus for quite different arguments and interest groups. Corner, Harvey and Lury (1994) have shown very convincingly how the British quality debate of the late 1980s and early 1990s mobilised a heterogenous crew. Programme-makers, the ITV companies and academics contributed to a debate in which little was clear except that everyone was 'for' quality. They also point to the neuralgic contradiction in the Thatcherite deregulatory project. For if, on the one hand, the nanny state must cede to market forces, on the other, who will then regulate for decency and Victorian values? Thus deregulation is accompanied by reregulation in the form of bodies like the Broadcasting Standards Commission. Chapter 9, which was written at the same time as the Mulgan collection on *The Question of Quality* (1990), was an attempt to open up some debate round the difficult word *quality*. Indeed, to some extent, it was an attempt to *practise* using it: to see what was entailed and whether 'quality' was redeemable from the strong sense of the class, gender and ethnic privilege which had traditionally informed the making of legitimate aesthetic judgement. My project was to think about how quality was thought about, not, as for example George Brandt has represented my characterisation of the '*Brideshead in the Crown*' version of quality, to provide a recipe for it (1993: 3–4). This particular debate has subsequently moved on. Now I think it is most productive in discussion to initially separate out assessments of the qualities of programmes and types of programming from discussion of the organisation and regulation of overall provision – although of course these are intimately connected. Thus there is one set of arguments to be had about the assessment of good and bad examples of particular programmes and examples of genres, and the appropriate criteria to be used. These arguments are about quality in an adjectival sense – high quality or low quality. This usage is different to 'quality television' in the generic sense, a category which seems much consolidated, with a rather heritage-worthy feel, by the debate round the 1988 White Paper. The point about this adjectival/generic distinction is that it makes it possible to think about bad 'quality television'. To give an example, I think *Ready Steady Cook* (Bazal Productions for the BBC, 1994), which is a rather cheap fast programme, initially made for daytime television, is rather good television. It uses the medium in a way which makes its liveness exciting, the design and concept is simple but well realised, it offers pleasures for both cook and non-cook and it values skills and competences rarely lauded in public. However, I don't think it is an example of 'quality television'. For that, in the genre cookery programme, we would need to turn to something like a Delia Smith programme, which has much greater use of post-production facilities, or a heritage version, like *The Wartime Kitchen and Garden* (BBC, 1993). (Delia Smith is Britain's best-selling cookery writer and has had several extremely successful television series with high production values. The particular virtue of her recipes and the programmes is that they are seen to be successfully reproducible by the viewer or reader). *Delia* may be 'quality', but it is, to my mind, a little bit too leaden to be good in the way that, say, Rick Stein's *Taste of the Sea* (Denham Productions for the BBC, 1995) is good.

However in Britain, at present, this discussion is actually provoked by the necessity for the evolution of new policies in a rapidly changing broadcasting environment. Here, as recipes go, John Mepham's three criteria seem particularly useful: 'High quality television is television which is excellent as measured by its faithfulness to these principles – the rule of diversity, the cultural purpose of telling usable stories and the ethic of truth telling' (Mepham 1990: 59). Mepham's concern with the ethical dimension of a judgement of quality does not, of course, tell us very much about what these programmes would look like, but he is very clear that his category of 'usable stories' includes television-specific forms such as the soap opera and the sit-com, as well as the more culturally legitimate forms of fiction. However, it is also clear that his conception of television in society is profoundly formed by a notion of public provision. Brian Winston puts the issue well in a period of accelerated deregulation prior to digitalisation:

> But to wish this [that the BBC were to die] is to ignore the fact that public service broadcasting – that is, crudely, non-commercial broadcasting – brings advantages for viewers and listeners that cannot simply be thrown aside. In other words, while it is true that the BBC was and is an institution insufficiently distanced from government, even by the standards of the liberal tradition of free expression, it nevertheless has constructed a broadcasting culture which, by every measure, better served more of its public than would have been the case under commerce. For it is quite simply a fact that the market-place in broadcasting, however it is organ-ized, has not provided a comprehensive range of programming, wherever it has been tried. It always has to be augmented non-commercially to fill, even partially, the cultural space available for broadcasting.
>
> (Winston 1994: 39)

It is not possible to predict how these arguments and power struggles – which in 1996 appear to be converging on the question of the privatisation of Channel 4 – will pan out. It is as a contribution to continuing debate that I reprint Chapter 9.

The 'Quality' essay (Chapter 9), though, was also commissioned for a very particular context, which was the first issue of *Screen* produced by the John Logie Baird Centre at the University of Glasgow (*Screen* had previously been produced in London by the Society for Education in Film and Television). Although the essay was in some ways occasioned by the 1988 government White Paper, its address was strictly academic and its concern was mainly pedagogic. Following on from the arguments made in Chapter 8, I wanted to argue that the disciplines of film and television studies were both dependent on, but disavowed, the making of judgements. I also wanted to raise a series of questions about the consolidating orthodoxies of the disciplines, in which a rather banal version of 1970s structuralist Marxism crossed with a range of politically correct moralisms appeared to be the 'theory' taught to a generation of Thatcherite students many of whom, far from wanting to change the world, wanted to do media studies as a route to becoming famous. A new period of *Screen*'s existence – perhaps the formative magazine for the discipline in the anglophone academy, and certainly the primary site for the translation of cine-structuralism in the 1970s – was a provocative place to put this argument.

The final essay in this section moves from the seminar room to the skyline. It was written in 1989 when satellite television first became commercially available in Britain. Rupert Murdoch's Sky television was widely advertised in this period, and the erection of off-white spherical dishes on the outside of houses and flats became an external sign of subscription to Sky. However the erection of these dishes also became the subject of considerable controversy in the local and national press. These taste wars, ostensibly about architectural appropriateness, in fact carried and condensed a much wider set of concerns, ranging from attitudes to official, legitimate 'BBC' culture to ideas of national, gender and generational identity. Chapter 10 sketches out the vocabularies in play in these debates and tries to think about the meaning of satellite television in Britain at this stage. I worked exclusively from newspaper reports, partly because, in a period of vogue for small-scale audience studies, I wanted to suggest that it was methodologicallly important to attempt to map the more general, public discursive contexts in and through which individuals understood and justified their own choices. I was in this sense pressing against the methodological implications of the radical particularism and contingency advocated as an analytic necessity by Ang and Hermes (1991) to suggest that any particular act of audience consumption, or account of it, always takes place in a macro- as well as a micro-historical context. So although I would agree with Ang and Hermes's argument against the too-easy connection of 'particular instances of meaning attribution to texts with socio-demographic background variables' (1991: 313), I would argue that it is impossible to interpret audience data without some sense of the significant vocabularies within which, for example, television taste is discussed, and the differential access of different groups of people to these discursive repertoires. My essay sketched out at an early stage what seemed to be in play as satellite television came to Britain. Shaun Moores's substantial ethnographic study offers much more detail and complexity in his accounts of the decision-making process for individual families in getting a dish (1993: 102–16; 1996). He shows how different the attitudes are within families to satellite television, and once again confirms that new technologies do not drop from the sky meaning-free but enter the home to become embedded in already existing familial and household routines and power structures, which in turn are articulated with regional and national maps of meaning.

These early arguments about the meaning of satellite television to national life have been much reinforced in the 1990s. Satellite television has become accepted as part of everyday British life, with pubs displaying forthcoming broadcasts of sporting events – particularly English football – as enticements to customers. BSkyB was floated on the stock market in 1994, the economics of Premier League football have been transformed and easy reference is now made to 'terrestrial television' which has stopped being ordinary 'television'. The debate, perhaps predictably, came to a head in Britain not over cross-media ownership or the diminishing value of the television licence but over who 'owned' certain national sporting events. The House of Lords, through a cross-party alliance in February 1996, established that the Derby, the Grand National, Wimbledon finals, the FA Cup Final, the Scottish FA Cup Final, the soccer World Cup, the Olympic Games and England's home cricket test matches constituted 'the crown jewels' of British sport and could not be sold exclusively to BSkyB. The paradoxes of the defence of public service broadcasting for someone like myself who is a feminist and neither sports enthusiast nor patriot become evident. Who is the public here, and why has the debate about broadcasting policy remained so resolutely masculinist? Why aren't women citizens yet?

Chapter 8
Aesthetics and audiences†

WHAT IS GOOD TELEVISION?

This has not been a very fashionable question for television scholars in the UK.[1] I want to think about some of the answers that have been given to this question, and to query its continuing banishment. In the process, I will make a series of observations about the progressive valuation of the television audience(s) over the television text (however conceptualised) since the mid-1970s. I am not arguing that the emphasis of television studies should be evaluative rather than analytic, but I am suggesting that there is something rather odd about the fascination with what 'real' (i.e., other, non-academic) people think about television when it is combined with a principled refusal to reveal what academics think about it.

This paper emerges from attempts to think through some of my own past practice – I do not hold myself exempt from these criticisms. Also, the focus of my remarks is on Britain. Apart from Janice Radway's 1984 work on the readers of romance fiction (which is in any case not about television), the long-term Katz and Liebes *Dallas* project[2] (which comes from a very different tradition) and the work of the Tübingen Soap Opera Project, I am not in a position to comment on any US ethnographic audience work.

We can start by outlining two traditional ways in which television has been seen to be good in Britain, both of which minimise its role or presence.[3] The first draws its legitimation from other, already validated art forms: theatre, literature, music. Television (by implication, not itself good) becomes worthy when it brings to a wider audience already legitimated high- and middle-brow culture. In this mode (the contradictions of which I shall discuss later), television can be good as a potentially democratic, or socially extensive, transmitter.

Written for the Blaubeuren conference, 'Rethinking the Audience: New Tendencies in Television research', organised by Hans Borchers, Gabriele Kreutzner, Ellen Seiter and Eva-Maria Warth at the University of Tübingen, 1987. This later version is from *Logics of Television* edited by Patricia Mellencamp (Bloomington and London: University of Indiana and the British Film Institite, 1990).

The other mode of legitimation, or set of discourses within which television is allowed to be good, poses a privileged relation to 'the real'. Although this mode does reference specific qualities of broadcast media, the qualities concerned – those facilitating the transmission of reports of live events – are precisely read as self-negating. Thus sports, public events, current affairs and wildlife programmes are 'good television' if we seem to get unmediated access to the real world, and are not distracted by thinking about television *as television.*

The other term constructed in opposition to 'good television' is not bad television; it is referred to as popular or commercial television, and its origin in Britain is usually, casually, dated to 1955 and the start of commercial broadcasting. This bad television, which is where we find soap operas and game shows, has another name – and that is 'American series'. In reciprocal moves, US ideas of British culturalness are confirmed by the broadcasting of imported British programmes to the small audiences of PBS, while American vulgarity is confirmed to Brits by the popularity of *Dallas, Dynasty* and imported game show formats. Dick Hebdige (1981) has discussed the sub-cultural significance of the American, and particularly of the discriminations made about design details such as streamlining among British working-class youth in the 1950s. Ien Ang (1985) has pointed to the significant anti-American element in what she refers to as the 'ideology of mass culture'. There are two points here. One is about the positive value, the appropriate-ability, of American mass culture – the way in which it has historically at certain points provided an escape route, a domain of cultural expression, for those excluded from legitimate national culture. The other – in some ways the same point differently inflected – is about the derogatory meaning, within legitimate cultural discourse, of 'American', particularly when coupled with 'television'.

So we have 'good television', so far, constructed across a range of oppositions which condense colonial histories, the organising and financing of broadcasting institutions, and the relegitimation of already legitimate artistic practices. That is to say, the dominant and conventional way of answering the question 'What is good television?' is to slip television, unnoticeably, transparently, into the already existing aesthetic and social hierarchies. (And it is, of course, because of this that television scholars within the culturalist tradition have eschewed judgement, but that is to open up another trail which I don't want to pursue at present.) This leaves out a lot of television and, perhaps more significant, denies a great deal of the pleasure that people get from watching and talking about television. This other television, which is endlessly produced and reproduced in the popular press – but precisely as news and gossip; there is no such thing as an *exclusive* critical insight – re-emerges within legitimate cultural discourse in the use of metaphors of addiction, and in features such as 'Schlockwatch' in the new *Listener.* In this series well-known personalities from within the high cultural field comment, usually in an unspeakably patronising manner, on a popular television programme they watch. The title of the feature says it all. Only within a frame which designates the programme as 'schlock' can there be a discussion of it. Indeed, it is only within this frame that viewing can be admitted. To put this another way, only when somebody you wouldn't expect (for example, Paul Theroux 1988) watches a genre programme, *Coronation Street*, is the programme interesting.[4] And what is seen as interesting is precisely how the author gets on with the not-good programme.

However, there is something else going on here which illuminates another way in which television exists in relation to, or is constructed by, or constructs the aesthetic field. This something else is the newsworthiness of certain categories of persons watching television at all. So we have a double structure of distinction. Firstly, we have the way in which, in British critical discourse about television, good television is constructed through reference to that which is other than television – already existing and validated art forms or 'the real'. Secondly, and here it is pertinent to remember Bourdieu's (1979) argument that the aesthetic gaze is constructed in and through an opposition to the naive gaze, we have the way in which, in much contemporary cultural discourse, television is *the* object of the naive gaze *against which* the aesthetic gaze is constructed. Television secures the distinction of all non-televisual cultural forms. At this deep level there can be no answer to the question 'What is good television?' because it is founded on an oxymoron. Thus bad cinema or theatre is designated soap opera, while video art barely makes it to the Arts pages of newspapers.[5] (And it is here that we can find the source of the contradictoriness of the 'transmitter' model of good television. Is the 'Ode to Joy' or 'I Heard It through the Grapevine' quite the same to the connoisseur if everybody sings along?)

This constitution of television as the bad cultural object creates a critical abyss when we try to shift the gaze, to look at television, not through it to the Real or High Art. To echo a formulation which has a different political and historical resonance to my own project, there is almost no elaborated discourse of quality, judgement and value which is specific to television and which is not derived from production practices or professional ideologies.[6] That is, if we forget 'Art Television' for the moment, what are the terms we can use to talk critically about that other television, terms which neither collapse pleasure and quality into each other nor constitute quality as the ghost of class, gender and national privilege? Can it be done, and should we, in this relativising age, wish to do it?

The third answer to the question of what is good television takes a sideways step away from the question, and says: forget these value judgements, let's look at what the people watch. I want to suggest that this sideways step is beginning to have the effect of merely inverting existing aesthetic hierarchy (the popular is good), leaving the power relations in place.

CAN WE HAVE A TELEVISION AESTHETIC, AND DO WE WANT ONE?

There are two main problems in thinking about a television aesthetic. The first, which I do not address substantially but which informs the endeavour of this paper, is part of the broader problem of popular aesthetics in general, and particularly popular aesthetics of mass cultural commodity production. This is to do with the suitability of the noun *aesthetics*, encrusted as it is with the meanings of high culture, in collocation with the adjective *popular*. Here some of the work done on popular music by people such as Simon Frith (1988a) and Dick Hebdige (1988), or on fashion by Angela McRobbie (1989), may be more useful than some of the existing ideological explications of popular television. The second problem, which is superficially more specific to television, has to do with the phenomenon of the rapidly disappearing television text. Or, to put it another way, how do we constitute the television text as an object of study?

Horace Newcomb, writing in 1974, argued for the use of criteria of intimacy, continuity and history in a television aesthetic, as well as for the importance of soap opera in the development of television drama.[7] Intimacy and continuity do seem important elements in characterising what is specific to television in certain textual modes. They are also, of course, characteristic of certain ways of watching television. The challenge of an adequate television aesthetic (if this is indeed what we should wish to call it) is not only that it must take a position on the relationship(s) between what we might call the institutional and the programme components of televisual discourse but that it must also address extremely variable and diverse ways of watching television.

By the former, I mean to indicate the critical and analytical importance granted to what we might temporarily call the television-ness of television, which can be taken as the dominant focus for analysis, as opposed to the more traditional concentration on single programmes. The classical site within British cultural theory for discussion of how the television text can be constituted as an object of study is the late Raymond Williams' (1974) formulation of 'flow', taken up by John Caughie (1977) in analysis of 'the world' of television, and John Ellis (1982) with the notion of the segment. In the USA, 'the viewing-strip' was proposed as the relevant unit by Newcomb and Hirsch in their 1983 essay. These attempts to theorise how we may both grasp the *continuousness* of television and integrate the *experience* of viewing into analysis can, I think, be most usefully supplemented by the deployment of the notion of 'mode of address', which allows us to specify, at a formal level, the way in which the television text is always constructed as continuously there *for someone*. The differing identities posed in these interpellations (child, citizen, hobby enthusiast, consumer, etc.) and the overlapping and contradictory ways in which we are called to watch form one of many sites for further research.[8] An insistence on the analytic importance of these moments – continuousness and mode of address – gives some access to the inscription of television's institutional basis in its formal operations.

The difficulty of defining or constituting the television text is accentuated by the privacy of television usage and the absence of an academy concerned to regulate both the production and consumption of television.[9] These factors tend to privilege the perception of diverse modes of engagement with the television text as a specific and defining feature of television viewing. There are two problems with this view. As Paddy Scannell (1988a) has argued, this is surely a feature of broadcast media rather than television as such.[10] Secondly, we should not forget that people have always engaged variously with all cultural texts. Many books bought are not read, many paintings in art galleries not looked at; much music is used as background – but the institutions of high culture, the academy, the museum, patronage, the auction room, have historically codified, both explicitly and implicitly, the proper mode of engagement with the text – be it a (sublime) mountain view or a lyric poem. Although many people may not engage in these proper ways, critical and aesthetic discussion is usually conducted on the assumption – or negotiation – of this type of engagement. This is not to polemicise for and against particular ways of watching television. It is to point out that, although the historical research of writers such as William Boddy (1985) and Lynn Spigel (1986) shows us that there was originally considerable uncertainty about how to understand the place of television in the home, the institutions of television are primarily concerned with maximising audiences and revenue, not with the codifying of proper ways to watch.

An aesthetic of television would thus, in some ways, have to be an anti-aesthetic to be adequate to its object and the practices constituting it. Engaging with the popular, the domestic and the functional, it undercuts the very constitution of classical aesthetic judgement.

The difficulty which I have outlined above of constituting the television text as an object of study is compounded by a series of critical shifts since the 1960s, which I now want to sketch before returning to these problems. I am thus arguing that there are qualities of television as a medium (and these can be qualities of usage, rather than essential qualities) which predispose one to abandon text for audience, and that this tendency has been much facilitated by a range of different, but obviously related, critical trajectories. The audience has come to dominance in Britain in five main ways: (1) through the changing paradigms in literary studies, (2) through the growth of cultural, and particularly subcultural, studies, (3) through particular logics in the development of film and television studies, (4) through the increasingly fashionable theorisation of postmodernity, and (5) through the impact of feminist methodologies on academic discourse. I will deal with these five areas more and less schematically.

THE MODES OF DISPERSAL OF THE TELEVISION TEXT

I wish here to examine what has happened to the television text as an object of study in recent years. I want to trace, very schematically, the different ways in which the television text as an object of study has been under assault, and to argue for the importance of retaining the notion of text as an analytic category.

Literary studies, and my next category, cultural studies, I want only to reference. Catherine Belsey's 1980 *Critical Practice* (and indeed, to a certain extent, the Methuen New Accents list), Terry Eagleton's 1983 *Literary Theory* and Raymond Williams's 1981 and 1983 accounts of the crisis in Cambridge English provide, in their shared references (which is not to equate their arguments), a patterning of the transformation of English and literary studies since the 1960s.[11] For our purposes, what is most significant is not so much the assault on the canon as the elevation of the act of reading, over the text, as the point of meaning production. The ascendancy of (different) theories of reading and reception has contributed to a radical devaluation of the notion of the text.

Ethnographic sociology and the study of subcultures, perhaps best exemplified by the 1975 Centre for Contemporary Cultural Studies' *Resistance through Rituals*, Paul Willis's 1977 *Learning to Labour* and Hebdige's 1979 *Subculture: The Meaning of Style*, also worked to validate the role of the cultural consumer in the construction of meaning. The apparent, obvious or intended meanings of a whole series of commodities were revealed as transformed within subcultural practice.

In relation to film and television studies I want to make my points through observations of trends at the two International Television Studies Conferences (ITSC) held in London in 1984 and 1986.[12] There are, of course, always ongoing debates in particular intellectual fields, which sometimes gel into apparently obvious sets of issues and concerns at particular historical moments in the academy. There are also always more and less fashionable and attractive areas for research. Although not the only shift in parameters of debate, there was, between the 1984 and 1986 conferences, a clear move in interest from what is happening on the screen to what is happening in front of it – from text to audience.

This is not in any way to underestimate the amount of research that has already been conducted into the behaviour and readings of the audience, both in Britain/Europe and in the United States. It is to suggest that the 1986 conference provides a convenient, if arbitrary, way of marking the entry of new and different interests into audience research. The 1984 conference took place just at the very end of a period of ten years or so of British culturalist analyses of popular film and television texts.

These analyses had, in the main, what one could call a political motivation.

For a range of quite complexly articulated reasons, including the (semi-) institutionalisation of film and television studies within the academy, the rightward shift in the British political scene, the ageing of the generation radicalised in 1968, not to mention the institutional convenience of textual analysis, we had in Britain the burgeoning of academic analyses of popular texts which sought to discredit both the left-pessimist despair over and the high cultural dismissal of mass and popular cultures. From the mid-1970s onwards, 'progressive' academics in these fields became increasingly involved in the production of what could be termed 'the redemptive reading'. Film noir, 1950s colour melodrama and television programmes such as *The Sweeney, Coronation Street* and *Crossroads* were among the texts addressed.[13]

The point about the 'redemptive reading' is that it is not a simple populist embrace of the entertainment forms of late capitalism. The purely populist moment – although of course there has always been a straightforwardly populist strain contributing to the arguments for this sort of work – comes at the end of this period roughly contemporary with the shift to the audience which I am describing, and, in popular cultural terms, with Madonna's rise to stardom. The redemptive reading is not populist in that it starts with an acceptance of the uncongenial politics of whatever cultural text – for it is primarily a political reading – and then finds, at the least, incoherences and contradiction, and, at the most fully articulated, subtexts of revolt. Partly because of the centrality of Hollywood to the constitution of film studies as a discipline, it is here that this form of critical practice is at its most sophisticated and elaborated. The notorious category 'e' of *Cahiers du Cinéma* ('films which seem at first sight to belong firmly within the ideology and to be completely under its sway, but which turn out to be so only in an ambiguous manner') (Comolli and Narboni 1969/1976: 27) is of course a category of reception ('If one reads the film obliquely, looking for symptoms . . .'), unlike all the other categories in their influential 1969 taxonomy. The famous account of *Young Mr. Lincoln* reveals what was at stake for cinephiles when ideological correctness became the principal critical criterion. The loved object, Hollywood cinema, which would have had to be jettisoned under the regime of the 'right on', could be retrieved if its textual (here standing for ideological) coherence could be demonstrated to be only apparent (Editors of *Cahiers du Cinéma* 1970).

The redemptive reading frequently meets with a certain scepticism, a doubt that *real* readers really read like that. The 1984 ITSC marked a suitable final appearance for the dominance of this type of textual analysis – the theoretical position had now to be supported by research into how non-academic readers read. In the 1984 ITSC the conference strand that was bulging at the seams was that of 'textual analysis'. In 1986 submissions to this area were radically reduced, and there was increased evidence of qualitative audience research. This 'new' audience work, which comes partly from the necessity of testing the type of textual hypotheses referred to above, and is often influenced by the ascendancy of reception theory in literary studies, met, often in ignorance, the older, more quantitative traditions of mass communications research. As Jane Feuer observed in her 1986 paper, the television text has been displaced by the text of audience – a much more various and diverse text – and the enormous conceptual and methodological problems entailed.

We are beginning to see a whole new body of research into how people view television, and this research functions to further disperse the text as an analytic category. We can now, following the work of, for example, Peter Collett, Ann Gray, Dorothy Hobson and David Morley (to take British examples), argue only that people watch television in extremely hetero-geneous ways. People watch alone, with intimates, with strangers. They watch while they're doing something else, even when they're in another room. The notion of 'flow', made less harmonious through practices such as channel zapping, has to be supplemented by the major variable of audience-presence-for-the-text. But how can we theorise this in a way which allows us to do more than accumulate an ethnography of particular practices?

With the 'everything is everything else' of 'postmodernity' we have also lost any innocent notion of what might constitute the television text through a recognition of the proliferation, across different media, of potential textual sites. At one level this is a phenomenon of marketing and product licensing, and of the international character of image markets, to paraphrase Mattelart *et al.* (1984), at another of the deep penetration of television into our daily lives. Thus we can buy videos of early episodes of *Coronation Street*, read novels based on any of the soaps, overhear and join in conversations about soap characters, and read about predicted narrative events in newspapers, as for instance in Brunt (1983). Again, what is posed for us is the question of how we organise our perception of these issues rather than the self-evident, textual destruction that some have found.

Tony Bennett and Janet Woollacott (1987) have done exemplary work on what they call 'the Bond phenomenon', in which they examine the many moments, textual existences and transformations of James Bond. They set out 'to demonstrate, in a practical way rather than just theoretically, that "the text itself" is an inconceivable object'. Their achievement, I think, is to prove not that the text itself is an inconceivable object but that the choice of what is recognised as constituting 'a' text, consciously or not, is a political as well as a critical matter. It is around this issue that the contemporary struggles to dominate the critical field will be fought.

Literary analysis has as one of its specialisms the identification of reference and allusion. Modernism was partly modern in its use of quotation and the assumed knowledge of other texts. But the intertextuality of television is in some ways more radical, without the central, organising drive of the author or, as I have argued earlier, the specific hierarchies of form given by an established aesthetic. This quality, the promiscuous and nearly parodic self-referentiality of television, is not quite specific to television in a way that could define the medium. It is a quality – along with others also attributable to television – seen as characteristic of a postmodern era.[14] The recognition of television and video as major agents of our understanding of contemporary time and space, indeed, along with the computer, of the transformation of these categories in everyday life, is essential, and potentially more useful than the analysis of single programmes as if they were poems. But I'm not sure that this perception requires that we throw up our hands and say, 'But it's all so ephemeral/such pastiche/without reference/depthless/intertextual that there's nothing to analyse.'

The final trajectory through which we can trace a dispersal of the text has its origins in feminist critical initiatives. This is of particular relevance because women have historically figured as preferred objects (I use the term advisedly) of audience research. Women soap opera viewers and listeners have proved particularly attractive to both commercial and academic researchers in ways that are relevant here.

If we accept that soap opera is in some ways the paradigmatic television genre (domestic, continuous, contemporary, episodic, repetitive, fragmented and aural), we have also to ask why it has received until recently so little serious critical attention. Soap opera has been neglected except, ironically, in terms of the investigation of its effects on audiences, because it has not been considered textually worthy. We find, in the massive research on the 'effects' of soap viewing, the repeated pathologising of the audience. Robert Allen (1985: 128–9) puts this nicely when he writes of soap opera viewers not being granted the capacity for aesthetic distance from the text.[15] Dorothy Hobson (1982) in particular has also argued for the key significance of the social status of soap opera fans in determining the aesthetic status of the form. Feminist criticism has taken an interesting path in relation to the genre.

Firstly, in a relatively short period, feminist criticism has moved from its initial repudiation of women's genres to the analysis and defence of traditionally feminine forms such as soap opera, melodrama and romance.[16] This process, as I have argued at greater length elsewhere (Brunsdon 1986a), has necessarily involved the attempt to analyse, and enter imaginatively into, the pleasures of these forms for their audiences. Sometimes motivated by a desire to defend the audience and its pleasures, sometimes concerned principally to use cultural texts as sites where the constitution of contemporary femininities can be analysed, this work necessarily demands the investigation of the responses of audiences or readers or viewers to the relevant texts. Thus, much of the new audience research to which I have already referred has been specifically concerned with 'feminine' texts, female audiences and feminist methodologies.

It is the notion of feminist methodology which points to the other important element contributed by feminist criticism. This is the use of autobiographical data and the validation of the use of 'I' in academic discourse. I am, of course, simplifying and generalising to make my point – the 'I' also enters academic discourse through other routes, and the exploration of subjectivities constituted in subordination has been essential to groups other than women and fragments the simple gender category. Here, however, the point is that the particular value set on the recounting and exploration of personal experience within second-wave feminism, and the recognition of the extremely contradictory nature of experience and identity, have worked to construct autobiographical data as 'proper' data.[17] Because the definition of feminist methodologies frequently involves particular political understandings of the way in which the researcher herself inhabits the gender category 'woman', we have in much feminist research a certain fluidity of pronouns, a blurring of the separation of the object and the subject of research. This blurring is also a feature of some sociologies; what I wish to do here is to point to the peculiar force that the first-person pronoun has in some feminist discourse.

This 'I' of some feminist discourse is a rather complicated affair in terms of to and for whom it speaks. Sometimes we have the simple use of autobiographical data, which are not explicitly articulated with either the assumed or researched experiences of 'other women'. Sometimes we have an 'I, the researcher' who sees herself as part of a larger category 'we women', *on whose behalf, for whose good* and *to whom* she will, at different moments and simultaneously, speak. There will thus be the validation of autobiographical material and a feminine 'I' over and above any unitary and inherent meaning of the text, but the status and identity for this reader or writer validated over the text fluctuate.

The point could be seen as a paradoxical one, in that feminist intervention in a particular academic field turns out to reproduce exactly the existing structure or patterning of the field. The traditional approach to soap opera within media research was to focus on audience rather than text. Although differently motivated, and ascribing different moral qualities to the two terms, *text* and *audience*, feminist research, also, has moved from the 'bad' text to the 'good' audience.

CONCLUSION

I am not trying to argue for the reinstatement of what we might call the pre-audience text. Through the different routes which I have tried to outline, I think we can see some of the reasons for the growth in ethnographic and qualitative audience research. These include the fundamental transformations of adjacent, and often formative, intellectual fields. The discrediting of a simple cross/tick political aesthetic of popular texts – as if that is all they merit – was overdue. The investigation of the activities of viewers reveals the variety of contexts and modes of viewing which prevent the television text ever being, in any way, a simple, self-evident object for analysis.

Similarly we have to accept the potentially infinite number or flow of textual sites. Together, I think these recognitions begin to lead us to the postmodern haven of insignificance, and I would, in this context, characterise the pursuit of the audience as a search for authenticity, for an anchoring moment in a sea of signification. Just like television, academics are obsessed with 'real people'.

So firstly, I want to argue that, difficult as it may be, we have to retain a notion of the television text. That is, *without* the guarantees of common sense, or the authority of a political teleology, and *with* the recognition of the potentially infinite proliferation of textual sites, and the agency of the always already social reader, in a range of contexts, it is still necessary – and possible – to construct a televisual object of study – and judgement.

Here I think we can most usefully learn from the practices of television itself. The broadcast world is structured through regularity and repetition. Time-shift video recording alters the viewer's position in relation to this regularity and repetition, but I'm not sure that it fundamentally transforms the broadcast structure of the day and week. Although it is tempting to start with a distinction between viewing alone and viewing with others (and recent research suggests that this might be particularly important in relation to understanding women's pleasures), the primary distinction seems to be between modes of viewing which are repeated on a regular basis and uncommon or unfamiliar modes of viewing (which thus incorporates the solitary/in-company distinction).[18]

The need to specify context and mode of viewing in any textual discussion, and the awareness that these factors may be more determining of the experience of a text than any textual feature, do not, in and of themselves, either eliminate the text as a meaningful category or render all texts the same. I may normally watch *Brookside* with one other person, and indeed prefer watching it in this familiar way, but I can still recognise the programme when alone or with a large group doing something else. The fact that the text is only and always realised in historically and contextually situated practices of reading does not demand that we should collapse these categories into each other.

Secondly, I do want to raise questions about the overall political shape or weighting of this concentration on what we might call the post-1960s audience. Although frequently informed by a desire to investigate, rather than judge, other people's pleasures, this very avoidance of judgement seems somehow to recreate the old patterns of aesthetic domination and subordination, and to pathologise the audience. Because issues of judgement are never brought out into the open, but always kept, as it were, under the seminar table, criteria involved can never be interrogated. It is for this reason that I wish to retain or construct the analytic category of the television text, for if we dissolve this category into the audience we further inhibit the development of a useful television criticism and a television aesthetic. This is difficult enough without collapsing bad programmes into bad audiences. I do not wish to argue that television studies should be devoted to discriminating between 'good' and 'bad' programmes, but I do want to insist that most academics involved in television studies are using qualitative criteria, however expressed or repressed, and that the constitution of the criteria involved should be the subject of explicit debate. To return to Bourdieu. Only the inheritors of legitimate culture, researching other people's pleasures, pleasures they may well share, can afford to keep quiet about the good and bad of television. They – we – through years of training have access to a very wide range of cultural production. Watching television *and* reading books about postmodernism is different from watching television and reading tabloid newspapers, even if everybody concerned watched the same television.

What we find, very frequently, in audience data is that the audience is making the best of a bad job. The problem of always working with what people are, of necessity, watching is that we don't really ever address the something else – what people might like to watch (and I don't mean to imply that these other desires simply exist without an object, but that is another paper). The recognition of the creativity and competences of the audience must, I think, be mobilised back into relation to the television text and the demands that are made on programme-makers for a diverse and plural programming which is adequate to the needs, desires and pleasures of these audiences. Otherwise, however well intentioned, our work reproduces and elaborates the dominant paradigm in which the popular is the devalued term. Having started with 'What is good television?' I would like to finish with 'What are we going to do about bad television?' Nothing, if we're not prepared to admit it exists.

Chapter 9

Problems with quality†

The British government's 1988 White Paper *Broadcasting in the '90s: Competition, Choice and Quality* (HMSO, Cmd. 517), published shortly before the 'opening of the (British) skies' to satellite television, has occasioned a rather unusual flurry of discussion about quality in television.[1] This seems to me both welcome and necessary. If, as a range of commentators have argued, one of the distinctive features of the White Paper is the disparity between its rhetorical aims, 'Competition, Choice and Quality', and its policy proposals, then public intervention by those committed to values opposed by this government is essential, and may actively shape broadcasting in the 1990s.[2] (In this connection it is worth recalling that the sustained campaign by the Independent Film-makers Association prior to the setting up of Channel 4 did have an effect on the eventual remit of the Channel, even though it may not have been quite what was desired.)[3]

The debate is currently joined mainly by 'interested parties' – broadcasters, the ITV companies, investors in satellite technology, etc. With broadcasting, however, we are all interested parties. My hypothesis here will be that 'progressive forces', particularly those working in the media or cultural studies fields, are severely handicapped in this debate by their eschewal of any interrogation of what is, and could be, meant by 'quality' in a discussion of television.[4] 'Quality', for some good reasons, has become a bad word. The consequence of this is that only the most conservative ideas about quality are circulating, and will therefore win the day.

I want to examine some of the available discourses of judgement in relation to television, and to try very schematically to point to some of the difficulties of entering this debate, while still arguing that it should be entered. I don't have answers to the problems I raise, but the White Paper has given an urgency to the formulation of issues in the development of film and television studies in Britain with which I have been concerned for some time.

I want to start with the juxtaposition of different practices of judgement.

†First published in *Screen* 31, 1 (1990).

PRACTICAL QUALITY 1

Example (a)

My local paper offers the following star system guide for films broadcast on television:

**** Excellent
*** Worth watching
** Video for a rainy day
* Forget it

Example (b)

In the production folder which they have to submit with a completed project video, some students I was involved in examining pointed out that nothing in their three years of study of film and television theory had indicated to them the criteria which would be likely to be useful in the assessment of their practical work. The examiners' discussion of the practical work was indeed marked by phrases which condensed aesthetic and professional assumptions, such as 'That's a nice bit of editing', 'Good use of sound', which one would be hard pressed to find in a volume of *Movies and Methods* or a copy of *Screen*. Our discussion of the student work was comparative and evaluative. We were concerned with the ambition and coherence of the original conception of each project, the organisation across audio and visual channels and the effective execution of the work. And we did indeed have opinions. But they were not opinions, particularly in the judgement of the execution of the videos, that the project of *Screen* in the last fifteen or so years could be said to have much refined.

These two instances of critical judgement in practice have similarities and differences. We could take the first as an abbreviated example of Bourdieu's 1979 'barbaric' taste code, in that there is a clear notion of function at work, articulated through an exchange of time spent for pleasure gained. This is clear, not so much from the extremes of the one- and four-star classifications, but from the 'Worth' of three stars, where the expenditure of time is clearly weighed, where we are in fact warned that we will notice time passing, instead of forgetting time as in the 'Excellent' films – there will be longueurs, but in the end it will be worth sticking with. In the two-star classification, the longueurs have left the television screen, and have moved into the viewer's life – 'a rainy day', from which the film may prove to be a distraction. So we have here that continuity between art and life, that demand that art should be useful, which Bourdieu sees as characteristic of the taste of the dominated classes. The particular use of film here is in its capacity to facilitate the forgetting of everyday life. This sense of weary time may also make it

7. The news studio: ITN for Channel 4 News. Channels 3, 4 and 5 will all be expected to show high quality news in peak viewing periods (paragraphs 6.11, 6.13, 6.21, 6.23).

8. Filming an independent production on location (Picture Palace Productions/Channel 4). The Government envisages that the role of independent producers will continue to grow (Chapter X).

9. BBC children's drama: "Chronicles of Narnia." The continuing special role of BBC TV services is described in paragraph 3.2.

Photographs by courtesy of the IBA, the BBC, the Cable Authority, BSB and Channel 4.

19 Page of illustrations from *Competition, Choice and Quality*

relevant to mention Conrad Lodziak's 1986 argument that it has been a mistaken endeavour for television and communication research to look to the analysis of television programmes to understand why people watch them. Instead, he argues, the statistical distribution of viewing can be understood only within a wider grasp of the differential distribution of disposable income and time. Crudely, the people who watch most television are those who can't afford to do anything else.

Jostein Gripsrud makes a related point, in an account of research into the reception of *Dynasty* in Norway (although in a quite different argument) when he emphasises that the international dominance of American television, and the production company's pre-broadcast publicity, rather than the specificities of the programme, could be seen as determinant in the success of the show:

> one might say that the introduction of *Dynasty* delivered a specific kind of *object* for an accumulated need or desire which in principle also might have been met by *other* conceivable objects, for instance an aesthetically and ideologically different form of serialized melodramatic saga.
>
> (Gripsrud 1988: 7–8)

Both these arguments may serve to remind us that high viewing figures do not of themselves tell us much about how and why programmes are watched. They also return us to the idea of function, which is an essential element in any exercise of judgement. 'Commodities of the fancy' serve different needs and desires, from killing time to stretching fantasy, but the commodities which currently do this are not necessarily the only ones which could. While newspaper television guides would not be very useful if they were endlessly hankering after unmade films and serials, it is a different matter for legislators, programme-makers and cultural analysts to construct policies which are based only on what is already on television, or to take the 'having-been-watched-ness' of a programme as a guarantee of the spirit in which it was watched.

The evaluation of student practical work is institutionally quite different. The exercise is located within higher education, one of the sites of the production of difference in taste codes, where what is most valued, in Bourdieu's argument, is that which is located furthest from the realm of necessity, or obvious function. The students were correct to point out that (non-practical) film and television studies orthodoxy in the British academy rarely explicitly engages with issues of critical evaluation, except perhaps politically in the varied guises and defences of the 'progressive' and the 'popular'. The evacuation of the explicit discussion of value does not of course mean that value is not taught. The turmoil over the canon in literary studies was precisely a dispute about the institutionalisation of value-judgements in syllabuses, courses and anthologies, an institutionalisation which requires no one, at any stage, to say explicitly 'white Anglo-American male writers are best because . . .'.[5]

The terrain is slightly more rugged in film and television studies because both media attract mass audiences, while their novelty and their industrial and technological infrastructures have functioned to disqualify them from the status of art. Thus the historical debates of film studies – 'Is film an art form?' 'In what does the essence or specificity of the medium inhere?' 'Should the director be seen as *auteur*?' – are partly debates about the extent to which the new medium can be understood within the traditional frameworks for the discussion of high art. Television studies faces even greater difficulties, particularly since the origins of much television scholarship lie in sociology and mass communications. The consequence of simply annexing film and television to traditional aesthetic discourse is to do extraordinary violence to any inclusive understanding of the media. This is the case, for example, when television is reduced to its plays and literary adaptations, and subjected to a sort of sub-literary criticism. The recalcitrance of these media (also apparent, of course, with photography) to traditional aesthetic discourse means that any canons are peculiarly hybrid.[6] It has also been one of the causes of quite fundamental transformation in aesthetic discourse, from 'The Work of Art in the Age of Mechanical Reproduction' to the dissolution of all distinctions in postmodernity – but that is another story. Here my point is that the hybrid and unstable canons of film studies could have led to the foregrounding of issues of taste, judgement and value in the discipline, but that, if anything, the move has been in the opposite direction, with these issues becoming increasingly illegitimate. The case is more pronounced in television studies, where texts that could form the canon are often ephemeral, and pre-video history is hard to come by. The marked populism which has partly sustained the discipline in recent years in Britain, which I discuss below, has contributed to a refusal of anything other than political evaluation.

To make my argument convincing I do, at this stage, need to construct a full history of the institutionalisation of film and television studies in Britain, written with a history of criticism in these fields, and the changing theoretical paradigms of the humanities, within a broader political history. I cannot offer this here, with its necessary attention to key books like *The Popular Arts* (Hall and Whannel 1964) and *The Long Revolution* (Williams 1961) or to journals like *Sequence, Movie* and latterly *Screen*.[7] Such a history would also chart the particular pressures exercised by the demand to demonstrate that the popular entertainment media are worthy of study, and the key, but different, roles of sociology and English in establishing a base; the influence of continental philosophical traditions on disciplines anxious to prove their difference from simple 'reviewing'; the importance of the British Film Institute's Education Department; the political impulse to study popular, not elite forms, to affirm that 'culture is ordinary'; the general shift away from explicitly evaluative criticism in both Britain and the USA; and the significance of the increasing employment market in audiovisual industries in underpinning growth in the study of the media. All I can offer here, however, is an hypothesis that it is the semi-institutionalisation of film and television studies which makes them exciting to teach, but that this novelty has its own paradoxes.

I can briefly expand this point by using Bourdieu's ideas to argue about the origins of film and television studies as disciplines. I am aware that there are problems with Bourdieu's formulations, particularly (ironically, for my argument) around his positive valuation of dominated taste.[8] I am more interested in the overall shape of an argument than whether it is watertight – I am sure there are lots of holes. I am also aware that film and television studies in Britain has developed in more than one way and differs accordingly. The attraction of teaching film was that it seemed to offer relevance and engagement to students. Precisely because it was not a legitimate subject, there was a chance of involving in discussion students who were normally bored or passive. For the purposes of the present argument, it was because students often held strong opinions about films – films, as opposed, for instance, to the Romantic Poets, represented a 'felt' realm of value – that films were attractive to teachers anxious to develop literacy, articulacy and powers of argument and analysis. But of course, to learn these things – to learn from films – this original value-laden universe must be left. It is functional as the point of engagement, but, once discussion is joined, new skills must be learnt, so that personal disagreements can be explored in impersonal ways. In Bourdieu's terms, only the student who learns to make the transition from barbarous to pure taste has truly learnt. As with the individual, so with the discipline.

I am not arguing that we should rewrite our syllabuses to re-install evaluative criticism as our central concern, but I do think we should pay some attention to the concealed ways in which we are teaching evaluation, and I feel an increasing concern about the types of orthodoxy which are developing in the as yet relatively young disciplines of film, television and cultural studies. Theoretical work which in the early 1970s was enabling, allowing students and teachers to see how their disciplines were constituted, is now installed in place of those critical orthodoxies which it once described and assaulted. Concepts like 'hegemony' are exercised hegemonically in higher education syllabuses. 'Bourgeois ideology', long banished by *Screen*, is dutifully deployed by students who want to work in advertising. The attack on liberalism, and the philosophical dispatch of humanism which accompanied much of the embrace of what in the USA is simply called 'Theory', have all too frequently involved a blindness to institutional power. As I have argued above, the absence of a canon that can be argued to be sanctified by centuries does not mean that judgements are not made, and the disciplines are sufficiently mature to have some explicit discussion about the history of criticism and the type of criteria in play. The fact that many of the impulses which propel the study of popular forms such as film and television also involve the repudiation of the class and cultural privileges which partly constitutes the history of high art (and thus aesthetic discourse) does not mean that judgements cannot be made on grounds other than the political.[9] It is not the exercise of judgement which is oppressive but the withholding of its grounds and the consequent incapacitating of opponents and alternative positions. We do not defeat the social power which presents certain critical judgements as natural and inevitable by refusing to make critical judgements.

SUBJECTIVE FACTORS

As the very title of the White Paper includes the word *quality*, some attempts at definition have had to be made. The recognition of what are generally referred to as 'subjective factors' has, however, proved a powerful inhibition. I want to look here at some of the available contemporary discourses in which quality figures, and, as a preliminary, I should like to attempt to unpick what is at stake in the notion of 'subjective factors', a notion which is often used to explain why there are disagreements about what would constitute quality in television. The type of usage I have in mind is exemplified by the report from *The Independent* (15 June 1989), in which there is a discussion of the possible legal ramifications of a quality requirement in the award of franchises. The imagined conjunction of legal and aesthetic discourse raises interesting issues, and (*contra* the views expressed in this report) is not without precedent: there are affiliations with both obscenity law (artistic merit) and compensation cases (loss of quality of life awards – so much for a limb, a sense, a spouse). What I wish to do here though, is to argue that there are always issues of power at stake in notions such as quality and judgement – Quality for whom?, Judgement by whom?, On whose behalf? – and that in certain instances the invocation of subjective factors (personal taste, preference, subjective judgement) as the ground on which judgements of quality cannot be generalised blurs the role of structural and institutional factors in the formation of these judgements.

'Subjective factors', which propose an equality of subjectivity for all individuals, are mobilised within a culture or society in which there is a differential distribution of the possibilities and capacities for individuals to generalise about personal tastes. So some subjective factors seem more subjective than others.

This first point, which does not stand alone, can be exemplified by the much-parodied British upper-class usage of the pronoun 'one' where less privileged individuals would offer 'I'. In this grammatical practice we see laid out for us a world in which certain forms of subjectivity exist in an impersonal, universalising form. This 'objective subjectivity' is paralleled by the invocation of transcendent and universal values within aesthetic discourse to produce a pantheon of great works over the ages.[10]

I don't at all want to deny that different individuals do have different tastes. As Simon Frith (1988b) has argued in relation to popular music, these tastes are experienced as integral parts of the individual's identity. But in addition to this recognition we need to articulate both a sociology of taste – there are demonstrable links between social origins or position or trajectory and taste sets (a fact that advertisers have had no difficulty with for many years) – and the existence of more and less arcane hierarchies of taste in every cultural field. As Bourdieu's work indicates, particularly his 'topographies' of distinctions made in cultural fields, these hierarchies, which are at their most elaborated in art forms with long histories – music, rather than cinema, for example – have an existence independent of subjective factors. Thus most people in western culture know that classical music is higher up the music hierarchy than reggae, whatever their personal tastes, or indeed their opinions about this ranking. In the contexts of taste provided by these hierarchies certain taste formations appear more eccentric – subjective – than others. To have preferences which run against the hierarchy involves people in endless self-justification ('I know it's rubbish but . . .'),[11] or else in the polemical assertions of other hierarchies (reggae as part of an international black music . . .). These assertions and justifications, in their very elaboration, reveal themselves as non-dominant, subjective judgements.[12] Speaking from the periphery, as Julien and Mercer (1988) have argued, requires more discussion of place than speaking from the centre, where it can be taken for granted.

So my first point is that there is more than one form of inequality between the subjects of subjective factors, and that there is more than one reason why some judgements are perceived as more subjective than others.

I would like immediately to juxtapose my unease with the formulation 'subjective factors' (a suspicion that it often involves the suppression of structural features) with a coinage of Barbara Herrnstein Smith's which may be more useful. In the context of a discussion about ideas of value within literary studies, and an argument to establish the radical contingency of all aesthetic value, Herrnstein Smith uses the notion of 'folk-relativism':

> It may be noted that the latter – that is, the normative mechanisms within a community that suppress divergence and tend to obscure as well as deny the contingency of value – will always have, as their counterpart, a *counter*mechanism that permits a recognition of that contingency and a more or less genial acknowledgement of the inevitability of divergence; hence the ineradicability, in spite of the efforts of establishment axiology, of what might be called folk-relativism: 'Chacun à son gout'; 'De gustibus . . .'; 'One man's meat is another's poison'; and so forth.
>
> (Herrnstein Smith 1984: 21)

The advantage of this formulation is that it is philosophically clearer with its invocation of relativism, and incorporates notions of power, although in a consciously archaic mode, in the use of 'folk'. Herrnstein Smith's definition makes plain that she understands the proverbs she quotes as bearing witness to the social and practical necessity of recognising different tastes in daily life. What I want to do is to dance on the pinhead which I think I can discern in the abyss of relativism. I want to argue that the debate about quality must be joined, not because dominant criteria of judgement are correct (or indeed that oppositional criteria, were we able to formulate them, would carry any objective guarantee), nor because texts necessarily have an ahistorical, intrinsic value, but precisely because, outside certain very limited fields, dominant criteria are in chaos, and because it is through debate and institutionalisation of ideas in, for instance, laws and courses, that ideas of quality are established. That there are no guarantees should function not to inhibit discussion but to predispose us to the promotion of variety and diversity as the single most important principle to extend and preserve – variety and diversity, that is, of both production and audiences. The extent to which this requires that certain sorts of programme-making be protected from the imperatives of the marketplace is one of the key issues for policy debates. Of equal importance is the question of the extent to which this type of protection can be extended in ways that are not paternalistic. These debates about policy cannot be entered without attention to the separate, but necessarily related, issue of cultural value.

If we take as a starting point, as Herrnstein Smith (1984) has argued, the idea that relationships between classification and function are a necessary element in the process of judgement – something that we all do whenever we channel-hop in search of an image or sound which we can identify as likely, or most likely, to satisfy – then it is clear that television, as a domestic medium, offers an enormous range of possibilities. Flicking through channels searching for something to watch involves a very speedy placing of images and sounds into generic classes.

Sometimes the identification may be more specific – a particular personality, actor or show – but the generic recognition is immediately functional: 'talk show, no; news, no; ad, maybe . . .'. Classification shapes expectation and allows judgement of the extent to which certain functions are being fulfilled. Sometimes the decision to stay with or return to a channel is made because it is not immediately clear what type of programme it is. Only after it is generically identified do we make the decision to stay or go, and there can often be a second decision as in 'Sit-com yes . . . (pause) . . . but not this sit-com, unless there is nothing better'. Here textual classification exists with contingent and personal functions for the audience member – the type of satisfaction any particular individual is looking for at any particular time. Thus the rejected sit-com may be watched because alternatives are generically or specifically unacceptable, even if, on traditional or professional criteria, the alternatives may be 'better'. There is a way in which 'folk-relativism' offers a model for desirable television schedules – the provision of a range of possibilities, of something for everyone all the time. Certainly propaganda for the proposed legislation stresses increased opportunities for choice. (This seems clearly desirable – whether it is likely is another matter.) My point, though, is that individual audience members (when they are able to) make their own judgements of quality, and that these are often highly context-bound and radically contingent. The proper place for notions such as 'All judgements of quality are subjective' is not as the justification for abandoning attempts to differentiate between programmes but as a reason why there should be a wide variety of different types of programmes to choose from.

There are thus two points to make. Firstly, as the broadcasters themselves argue, the generic diversity of television must be taken into account in discussions of quality, but not in ways which makes quality 'genre-specific', creating certain 'sink' or 'trash' genres of which demands are not made. Secondly, that in answer to the question 'To what is the judgement of quality to be ascribed?' we should privilege the overall provision rather than individual programmes.

DISCOURSES OF QUALITY

What is of interest when thinking about established canons and criteria of value in relation to television is partly the novelty of the medium, and partly its dependence on other art forms. It is this novelty – and the accompanying absence of an institutionally and academically ratified tradition and a history – which contributes to, for example, the legal quagmire predicted above. I doubt there would be quite the same problem if judgement was sought on the relative quality of Mozart and Bros. I don't mean to dismiss fifty-odd years of programme-making at a stroke – but, compared with Milton studies, sit-com studies has a long way to go in terms of institutional presence. I have argued at more length elsewhere about television's peculiar place in relation to established aesthetic discourse (see Chapter 8). It is both excluded from these discourses and formed by them. Thus jostling to define quality television we have several main contenders, which can be outlined schematically.

Traditional aesthetic discourse

This tends, for obvious reasons, to concentrate on televised opera, dance, drama and music, with excursions to arts magazines or profiles.[13] There are conservative and avant-garde variants of this strategy and I discuss the former in the section *Brideshead in the Crown* below.

Professional codes and practices

These are highly internally differentiated. While I cannot discuss them here fully, available production studies allow us to hypothesise that there would be institutional and generic differentiations (BBC, ITV, Channel 4; current affairs, soaps, light entertainment, etc.), with very fine appreciations of what has been achieved with what production constraints in what circumstances.[14] Within these differentiations I think it is possible to separate out some key hierarchies and sites of judgement. Thus there are generic hierarchies in which current affairs programmes are 'more important' than soaps, and ratings can signify 'quality', or its opposite. Much of British television is dominated by a sub-naturalist aesthetic which seems to be partly function-led (crudely, good sound is clear sound).[15] This category also encompasses more strictly technical discussions which condense aesthetic assumptions – for example, the relative virtues of film and video for drama production, or the innovatory use, in 1982, of steadicam in *Brookside*. The trade magazines are a main source for the establishing of the main contours and changes in these discourses. The involvement of broadcasters in the Campaign for Quality Television has provided one site where these discourses have been given a more public form.[16]

Realist paradigms

By this I mean the discussion of anything from news bulletins to sport in which key criteria are those of adequacy, objectivity, immediacy.[17] This paradigm is used by professionals, 'the general public' and academics. Thus, for example, much work in mass communications research and television studies is within this paradigm: 'Is the news biased?' 'Does it show us only effects not causes?', etc. I would see the work of the Media Studies Group at the Birmingham Centre for Contemporary Cultural Studies, including the *Nationwide* work (Brunsdon and Morley, 1978), as being mainly within this paradigm. Criticism of the 'representation' of particular social groups (striking miners, working-class communities in soap operas, black characters in crimes series) is also frequently within this paradigm.[18] Thus, although its philosophical home is with non-fiction programming, it is frequently the central critical criterion used in discussion of fiction pro-grammes, and is one of the dominant common-sense aesthetics of this culture – as in 'But I come from the East End, and it's not a bit like Walford'.

Entertainment and leisure codes

These are more difficult to locate, mainly because of their lack of elaborated legitimacy. This lack of legitimacy may be due to the fact that many of these judgements are made casually, in speech, rather than in writing. Paddy Scannell (1988b) touches on this in his discussion of 'The communicative ethos in broadcasting' when he discusses the social currency of the question, 'Did you see?'. Ien Ang (1989), discussing the role and pleasure of fantasy in television viewing, opens one way of approaching areas quite untouched by political and realist criteria. Richard Dyer (1973 and 1985), whose work on utopia uses non-psychoanalytic frameworks, has consistently tried to address light entertainment, as has Andy Medhurst in his columns in *The Listener*. What has perhaps produced more comment is the way in which these codes are increasingly being collapsed into and constructed as the practices of consumption, and so magazines like *Marxism Today* have become associated with notions of culture as 'enlightened consumption'. I attempt a preliminary excavation of some of the criteria in use by looking at the newspaper television guides below.

Moral paradigms

Here I would locate the famous imperatives of public service broadcasting, notions of impartiality and the justification of censorship and controls on broadcasting. It is this discursive formation which is partly in crisis in the White Paper, as others have observed, because of the contradictions between views of the citizen inscribed within the notions of the Broadcasting Standards Council, and that of the citizen as consumer. Historically, moral arguments are often presented as, or justified by, realist ones. Although this strategy is present within the document, one of the noticeable features of the White Paper, as with the Peacock report, is the way in which the moral arguments are conducted as arguments about consumer protection:

> Programmes should not offend against good taste or decency, or be likely to encourage or incite to crime or lead to disorder, or be offensive to public feeling. . . . The consumer protection obligations need to be properly enforced so that the quality of programming is maintained and the power of television and radio is not abused.
>
> (para. 7.2)

This typology allows us to see quite clearly that the White Paper offers only realist and moral discussion of 'quality' television, and that discussion is brief.[19] The relevant paragraphs are 6.10 and 6.11, which deal with the regime for Channel 3, and, by extension, Channel 5; paragraphs 6.23–6.27 which deal with Channel 4 (and may have already been modified); and Chapter 7, which deals with the Broadcasting Standards Council. The problem is not so much that the White Paper *should* specify what quality television will be – in current circumstances the less said probably the better. Rather the problem lies in conceiving of cultural texts solely or primarily in moral or realist terms which remove the possibility of what we might call 'the aesthetic defence'. To give an example: there is a scene of 'explicit sex' in *The Singing Detective* (BBC, 1987) which was objected to as obscene. The scene was defended on the grounds that it was part of an aesthetic whole, and that it was therefore inappropriate to isolate it. Whatever we may feel about the scene, the play or the cultural assumptions which underpin the defence, we should also be concerned that such an 'aesthetic defence', given the remit of the Broadcasting Standards Council, may not be available in the future. This has implications for the future of innovative work on television – which is of course going to be under stress anyway.

PRACTICAL QUALITY 2

It is in this context that we can move to a discussion of some of the ways in which judgements of quality are made about television.

Newspapers: the broadcast schedules

Newspaper and journal reviewing, sensible places to start when thinking about the critical judgements made about television, have been substantially discussed in *Screen* by Mike Poole (1984) and John Caughie (1984), and more briefly elsewhere by Kathy Myers (1984) and Colin McArthur (1980). Critics such as Clive James (1983) also offer some comment on their role and practice in collections of their work. McArthur makes the point (in 1980) that the function of television reviewing is less clear than that of film and theatre reviewing, in that reviews usually appear after one transmission: 'Given the absence of a clear use-value', he says, 'the strong tendency . . . towards personality flashing is writ large in the television columns of both the popular and the heavy press' (McArthur 1980: 59).

The increased use of the VCR in the 1980s may have increased the use value of reviews since this was written, but it is still the case that clearly 'voiced' comment is typical of much television criticism. I want here to look briefly at what is often offered as a less voiced coverage of television, the broadcast schedules in the daily press.

The asterisk system discussed at the beginning of this article is a fairly typical approach to the classification of films shown on television within the British tabloid press, with the *Star* offering a rather enterprising one-star classification, 'Ring up and complain'. Of broadcast material, only films get this symbolic evaluation (although *The Sunday Correspondent* has started life with ticks for approved television programmes). The assessment of television programmes occurs sometimes in the listings and sometimes in a separately boxed daily selection.

I want to examine the assumptions and values found in these listings. I have worked with the weekday press only, choosing Friday as my sampling day, and the survey has no pretence at rigour. I was interested in the listings, rather than the reviews, because there is a clear aim to provide information about what is on, while the listings compiler is also usually expected to provide details or comments which will allow the readers of that particular newspaper to make their viewing selection. I refer to the newspapers by size as tabloids or broadsheets, recognising that *The Daily Mail* and *The Daily Express* are not generally considered connotational tabloids, and that 'tabloid' carries associations usually matched by referring to the broadsheet press as 'the quality press'. For obvious reasons that name won't do here.

The tabloids generally separate films from the broadcast schedules (partly because of network schedule differences, and their commitment to comment on all available films) and offer one- or two-sentence synopses, usually with some evaluation. *The Sun*, which keeps film comment within the schedules, offers a '*Sun*-rating', which is often alliterative, as in, for *The Day it Came to Earth*, 'More of a hoot than a horror', or 'Hairy hot-rod action' for *Burnout* (25 August 1989). Tabloid layout often places the Film Guide box with the news of video releases, frequently on a page with a general show biz emphasis, facing the schedules. *Today* provides bar codes for timer video recording of films, programme details for cable television, and gives the most space to satellite programmes. The space given to satellite programmes exemplifies the way in which page layout condenses complex interrelations of reader profile, corporate ownership and aesthetic evaluation. Thus while it is not surprising, given Murdoch's ownership, that *The Times* is the only broadsheet to give full satellite details (only *The Guardian*, with its high media profile, of the other broadsheets even mentions satellite), it is not immediately predictable that it should be *Today*, rather than *The Sun* (also owned by Murdoch) which should give most tabloid space.

The television and radio schedules, then, their place within the newspaper, the detail and typeface used, testify to a series of assumptions about the place and function of broadcasting within the readers' lives (and the ownership of the newspapers). Thus, on the one hand, *The Financial Times* offers a small section of its Arts page, with brief complete listings, in very small print, of the four terrestrial channels, and more extended daily television selections, usually by a 'name' critic, Christopher Dunkley. It offers no listings for Radio One and Radio Scotland but the World Service is given in full. *The Sun* on the other hand, gives programme listings for BBC2 and Channel 4 in a smaller type face and space than that for BBC1 and ITV, and with a more cramped spacing than that used for the main Sky channels. There are no radio listings. In general terms the tabloid press tend to stretch BBC1 and ITV, shrinking BBC2 and Channel 4, while the broadsheets may give equal column length to all channels but are rather cavalier with ITV regions.

Throughout the tabloid treatment of both films on television and the television schedules, there is a fairly snappy feel to the judgements being made. Television is placed within a wider entertainment or show biz context, but in choosing viewing, whether broadcast or pre-recorded, the reader is encouraged and expected to make choices. This exercise of (consumer) power can be contrasted to the role of witness or eavesdropper offered in much of the show biz coverage in the same papers, where the reader is the recipient of gossip about stars and shows.

There seems to be a fairly clear notion of function in these television guides. The reader wants to make choices that will result in the most enjoyable viewing, and the central criterion seems to be 'Does this entertain in recognisably pleasurable ways?' For feature films there is a relatively limited code, the most significant recurring elements of which are 'over-rated', 'far-fetched', 'zany' and 'touching'. 'Touching' seems clearly gender-coded, while 'over-rated' (used for example of *Chariots of Fire* by *Today*, 1 September 1989) signals the disparity between wider critical reputation and that paper's readers. It is precisely this type of targeted aesthetic judgement which is useful to readers – so long as it proves accurate. The same kind of specific address is also apparent in *The Independent*, where what is repeatedly revealed is ambivalence about entertainment television. This appears through a rather dead-pan reproduction of programme synopses in a context which makes them read like pastiches of the same details in the popular press. Obviously, to draw any conclusions, it would be necessary to conduct research over a long period, with attention to any types of patterning that might recur in the giving of details and judgements: patterns of channel preferences, genres, slots and evaluative terms. The point here is that different taste codes and expectations of television are daily inscribed in newspapers in ways that casually employ targeted, but rather mixed, criteria of judgement. If the government, in the White Paper, speaks mainly of television in moral and realist terms, potential 'consumers' are given informa-tion in ways which mix discourses of leisure, conventional aesthetics and a little bit of realism.

Brideshead in the Crown

One of the ways of side-stepping the difficult critical arguments about quality television, while still being able to attest to its existence and virtue, is to refer to specific programmes, which can then function as shorthand for taken-for-granted understandings of 'quality'.

Thames Television used and parodied this strategy in the series of full-page advertisements in the national press in July and August which declared, 'To celebrate our 21st anniversary, we're going to be re-showing several of our better programmes over the next few weeks', below full-page images from named shows. The ads clearly seek national popular recognition for Thames as the originator of successful and remembered programmes, as well as making a bid for a definition of quality which includes funny, audience pulling programmes within a notion of diversity – all human life is here in (on) the two sides of Thames. Thus in the ad which uses a still from *Bless this House* (Thames, 1971–) the headline 'Throughout our programme-making history, Thames Television have always been involved in serious social issues' is placed above a very *Carry On* image of Sid James holding up a bra. In a way, the ad recruits Sid James, and that whole tradition of British comedy, to say 'Bras to (franchise winning) serious social issues'. Simul-taneously it provides a very heterosexual cover for a plug for one of Thames's

21 'Serious social issues', Thames Television advertisement, British national press, 1989

award-winning plays, *The Naked Civil Servant* (Thames, 1975) which, as the ad reminds us, 'dealt with homosexuality'.

It is unusual, outside professional discourses, for popular programmes such as *Bless this House* to function as synonyms for quality, and here it is precisely the juxtaposition with *The Naked Civil Servant*, producing a transaction of symptomatic significance in which each covers for the other. *The Naked Civil Servant* is of course a much more traditional choice (single play, name adaptation of known author, professional recognition) to signify quality. By placing together the popular and the esoteric the ad gives us quality as variety. This 'quality as variety' strategy is recurrent with the ITV companies, with the national ITV ads, 'ITV? It's all game shows and soaps', in March 1989 (*The Independent*, 8 March 1989), and the current (October 1989) Yorkshire ads, which use a headline 'From the people who bring you *Emmerdale Farm*' below an image of a family fleeing from the My Lai massacre taken from a Yorkshire documentary.

22 'From the people who bring you "Emmerdale Farm"', Yorkshire Television advertisement, British national press, 1989 (Young and Rubican)

More commonly, to signify quality the single play is invoked alone, often as 'The Wednesday Play' (which dates the legislator's interest in television). Other programmes too have functioned historically – *Civilisation, The Forsyte Saga, Cathy Come Home* – but the recent debate has seen two programmes repeatedly invoked to carry the meaning of quality television:

Brideshead Revisited (Granada, 1981) and *The Jewel in the Crown* (Granada, 1984). Thus with a blithe disregard for production companies (there is a significant and common misattribution of the two programmes to the BBC), the attack on the White Paper by John Mortimer in *The Mail on Sunday*, 13 November 1989, under a trail declaring 'White Paper is death sentence for the BBC' was headed 'Selling off television's jewels in the crown'. Alan Coren, in a column in *The Times* (10 November 1988) which satirically welcomed the White Paper pointed to the ubiquity of this characterisation of quality: 'I was much cheered to hear the ululations rising over Hampstead Heath and Camden [*sic*] Hill on Monday over the imminent Qualität-sdammerung [*sic*], as smarties kept chanting that this was the end of *Jewel in the Crown* and *Brideshead Revisited*, which seemed to be the only two examples they could think of.'

Brideshead and *Jewel* have come to figure, within discussion of television's fictional output, as the acme of British quality. I want to offer some hypotheses on the 'quality components' in these particular programmes, and some thoughts on the likely consequences in the current debate.

Firstly, literary source. The power of the legitimating force of the Evelyn Waugh novel should not be underestimated. At the same time, the exclusion of the novel from the highest echelons of the literary hierarchy probably also works in favour of its literariness being lent to television. The adaptation of Evelyn Waugh (or Scott Fitzgerald, or Anthony Trollope, or Daphne du Maurier) does not occasion quite the rumpus we get with Jane Austen. 'Middle-brow' literature (to use an old-fashioned but rather useful term) is not itself spoilt by the vulgar medium of television, and indeed enhances the upstart with a little culture. In this context Dickens, a popular serialiser in his day, is an interesting case, and Paul Kerr, in his discussion of adaptations and classic serials in 1982, points out that there have been more than thirty Dickens adaptations on the BBC since 1950.[20] With the Scott novels, despite (or perhaps because of) the Booker prize, contemporaneity seems to function in a similar way.

Secondly, the best of British acting. The presence of name theatrical actresses and actors adds the international dimension of British theatre to the programmes. Again, the point here is not whether British theatrical acting as exemplified by Dame Peggy Ashcroft or Jeremy Irons, is better than other traditions of acting, but that there is a comfortably established international (hence, foreign sales) body of opinion to this effect.

Thirdly, money. Like MGM musicals, both these series cost a lot, and, as importantly, looked as if they cost a lot. As the comparison reveals, though, high production values can be deployed across different taste regimes. Throwing money at a project doesn't guarantee that it will look expensive, and it is the combination of restraint and uncommon spectacle which is the key signifier here.[21] These were expensive productions in which the money was spent according to upper-middle-class taste codes whether to represent upper-class lifestyles or exotic poverty. 'Quality' has an archaic provenance, as Rupert Murdoch has been quick to point out: 'Much of what passes for quality on British television is no more than a reflection of the values of the narrow elite which controls it and has always thought that its tastes are synonymous with quality.'[22] 'Quality' is semantically opposed to the common or the vulgar – these are expensive tales about 'the quality'. It is significant that it is *Brideshead* and *Jewel*, rather than *Boys from the Blackstuff* (BBC, 1982) (which had the quickest repeat in television history, and national popular acclaim)[23] which have come to signify quality television. In another old fashioned usage, the way that money is spent in *Brideshead* or *Jewel* is fundamentally 'nice', even, or especially, when dealing with horrid subjects like rape, racism, alcoholism, homosexuality and suicide by fire.

Fourthly, heritage export. As many commentators have pointed out, these series produced a certain image of England and Englishness (with little reference to the rest of Britain), in which national identity is expressed through class and imperial identity.

The widespread acceptance of *Brideshead* and *Jewel* as signifying quality thus condenses several sets of power relations. Crucially, they have come to function as *uncontroversial* indicators of quality. There is here no trouble with subjective factors, as there would be, for example, if *The Singing Detective* (BBC, 1987), which has been one of the preferred tokens of those with more avant-garde tastes, was used. In the current linguistic usage of these programme names, television is seen to have established a canon, which is perceived to be independent of personal taste. We see this most clearly in the cases of writers like Richard Collins (1989) or Paul Kerr (1989), who are reluctant to be complicit with the ideological baggage entailed but have to recognise the semantic currency these programme names now have. *Brideshead* and *Jewel* are uncontroversial signifiers of quality mainly because they incorporate already established taste codes of literature, theatre, interior decoration, interpersonal relationships and nature. Formally unchallenging, while nevertheless replete with visual strategies that signify 'art', their only specifically televisual demand is that the viewer should switch on at the right time and watch. Just like the National Trust and advertisements for wholemeal bread, they produce a certain image of England and Englishness which is untroubled by contemporary division and guaranteed aesthetic legitimacy. In 1971 Raymond Williams calculated that 'the median date of current show pieces of English television' was 1925 (O'Connor 1989: 135). He begins to provide an answer to the question of why this should be the case in an earlier essay on a programme called *An Englishman's Home*, when he observes 'the past is all art and buildings, the present all people and confusion' (O'Connor 1989: 58).

ACADEMICS WATCH TELEVISION

Reading, in 1989, O'Connor's collection of Raymond Williams's television criticism from *The Listener* which was written between 1968 and 1972, I have been struck by his enthusiasm for BBC2. It is the channel he chooses when trying to give an analysis of what has become known as 'flow', and also the one which scores highest in his 'serious television' stakes. As a critic, Williams is always attentive to class sleight of hand, quietly restoring the social context to a 1970 episode of *Survival* which dwells on the disappearance of the marshland bird, the bittern, with the 'of course' in this sentence: 'Before clearance and draining the bittern may have been more widespread, of course' (121). Or calculating that six or seven hours a week on the pools would be necessary to balance the unembarrassed coverage of stocks and shares in *The Money Programme* (142). Williams likes BBC2 best most of the time because he finds it interesting and challenging. His political and class allegiances are clearly articulated throughout these essays as the basis from which he thinks about other things. Often, the thinking about other things from a socialist perspective brings him back to reflecting on the determining nature of class division. There is here no fear that to exercise judgement, to make discriminations, is elitist. Engaging critically with presentations, issues and stories is seen as emancipatory.

In a 1971 piece Williams attacks the definition of serious television advanced the previous week by Paul Fox, then Director of BBC programmes. Williams applauds the inclusion of fictional programmes within Fox's definition, but deplores what he sees as a utilitarian bias in which serious broadcasting has to be instructional in some way. However Williams is serious about the adjective 'serious', and retains a notion of hundred per cent attention in his own category, commenting approvingly that a *World About Us* 'could hardly be casually watched'. Williams's own definition of 'serious television' – 'programmes that looked as if someone had successfully meant something in making them, rather than simply slotted them into a market' (129) – is insistently cross-generic, including *Match of the Day, Monty Python, Z Cars, The Money Programme*, and, rather grudgingly, *Panorama* and an *Omnibus* on T. S. Eliot. He cavils at the *Omnibus* because of its intellectual naivety, and consistently searches for, and applauds, programmes that utilise the resources of television to their full extent. 'Serious' is, throughout these essays a term of approbation, but is frequently withheld from his contemporary equivalents of *Brideshead* and *Jewel*, programmes like *Civilisation* or an adaptation of *Jude the Obscure*. This is partly because Williams is constantly searching for criteria which are specific to television in making his judgements. 'These are programmes within the present real limits of television, and above all, they were not confused by the residual power of other art forms' (135).

The aesthetic Williams develops, then, is formed within the two major cultural traditions of the West. It is a profoundly realist aesthetic, in that he believes strongly in the capacity of television to tell us about the world we live in, to extend our knowledge of cultures not our own and enable us better to understand our own. Sometimes he can be very sharp about the way in which the medium which he conceives as potentially democratic and socially extensive is used: 'All I have to say, there, is that nobody would believe there are 56 million people in Britain: we see and hear so few of them' (42). However, it is also a modernist aesthetic in that it demands that form should follow function and that television should develop its own specificity. Williams has least time for productions which merely reproduce existing cultural habits and values.

Williams's class confidence, and his belief in the value of education and argument, lead him to the new minority channel, BBC2, without embarrassment. I think I was struck by discovering how much he liked this channel because I have, in the 1980s, become accustomed to a type of academic populism in relation to television. It is not that I want to go all the way with 'serious television' if it means I can never watch television casually, but I like the construction of a cross-generic category which takes leisure and pleasure seriously, which makes demands on the programme-makers – however I choose to watch. Williams writes in another essay of 'the small programmes which make up so large a part of decent television' (173), and 'decent' seems, in 1989, a word difficult to find, let alone defend. In the current context, Williams's own work on the construction of ideas of the countryside, and the class history of pastoral, makes it perhaps appropriate to use Bourdieu's comment on the role of populism for artists and intellectuals:

> The essential merit of the 'common people' is that they have none of the pretensions to art (or power) which inspire the ambitions of the 'petit bourgeois'. Their indifference tacitly acknowledges the monopoly. That is why, in the mythology of artists and intellectuals, whose outflanking and double-negating strategies sometimes lead them back to 'popular' tastes and opinions, the 'people' so often play a role not unlike that of the peasantry in the conservative ideologies of the declining aristocracy.
>
> (Bourdieu 1984: 62)

Although there is frequently a strongly democratic and egalitarian motivation for the installation of 'the people' as the subject of a positively endorsed 'mass culture' aesthetic, I think that there are problems, of the type Bourdieu suggests, when this is the *only* aesthetic endorsed, and particularly when it is espoused in this fashion, within academia, by those most educated in other (implicit or explicit) aesthetics. Meaghan Morris, in a recent essay on 'Banality in cultural studies', argued that 'the people' seem increasingly to function as the 'textually delegated, allegorical emblem of the critic's own activity' (Morris 1990: 23). This can be related to Jostein Gripsrud's discussion of the position of academics studying popular culture, and his argument that there is a danger of mystifying – forgetting the privilege of – the academics' own position. Gripsrud is partly in dialogue with Michael Schudson's 1987 essay 'The new validation of popular culture: sense and sentimentality in academia', in which he calls for a recognition of the significance of formal and informal education in affecting responses to texts, and posits that:

> The challenge is not to deny a place for judgement and valuation but to identify the institutional, national, class, race and gender-bound biases set deep in past judgements, and to make them available for critical reassessment.
>
> (Schudson 1987: 66)

It may be the case that the political climate of the early 1970s made Williams's aligned practice of discrimination easier than the equivalent practice would be today. More important though, I think, is his confidence in the empowering and enfranchising potential of talking about ideas. It is not a sense of ease, or complacency, that these essays give, but of the value attributed to the often difficult task of thinking seriously about an everyday ephemeral medium.

I have argued here and elsewhere that television does not 'fit' into established aesthetic discourses. This lack of fit, the generic diversity of the medium, and the particular paradigms which have formed and dominated television studies make it peculiarly difficult to oppose coherently and democratically the highest-bidder award of commercial television franchises through the defence of 'quality'. This is particularly the case when the most currently accessible idea of quality, which I have designated *Brideshead in the Crown*, so clearly represents the historical and cultural privilege with which aesthetic judgement is encrusted. However, I hope I have also shown that it is not a category that can be dispensed with. Judgements about the quality of television are made in a great many ways all the time – in speech, in newspapers, in practice – and on television itself.

The value audience members ascribe to, or gain from, particular programmes does not necessarily correlate with traditional ideas of quality. It does not follow from this that it does not matter what television is available, rather that the issue is considerably more complex than the government is currently suggesting. It is not possible to enter into discussions about quality unless difference is significant. Aware that in so many instances significant difference is made from and through social inequality, we stand in overcompensatory danger of refusing to recognise it. In this context, I have tried to argue, television scholars must engage with television in a way which recognises the contradictions and paradoxes of the study of popular forms in the academy. This process is necessarily an historical one – there is a history, as well as a sociology and politics, of taste and value. It is also a self-critical one which requires the re-opening of debates, particularly those around cultural values, which were closed off in *Screen* some years ago. Judgements are being made – let's talk about them.

Chapter 10

Satellite dishes and the landscapes of taste[†]

INTRODUCTION

This paper was originally written for an interdisciplinary conference on the study of the audience held at the University of Illinois (Urbana-Champaign). In that context, where the disciplinary origins of my contribution would be seen as part of a 'cultural studies' grouping – as opposed to, for example, psychology or mass communication – I wanted to use an analysis of a particular, historical 'taste war' to pose questions about the relation of individual audience practices to a wider social. This was, by implication, to raise questions about how we understand the 'new' small-scale ethnographic studies which are coming out of research projects influenced by cultural studies.[1] These were not questions about the generalisability of the findings traditionally posed to this type of research, but questions about the very constitution of the social at a theoretical level. Methodologically, as Ang and Hermes (1991) point out, this is partly a problem of the construction of interpretative categories, such as class or gender, 'whose impact as a structuring principle for experience can only be conceptualized within the concrete historical context in which it is articulated' (314).

The way I address the issue is partly through a kind of pun about the social and British public space which enables me to argue that there is a spatialisation of debates about British broadcasting policy apparent in the seemingly minor public spats about the siting of satellite dishes. Focusing on an audience practice, the erection of satellite dish aerials, and the ensuing taste wars, also allows me to move away from a concentration on the verbal.

However, it is also clear that the paradigm I am using is most familiar from cultural studies subcultural work of the 1970s, 'resistance through rituals'.[2] This work, with its stress on the transforming agency of members of subcultures – or audiences, in its media studies incarnation – has, despite appearances, a strongly formalist element, a certain insouciance about 'content'. At a time when the expansion of satellite broadcasting has

---

[†]Written for the conference, 'Audience', organised by Larry Grossberg, James Hay and Ellen Wartella at the University of Illinois in 1990. First published in *New Formations* 15 (1991).

dramatised many of the issues constituting the crisis in European public service broadcasting, these paradigms for the analysis of subcultures fit very uneasily with debates about policy. It is this uneasy fit which retrospectively seems the most urgent subject for debate.

I

'I like to like what's better to like.'
Billie (Judy Holliday) in *Born Yesterday*
(Columbia, George Cukor, 1950)

This case study of the newspaper coverage of the erection of satellite dishes in Britain in 1989–90 offers a series of more and less implicit points of theoretical engagement with current research into the television audience. I try to show the way in which the personal tastes and preferences experienced and articulated in the domestic context to which ethnography gives us some access, while always being *personal*, are always also profoundly *social*. While this issue is an acknowledged focus of ethnographic concern, it is not usually discussed in the way in which I wish to address it, but more commonly forms a site for a recognition of a certain kind of trouble for the ethnographer.[3]

Ellen Seiter (1990) discusses this lucidly in her reflection on the Tübingen/ Volkswagen project 'Case study of a troubling interview'. She points to the way in which the different social statuses of those involved in the interview, as well as their contrasted approach to, and desires for, the occasion structures the interaction, and indeed could be considered the substance of the interview. Basically, the two interviewees involved do not want to offer detailed textual readings of television programmes to two university professors because of their attitudes to television in general, and their sense of what is appropriate to discuss with professors. These views, to Seiter and Borchers's discomfort, they are happy to expound. Seiter's account directly addresses and reads this trouble in the interview, this failure to gain the data envisaged in the original research design. It is these failures, these gaps, these pauses – the moments when an interviewee changes tack in the middle of a sentence – with which I am initially concerned, for these seem to me moments in which we can locate the often unconscious recognition and negotiation of cultural power, in that we see here the struggle of an individual to locate themselves in relation to already circulating discourses of taste. In Billie's words, 'to like what's better to like'.

Ang (1985) addresses this directly in her *Dallas* study, and it leads her to her formulation of the 'Ideology of Mass Culture'. It is thus that she designates the cultural attitudes with which her respondents have to negotiate when recounting the experience of watching *Dallas*. She had actively solicited this self-referential reflection in the formulation of her original advertisement: 'I like watching the TV serial *Dallas* but often get odd reactions to it', and offers a sophisticated analysis of the different discursive strategies whereby her respondents incorporate the recognition that the object of their pleasure is not culturally prestigious. As her respondents sometimes repudiate and disavow any pleasure, Ang also touches on the very complex relation of conscious and unconscious desire, something which has hardly been touched in empirical audience studies.

Janice Radway becomes concerned with the issue of readers' under-standing of the cultural value of their pleasure in her 1984 study *Reading the Romance* when she investigates the connotations of reading 'to escape' for her readers. Although they recognise that this is what they do, Radway insists: 'if given another comparable choice that does not carry the connotations of disparagement, they will choose the more favourable sounding explanation.'[4] Later she continues:

> In an effort to combat both the resentment of others and their own feelings of shame about their 'hedonist' behaviour, the women have worked out a complex rationalisation for romance reading that not only asserts their equal right to pleasure but also legitimates the books by linking them with values more widely approved within American culture.
>
> (1984: 90)

Although it is not her central concern, Radway gives clear accounts of the way in which romance reading is legitimated through recourse to less controversial benefits like 'learning about other countries'.

In what might be taken to be a quite similar case, the reactions of fans to *Gone with the Wind* (*GTW*), we find rather less tortuous work done by the women to justify and explain their pleasures. Helen Taylor (1989) points to the way in which the celebrated 'legendary' status and commercial success of *GWTW* functions partly to legitimate her correspondents' pleasure to themselves, as well as to her. So 'what's better to like' is not generically given, although there clearly has been an historical association of feminine genres like the novel, melodrama, soap opera and romance with the downside of taste. But, as in the case of *GWTW*, a certain kind of success can lead to a change of category, just as different media – the novel, cinema, television – have all in their time been seen to seduce the (non-masculine) feeble-minded (Lovell 1987).

Andrew Ross (1989), in his reading of contemporary US responses to the Rosenberg letters, points to a related process, when the cultural legitimacy – or otherwise – of tastes and vocabularies determines their reading so thoroughly that it can be quite invisible to researchers and commentators. He compares the relative failure of the published letters to gain the Rosenbergs any support from the erstwhile left intelligentsia with the later reception of George Jackson's letters. He argues, most persuasively, that the revelation of the intimate sensibilities of the Rosenbergs, their quotidian middle-brow tastes, and, specifically, the fluctuating expressive register of Ethel Rosenberg's style, which mobilises all her 'ordinary' cultural resources to write these (public) private letters, were profoundly embarrassing for the more mandarin tastes of (anti-Stalinist) intellectuals. The letters – indeed the lives of the Rosenbergs – were too centrally formed within a petit bourgeois aesthetic to be readable as authentic by legitimate intellectuals – unlike the authenticity incarnate of the Jackson's 'otherness'. Ross's reading of the letters attempts to address what is specific to these letters, rather than what they are not, and argues for their continuing capacity 'to compromise every possible canon of "legitimate" taste' (29). Ross concludes this part of his research by arguing that it is the 'untidy problematic of lower-middle class culture' which is most neglected in cultural studies.

My case study is the erection and reception, in England in 1989–90, of dish aerials to receive satellite television. Available figures suggest that these dishes have been overwhelmingly bought and rented by those in social classes Cl (19.3 per cent of sales), C2 (35.3 per cent) and D (20.3 per cent).[5] The dishes, which are about 2 ft across, first easily became available to the private purchaser in 1988, shortly before the launch of Rupert Murdoch's Sky television in February 1989. Cabling is the exception rather than the rule in Britain, and a different dish (the squarial) was necessary to receive British Satellite Broadcasting (BSB), the more upmarket satellite channel, which started broadcasting in May 1990.[6] There has been a certain amount of public discussion about satellite dishes, and it is on this, mainly as reported in newspapers, that I wish to concentrate. I want to argue that in this one example we see condensed a complex set of issues, including a conflict of taste codes which is illustrative of the history and status of different taste formations in Britain. The argument about who has the right to put satellite dishes where provides, if you like, a *mise-en-abyme* of current conflict about broadcasting policy in Britain (see Chapter 9). More germanely for this context, it provides a site within which we can trace the vocabulary and discursive contours of 'television tastes', within which individuals experience and articulate their own preferences, which in their turn redefine, extend and reinforce the conflicting fields and their relation to each other.

Like channel selection, or programme watching, but unlike giving an account of either of these two activities, erecting a satellite dish is not necessarily a verbal activity. Buying or renting a dish can I think legitimately be read as an act which signals a desire, a connection with something that these dishes are understood to mean, or connote, or promise.[7] However, unlike channel selection, or programme watching, which are activities performed in the privacy of the home, erecting a satellite dish is done outside the home. This audience practice is, among other things, a non-verbal signifier of taste and choice – or, as an article in the *London Evening Standard* put it:

> So far in London, take-up of Sky has been slow. If, however, you actually welcome the round-the-clock rubbish being beamed out the problem is that you can't watch it discreetly.

Under normal circumstances if your tastes extend no further than Neighbours, Capital Radio and Dynasty at least you can indulge yourself without the whole street knowing about it.

(Mark Edmonds, 'Fright on the tiles', 12 July 1989: 23)

This passage uses a structure common in discussion of taste, one which is present in the negotiations with the researchers in work I have cited earlier. This is a distinction between a private and a public taste, an indoors slippers and dressing gown and a Sunday Best of taste. The invocation of a known hierarchy of 'what's better to like', from which ordinary mortals fall away. For this writer, the problem for those who like 'round-the-clock' rubbish from space is that they can no longer indulge secretly.

However, this private/public distinction can work more than one way with satellite dishes – people can have quite different attitudes to acknowledged hierarchies of taste. Ondina Fachel Leal (1990) uses the idea of the television 'entourage' to discuss the customary decoration of the television set in Brazilian homes. In fact, as her work shows, the notion of the entourage – the doilies, plastic flowers, photographs of loved ones carefully arranged on the television set – is appropriate only in the case of lower-class homes. The upper classes, instead of decorating and celebrating the television, enshrining it as the centre of family life, often give it a room of its own, and always leave it unembellished in its techno-austerity. The case of satellite dishes, and the question of their siting, has similarities with the creation, or not, of a television entourage, but also substantial differences. Leal demonstrates that the television in working-class homes must be placed in such a way that passers-by can see that the family possesses a television, so the difference between the two is not simply that the entourage is in the home, while the satellite dish is outside it, although, at the same time, the public siting of the dish is exactly what is at issue, and it is this which I wish to explore.

II

'It's a nice extra, like a jacuzzi, that I'm sure would interest a lot of people.'
(Mark Goldberg, Hamptons Estate Agents, quoted in the *London Evening Standard*, 12 July 1989: 23)

Press coverage of satellite dishes in Britain can be divided into three categories, if we exclude the trade press and advertising features generated by Sky television and BSB themselves. This distinction is not always easy to maintain, as can be seen by investigating the first category, business or industrial coverage of satellite television. This necessarily, and properly, entails the reporting of satellite television within discussions of Rupert Murdoch's communications empire, as well as smaller-scale coverage of employment in dish-making factories, and individual entrepreneurs of the dish revolution, like Liz Stewart, 'a bubbly brunette from Fife', who, reports the *Sunday Express*, designed a system which 'dishes out a blow to satellite giants' (16 October 1988: 25). However, in early 1989, it was noticeable that it is the Murdoch-owned papers. *The Times* and *The Sun*, which carried news reports about the increased demand for satellite dishes. For example, *The Sun* reported in January, shortly before Sky opened, that there were 'THOUSANDS IN DASH FOR SATELLITE TELLY DISHES', and quoted a spokesman ostensibly from Dixons, an electrical goods retailer, saying: 'The fantastic range of programmes being offered by the Sky station has really caused a stir' (5 January 1989: 5). Similarly in February *The Times* reported that 'Sky launch boosts demand for dishes' (4 February 1989: 3) and a couple of days later, 'Satellite dish firm expanding' (7 February 1989: 2). The earlier of these two articles, which includes a statement from the Council for the Protection of Rural England, offers an early formulation of 'satellite dishes as a threat to the environment' with which I will be centrally concerned in my third category. Thus although there is a certain fuzziness, particularly in some newspapers, about this category, we can still legitimately distinguish it from the other two, 'consumer guides' and 'dish-siting controversy'. However, it should be noted that it is *The Independent* which has given most prominent coverage to the latter controversy which has been covered almost exclusively by non-Murdoch titles.

The consumer guides are fairly self explanatory and were mainly a feature of the immediate pre- and post-Sky launch period. For our purposes what is

23 A 'functional' satellite dish outside a bookmaker's in Kings Heath, Birmingham, July 1990

24 Dishes, and an empty dish bracket, on a council housing block in Balsall Heath, Birmingham, July 1990

significant is the way in which the choice of what to buy or rent is presented solely as an individual consumer purchase – a private, domestic matter which is treated appropriately by different newspapers with their different images of the type of consumers their readers are. Thus *Today* (4 February 1989) makes no mention of BSB and addresses '[t]he big question facing viewers keen to wire up to satellite television [which is] whether to rent or buy' (22), while *The Independent* (1 February 1989), in an article called 'The cost to the viewer' consults a range of experts and mentions BSB and W. H. Smith Television (Astra). Here the reader is regarded not as a potentially 'keen' viewer but as more distanced – 'curious' – as in 'For the curious consumer, the message seems to be: tread carefully' (13). There are no mentions in any papers of planning restrictions – or indeed of the fact that these dishes will be put on the outside of houses. It is only in the third category of coverage that this private consumer choice is seen to have public consequences. It is the formulations of these consequences that are of interest to us here, articulating as they do a range of oppositions:

private: public
consumer: citizen
entertainment: culture
supranational: national
future (innovation): history (conservation)

25 A dish on a terraced house with stone cladding, a new red-tiled roof (slate is normal here) and a replacement downstairs window (removing a bay window). On the right, the house has been pebble-dashed and the bay has been replaced and a porch added. To the left, the upstairs window has been replaced and the brickwork patched. Kings Heath, Birmingham, July 1990

26 A dish on a house in a street where most maintenance is 'in character'. The new roof is imitation slate and the original decoration on the plaster work has been accentuated. Note the prominent terrestrial television aerials and wiring. Kings Heath, Birmingham, July 1990

The controversy about the siting of satellite dishes, peculiarly resonant as it is in 1990 against a decade of 'heritage enterprise' in Britain, also reworks and re-presents founding historical conflicts about broadcasting, some of which have simultaneously been articulated in the debates over the quality threshold in the 1990 Broadcasting Bill. Indeed, the BSB/Media Education pack aimed at those taking GCSE Media Studies draws attention to the hostility in some quarters which greeted changes in broadcasting from the 1920s through the juxtaposition of a series of (unattributed) hostile quotations from 1922 to 1982, asking, 'Knowing when these comments were made, and the ways in which all of the developments referred to are now part of everyday life, how far do you think people are justified in criticising satellite television?' (Wall and Chater, undated: 12). The false ingenuousness of this question is to some extent redeemed if we consider the most obvious historical parallel to the satellite dish, the television aerial in the 1950s.[8] Oral history and historical ethnographic research such as O'Sullivan's (1991) confirm that there was public controversy about the erection of television aerials in the 1950s, although there is no trace of this controversy in the standard histories of the BBC and Independent Television (Briggs 1985; Sendall 1982), nor in standard textbooks on planning such as Cullingworth (1964/1988) or histories of planning such as Punter (1984, 1985) or Cullingworth (1979). The traces of this history can be found in repetitions, such as the fact that many of the places that have banned satellite dishes, like the Joseph Rowntree Trust village, New Earswick in Yorkshire, also have bans on outdoor television aerials,[9] or the inclusion of television aerials within the strict national restrictions on any alterations to Grade I and II listed buildings. New towns like Milton Keynes, built in the 1960s, were cabled throughout, partly to avoid exterior television aerials. It is noteworthy that the public debate about aerials in the 1950s coincides with the more general debates about the Americanisation and commercialisation of British culture of the period which are particularly focused by the opening of commercial television in 1955. Tim O'Sullivan (1991), conducting interviews with people about their memories of first getting television, shows the way in which to some the television aerial symbolised a proud stake in modernity. As Charles Barr (1986) and John Hill (1986) have shown, in British cinema of the 1950s and early 1960s commercial television functions metaphorically to condense a set of attitudes to the commercial, the American, the mass-produced. Raymond Williams, in his 1960 essay about advertising, dates the battle for the skyline much earlier, to the 1890s 'with "taste" and "the needs of commerce" as adversaries' (Williams 1980: 177). The point about history repeating itself in this way, now that television aerials have, in the main, become accepted as part of the urban landscape, or as the BSB pamphlet puts it, 'part of everyday life', is partly the significant differences (Sky television, rather than television as such, etc.). But it is also the way in which the

similarities of some of the debates and discursive figures, encrusting or
constituting a new object, the satellite dish, reveal that new ideas don't drop
from the sky, but indeed, as others have argued about the television set itself,
are constructed as meaningful within networks of relationships and discourses which pre-exist the technological innovation (Lull 1988, 1990;
Morley 1986; Gray 1987).

Thus much of James Lull's work has been concerned to explore the way
in which the television set is used within the familial domestic context. He
uses the concept of extension to conceptualise the relationship between the
set and the already existing dynamics of interaction within the family. In a
1988 piece he argues that McLuhan's original notion of the mass media
extending the human senses through technological capability can be re-
vamped to allow us to classify extension at three levels: the personal, the
familial and the cultural. I have some reservations about a certain un-
contradictory quality of this concept, but would here wish to propose that
satellite dishes, as well as being literally extensions, also condense familial
and cultural extensions. The several instances of men erecting, and indeed
inventing, their own dishes further suggest that this new technology may have
a particular place in the gendered division of labour – and personal
extension.[10] Recent ethnographic work offers specific instances of the
mapping of gender and generation across and through domestic technology
(Morley and Silverstone 1990; Gray 1992; Seiter *et al.* 1989). Thus Tim
O'Sullivan (1991) finds that the final decision to buy a television set in the
1950s often rested with the man of the household, who frequently also
installed the aerial, and sometimes retained a residual proprietorial power
over the on/off switch. Moores (1991a) maps the fluctuating gender and
generational conflicts around satellite television, in which different family
members occupy different positions at different times to different others in
relation to the 'same' equipment – for example, a woman unhappy with her
spouse's purchase of satellite television defending that same purchase to her
parents. These fluctuating identifications should make us cautious about
ascribing essential qualities to technology and technology use, while still
being alert to the patternings of power in specific historical divisions of
labour, use and attitude. Here it is useful to recall Ang and Hermes's
theorisation of the interplay of gender and generation in the Meier household
recorded by Bausinger (Ang and Hermes 1991; Bausinger 1984). Ang and
Hermes observe, at the beginning of their article:

> Mr Meier, the male football fan, ends up not watching his favourite team's
> game on television, while his wife, who doesn't care for sports, finds
> herself seating herself in front of the TV set the very moment the sports
> programme is on. Gender is obviously not a reliable predictor of viewing
> behaviour here.
>
> (1991: 307)

They proceed to argue for a postmodern feminist understanding of gender, in which the concept of articulation is central. They conclude, 'we must accept contingency as posing the utter limit for our understanding, and historical specificity as the only ground on which continuities and discontinuities in the ongoing but unpredictable articulation of gender in media consumption can be traced'. Ang and Hermes include within the logic of their argument about gender a similar critique of the way in which class (and race or ethnicity, although this is not developed) can be used within ethnographic accounts, as pre-constituted and pre-emptive explanatory factors.

The public debate in Britain in 1989–90 about the siting of satellite dishes offers us a particular, national, historical example of a conflict of values, which, because it is staged on the skyline, gives us some access to non-verbal audience practice. Working as I do here from one source, national newspapers, will obviously provide only one kind of outline of this debate. I think it offers an account of some of the discourses in play. How individuals position themselves in relation to these differentially available circulating discourses at particular times and in particular contexts cannot be deduced, and can only be investigated through particular ethnographies of the type that Ang and Hermes advocate. However researchers cannot do anything with these particular local knowledges unless there is also an attempt to apprehend a wider discursive field. To 'place practices of media consumption firmly within their complex and contradictory social contexts' (Ang and Hermes 1991) requires some mapping or constitution of these contexts.[11]

It is in relation to this argument that I wish to place a discussion of the third category of press coverage of satellite dishes, 'controversy about siting'. Working from a corrupt and rather random corpus – national, non-specialist newspaper coverage of rows about the siting of dishes – certain patterns emerge with striking clarity.

Firstly, there is the question of who speaks. Two categories of persons appear in these reports, 'Anti-dishers' and 'Dish-erectors'. Coverage is overwhelmingly dominated by anti-dishers, who are always professional – graphic designers, professors, etc. – and nearly always *representative* – councillors, spokespeople for trusts or estates, residents' associations. Often of course, they will have initiated the news item as part of their campaign to get a dish removed, but for our purposes what is significant is the way in which they never represent themselves as speaking on their own behalf. Anti-dishers, who in Bourdieu's terms are the possessors of, indeed propagandists for, legitimate cultural capital act and speak at a general social level about a matter of public concern (Bourdieu 1984).

Dish erectors, on the other hand, are always particular individuals; for example, the Radford family of Norton-sub-Hamdon, in Somerset, who won a dish in July 1989. I quote:

John Radford a building worker, pinned it proudly and prominently to the wall of his little cottage, a Grade II listed dwelling and settled back with his wife Jean, a cheese packer, to watch Mr Murdoch's old movies dropping in from outer space.

('Sky dish is the limit for listed village', *The Independent*, 25 October 1989: 3)

Here we have a construction worker and a cheese packer. In February 1989 we had Steven Davenport, a forty-two-year-old unemployed disabled man:

A disabled TV viewer has been ordered by town hall planners to take down his rooftop satellite dish in a test case which could affect the future of satellite broadcasting in Britain.

Steven Davenport was stunned by the council decision. . . .

('Satellite TV dish banned as "eyesore"', *Sunday Express*, 19 February 1989: 17)

Most interesting, though, is the case of dish-erector Maggie Brown, who is also the media editor of the national newspaper *The Independent*. Unlike all other reported dish erectors she is a well-paid professional with access to the media, a profile more common in anti-dishers. Furthermore, despite her designation of her own house as 'undistinguished', given that it is administered by Dulwich College, it must certainly be within reach of the most desirable areas of south London. Reported dish controversies have taken place either within villages, where there may still be local working-class occupancy of desirable cottages, or in areas of terraced urban housing. The erection of dishes on secluded detached houses has aroused no comment.[12] Similarly the extensive dishing of the river frontage of luxury dockland apartments on the north Thames bank also appears to be uncontroversial. Although as Muthesius (1982) traces, the terraced house, in England was built for and is occupied by all classes of society, it is not in the very prestigious terraces, of, for example, Bath, Brighton and Leamington Spa that there has been dish controversy. Nor in the inner city, where there is usually a mixture of terraced housing and newer council blocks, despite the fact that the satellite dish has come to signify the conspicuous consumption of a certain kind of poverty, as in this commentary on a Gallup poll for *Moneywise* which voted Nottingham the most desirable place to live: 'There is relatively little difference between rich and poor in Nottingham; the way to tell the middle-class area from the council estate is that the council houses all have satellite dishes' ('Life is not so bad and that's the bottom line', *Independent on Sunday*, 26 August 1990: 3). The controversies have taken place in areas which have a more mixed occupancy, where what section 4 of the 1971 Town and Country Planning Act refers to as 'the essential character of the area' is a matter of continuous everyday struggle. The character of the docklands development is in some ways perfectly homologous with the character of the satellite dish. Thus although Maggie Brown has many characteristics of the anti-disher, she, for professional reasons – and she is careful to point out the professional necessity of having a dish – is a dish-erector, and her case-study,

'My dish did not go down well' (*The Independent*, 8 May 1990: 14) conforms to the individuated format of all dish-erectors, which is particularly interesting given that she has written it herself.

The very contradictoriness of 'My dish did not go down well' allows us to outline the contours of anti-dish discourse, which is remarkably uniform. Dish-erectors, in contrast, are normally marooned in the personal, specific and concrete.

Firstly, anti-dishers generally make no reference to television programmes. Brown, whom we could describe as an anti-disher with a dish, illuminates this point because she wants to have both BSB and Sky. Generally, though, anti-dishers discuss dishes quite formally as alien protuberances perversely attached to the outside of houses by untutored DIYers.

Secondly, reference is always made to architectural provenance – often with some precision 'perfectly good late Victorian terraced house' (*The Independent*, 14 July 1989); 'villages built of lovely honey-coloured hamstone' (*The Independent*, 25 October 1989); 'terraced Edwardian House' (*Daily Telegraph*, 7 October 1989) or, in Maggie Brown's case, 'the front of my Victorian house'.

The contrasted repertoires of knowledge, television versus architecture, are, evidently, contrasts between less and more culturally legitimate forms.

Thirdly, some knowledge of the relevant environmental regulation and town planning acts is often displayed. Anti-dishers often express regret at the lack of legal restriction, particularly for unlisted buildings. Thus, of Queen's Park, London:

> A classic late-Victorian suburb, the district is supposedly a protected area of 'special architectural or historic interest', a place where the writ of the home-improvement brigade should not run unchecked; where picture windows, stone cladding and television dishes are outlawed. Does it work? 'This may have been declared a conservation area' but my answer is 'so what?'
> ('Battle against blots on the townscape', *The Independent*, 14 July 1989)

The law, for anti-dishers, is not in these matters strong enough and is not enforced satisfactorily.

Fouthly, certain evaluative phrases reoccur. The favoured written adjective is 'unsightly' which is such a normative word that it does not exist in the positive 'sightly'. 'Eyesores', 'Blight/Blot on the landscape' are also favoured, often as a headline (see above). This phrase in particular has been offered to me quite unsolicited by many passers-by when I have been out photographing houses with dishes, and was also volunteered by the lab which develops my films.

Fifthly, value. Apart from the estate agent who provided my opening epigraph – which, with its comparison of satellite dishes to jacuzzis, items of conspicuous consumption of a very particular provenance, sees dishes as potentially valuable home-improvements – the consensus among the anti-dishers, the worry which underlies the articulated, public-spirited architectural concern for the integrity of the buildings is one about value. This is not necessarily simply house prices, but for example in villages is to do with a more generalised 'heritage' value. Thus of Norton-sub-Hamdon:

A council spokesman said: 'We'd be absolutely appalled if this became widespread. Somerset's value as a tourist venue relies on the character of its historic buildings and villages.'

(*The Independent*, 25 October 1989: 3)

In London though, things are harsher:

And apart from the effects on the skyline, who knows what will happen to house prices once dishes start sprouting in earnest from our roofs and walls?

(Mark Edmonds, 'Fright on the tiles', *Evening Standard*, 12 July 1989)

Mr Tyler believes most householders appreciate the benefits of following the rules. House prices in a conservation area can be significantly raised.

'People who buy houses round here tend to have regard to the ambience of the area as a whole'

(Michael Durham. 'Battle against . . . ', The *Independent*,

14 July 1989)

The dishes have to face south, and a view of a south-facing facade with satellite receivers along part of it is not going to make a house on the opposite side of the street easier to sell.

(Tim Rowland, 'The blight of the satellite dish', *Daily Telegraph*, 1 October 1989)

It is, in the end, not what the dishes look like that matters – it is what they mean. And what they mean is both very simple and very complex. It is not necessary to be reductive, to say, well it's all about house prices really, because this move is made so spontaneously by the anti-dishers themselves. It is not made by all of them, and I'm sure most would protest if this was offered, say by an audience researcher, as a primary motivation. Sometimes, indeed, mention of house prices figures as a rhetorical last resort, an attempt to speak the language of philistines – or to recognise the values most endorsed in Britain in the last twelve years. Furthermore, financial gain does not have to be a primary motivation, if we follow Bourdieu's arguments about the disinterestedness of the inheritors of legitimate culture, for financial reward to result. There is a vision inspiring many of the anti-dishers, a vision of a particular England, as Patrick Wright (1985) puts it, of an old country. This harmonious, orderly community is self-policing because of its shared values and assumptions, vigilant against the autodidacts of the environment. To continue the quotation I began above:

'People who buy houses round here tend to have regard to the ambience of the area as a whole,' he said. 'By and large they are not the kind of do-it-yourselfers who think it's the bee's knees to put in a mock Georgian frontage, or go down to a DIY superstore to pick up a timber cladding front porch. They tend to stick to traditional styles, though we still have to be vigilant – there are exceptions.'

> (Mr Tyler, quoted in Durham, 'Battle against . . .' *The Independent*, 14 July 1989)

The shifts in this speech, 'People who buy houses round here. . . .' 'They' . . . 'We' . . . trace the fragility of this community of natural taste, the way in which it is made through vigilance as well as born. There is here a particular characterising of the relationship between the public and the private, which, as I argued earlier, is a significant division within discourses of taste. Judy Attfield (1989) provides a fascinating example of conflict over this distinction in her account of the net curtain war between tenants and architects in Harlow New Town in the 1950s. In this, in some ways analogous, public conflict the architects repeatedly complain that tenants ruin their open-plan picture-window dwellings in a quest for cosiness pursued through the obstructive placing of furniture, heavy curtaining and nets. Attfield observes, 'Through the appropriation of privacy by the concealment of the interior from the uninvited gaze, people took control of their own interior space and at the same time made a public declaration of their variance from the architects' design' (228). This example provides another indication of the way in which public and private are constructed spaces, perceived differentially and differently accessible to different persons. Mr Tyler's speech above is the discourse of the unselfconscious inheritors of public space who accept external uniformity in the absolute confidence of internal, private uniqueness. This vision of Britain has to be set against the aggressively downmarket image of Sky. As Mark Edmonds put it nearly a year before:

> But unless Sky changes tack and goes for a more upmarket audience, a satellite dish protruding from the front wall will do about as much for your standing in the neighbourhood as a visit from a rat-catcher.
>
> (Edmonds, 'Fright on the tiles', *Evening Standard*, 12 July 1989)

Dish-erectors defend themselves with considerable resignation, in vocabularies of the personal, which hint at other meanings for dishes. Thus Mr Bolton of New Earswick:

> 'The village is beautifully kept and a much more desirable place to live than most council estates, but the people who have a big say in our lives tend to be old folk with old-fashioned ideas. Like it or not, satellite TV is here to stay and it's frustrating to be denied it.'
>
> ('TV dish ban in "Quaker" village', *Daily Mail*, 4 December 1989: 15)

or Mrs Kidd of the same village, quoted in another newspaper:

'We saved up £130 to buy the dish. We have three kiddies who love the films.'

('Village bans TV satellite dishes', *The Guardian*, 4 December 1989)

Or the Radfords' son, Colin:

'I know all my friends would like one. I also know what they're saying about spoiling the village. For me it's rather *boring*.'

('Sky dish is the limit. . . .' *The Independent*,
25 October 1989)

The dissatisfactions which leak out of these plain statements, the half-expressed desire for another order, one more modern, or more fun for the kiddies, less *boring*, are of a quite different type to the confident, regulatory public-spirited complaints of the anti-dishers. Dishes are a DIY chance of a better environment of satisfaction. In the classic privatised consumer transaction, you pays your money and you takes your choice. The fact that the choice itself may be less than anticipated, or that the quality of what is available may be disappointing, is another matter. The discursive context within which this choice is made, the double jeopardy of satellite television in the terms of legitimate culture, militates against elaborated defence or critique. The *Daily Telegraph* (13 April 1989: 23) epitomised this point in heading an article about a man who made a dish from a dustbin lid, 'The man who cannot complain about trash on TV'. For the anti-dishers though, each 60 cm platter, 'scarring rows of houses at exactly the level where their uniformity remains most intact' (Rowland), signals an opting out of, an impediment to a certain public vision. And it is this, as I have argued which is the hegemonic taste code, this which constitutes dish-discourse, which frames the terms and reporting of dish conflict, and will therefore also provide one of the contexts in which dish erectors articulate their defences. It is thus that the non-verbal aspects of the practice become significant. We could say actions speak louder than words. Certainly at a general level the dishes can be approached as conspicuous consumption, and, classically, conspicuous leisure consumption. But the erection of a dish is also historically specific, a particular act, a concrete and visible sign of a consumer who has bought into the supranational entertainment space, who will not necessarily be available for the ritual, citizen-making moments of national broadcasting (Scannell 1988a; Chaney 1979). Who is abandoning the local citizenry and the national landscape of heritage and preservation (Morley and Robins 1989). Erecting a satellite dish on the front of your house is partly a declaration of not being bothered 'to like what's better to like'.

APPENDIX

In discussion at Champaign I argued that one hypothesis that could be advanced from the research for this paper was that British Satellite Broadcasting (BSB), the 'quality' satellite station broadcasting to Britain, was unlikely to survive because its target audience was precisely the people who, for the reasons outlined above, would feel most reluctant to erect satellite dishes on their homes.[13] Since then, on 2 November 1990, British Satellite Broadcasting (owned by a consortium of mainly British media interests, including Pearson, Granada, Chargeur and Reed International) has been merged very suddenly with Sky (News International) to form British Sky Broadcasting. Despite the retention of the BSB acronym, most commentators, including, for example, Anthony Simonds-Gooding, the head of BSB, regarded the deal as a Sky coup which finally gave Murdoch (a non-EC citizen and a British newspaper owner) an (unregulated) place in (regulated) British television.[14] Murdoch's other media interests were incompatible with this in terms of the 1990 Broadcasting Bill, a problem evaded in the use of the older Astra (Sky) satellite which is regarded as Luxembourgian not British. Certainly, the nationwide posters which herald the merger at present (November 1990), read: SKY AND BSB MERGE, THE BEST OF BOTH WORLDS – SKY, and two of the five BSB channels have now stopped broadcasting. It is not clear yet whether there will be any intervention by the Office of Fair Trading or the Independent Broadcasting Authority.

Of course, the reasons for the failure of BSB are complex, and must be seen alongside the massive losses sustained by Sky since inception. Satellite television in Britain is not yet profitable for anyone.[15] However, in all the retrospective discussion of investment levels, multi-media support, etc., I would still argue for the significance of the taste codes discussed below as one element in the final outcome. My argument above is exclusively concerned with the erection of Sky dishes. This is partly because Sky started broadcasting earlier than BSB, so all press coverage was initially about Sky and satellite dishes meant Sky. It is also because there are very many more Sky dishes easily visible.[16] This fact is not in and of itself an explanation of why Sky survives. It is a fact which also needs explaining. This I hope the paper makes some moves towards.

Part IV

Feminist identities

Introduction

The final part of this book returns to many of the concerns with which it opened. These two chapters were written a good ten years after the early work on soap opera, and offer, in different ways, reflections on the institutionalisation of feminist film and television criticism in the academy. If many of the concerns recur – notions of a gendered audience, the aesthetic place of women's genres and the difficult relation of feminism to femininity – what is perhaps more interesting is the way in which the same characters persist. 'The feminist' is a character with a long history. A politics based on gender identity has been differently inflected through other contemporary political concerns. As historians of feminism such as Lucy Bland (1995) and Vron Ware (1992) have shown us, feminism has never been a unitary phenomenon, and its politics and allegiances have been extremely diverse. The feminist, if we can speak of such an abstract figure, has both honourable and dishonourable inheritances. She has fought against slavery and for eugenics, for the right of married women to own property, for and against the veil and for votes. She has come to historical prominence at different periods in different contexts with different meanings and profiles. My concern here has been with the particular coming-into-being of this figure in relation to the academic disciplines of film and television studies. That these disciplines too are only emergent in this period from the mid-1970s both complicates the picture, and suggests that these disciplines may be porous to concerns around gender precisely because they themselves are only semi-institutionalised.

This particular incarnation of the feminist, as suggested in both Chapters 11 and 12, partly constructs herself in a contradictory and ambivalent relation to one of the more significant modern female personae, the feminine consumer of mass culture. Terry Lovell (1987) has shown us the way in which the moral attack on the English novel concentrated on women as readers; Janice Radway (1994), more recently, has demonstrated how attacks on the pretension of the middle-brow consumer in the USA have been persistently gendered. Research on television soap opera, as Robert Allen (1985) has recorded, repeatedly characterises its pathologised viewer as female. These essays explore the way in which the 1970s feminist is partly defined as 'not that woman', but on the other hand, constructs as her unique field of study precisely those despised women's genres (see Hallam and Marshment 1995 for critical discussion of this argument).

A range of critics have commented on the 'self-limiting address' of feminist media theory (Schlesinger *et al.* 1992: 8). Liesbet van Zoonen, who has herself conducted research on women as newsmakers, has used a formulation of John Corner's to characterise the predominant emphases of feminist media work. Corner discusses a distinction within the newer reception-orientated media studies between a 'public knowledge project' and a 'popular culture project' (Corner 1991b: 268). Van Zoonen points out that this distinction also tends to be a gendered one, with feminist work, with its emphasis on taste and pleasure, clustering in the 'popular culture' domestic corner while citizenship, knowledge and the politics of information occupy the main square (van Zoonen 1994: 9). Similarly, Christine Geraghty, using the colour coding employed by Ann Gray (1992) in the gendering of domestic technology, points out that in recent media scholarship 'issues of consumption, audience and pleasure are relatively pink but work on media ownership, control and regulation is deepest indigo' (Geraghty 1996: 320). This history and emphasis is undeniable. Feminist media scholarship has concentrated on the representation of, and reception by, women, in and of genres and media marked as feminine. These histories are recounted, in different ways, in both Chapters 11 and 12. Here I want to sketch out what might be at stake in this reproduction, within the very structures of the discipline, of the gendered private/public distinction so fundamental to the organisation of western bourgeois culture.

There are two main issues. One is the domestication and privatisation of feminist work, the overdetermined location of this work in engagement with the feminine and femininity. Second is the kinds of femininity that are valorised. In both cases we can see the reproduction of existing relations of power. In 1988 Isaac Julien and Kobena Mercer co-edited an issue of the journal *Screen*. Wittily, but with the serious thrust of good wit, they called it 'The last special issue on "race"' (*Screen* 29, 4 (1988)). Their choice of contributors was international and anti-essentialist: they were making a point about the urgent necessity of everyone paying attention to "race", while suggesting that it is the quality of the attention, not the origins of the attention-giver, which is most significant. But the title was also about the failure of the project of attention to 'race' to move into the mainstream, remaining instead the special preserve of those ethnicised or racialised by Anglo-American white culture, framed, every so often, in a special issue. This has relevance in both areas I want to discuss. Firstly, it points us to what we might call the 'women', 'race', 'Third World', 'queer' special issue or chapter story. This is a story with which many scholars will be familiar, which is that of being invited to contribute to a collection because of one's type: what identity one represents. Now of course, in some ways, this is a story of political gain. At

least the textbook makers, the gatekeepers – and I don't exclude myself from
this category – do quite often recognise that they have a problem. New
chapters and special issues are commissioned, and the commissioned work
is often ground-breaking. I think here, for example, of the 1984 *Feminist
Review*: *Many Voices, One Chant: Black Feminist Perspectives* (*Feminist
Review* 17), or the 1986 issue of *Communication*: *Feminist Critiques of
Popular Culture* edited by Ellen Wartella and Paula Treichler (9, 1). We can
even point to a chronology which gives us a rate of frequency. 'Women' now
get in quite often (although, as Chizuko Ueno remarked, feminism has gone
out of fashion without ever becoming mainstream), the problematic of 'race'
is no longer invisible (although indeed, a little difference goes a long way),
while 'queer' is just breaking cover (in terms of anthologies). This chronology has its own bizarre consequences and logics of power, with the
differential construction of successive differences against each other. Thus,
for example, as is now well documented, the 'woman' constructed by 1970s
feminism was generally an unconsciously '(white straight western) woman',
and while black women might get a look in under 'race', this was not
necessarily the case. Here theories of the postcolonial have seemed more
welcoming. But before considering a little more the content of these chapter
identities – 'we just need a summary of the current state of thinking and
something about new work by category X' – it is important to spend a little
longer with the chapter or special issue phenomenon itself. For its persistence
points to the quite elaborated existence of what we might call academic
parallel universes.

For the irony of course, is that quite often the scholars invited to write these
'women/race/queer' chapters do indeed specialise in articulating something
of the dynamics of the particular identity in the chosen field. And also retain
a certain ambivalence about 'others' appropriating their object of study. It is
quite reasonable to invite me to offer a survey of feminist film and television
criticism: it is the area in which I have specialised. But while I have been
doing this, I turn out to have been working in a girlzone, a subordinate field
which although it has had to transform its own foundational category,
'woman', and has produced a quite substantial literature, still seems to have
had remarkably little impact on the wider contours of the discipline. This is
most vividly presented to me whenever I visit my favourite bookshop in
London. Here the basement has traditionally been the home of philosophy,
critical theory, film, media and cultural studies. Feminist work was introduced in a small section on the ground floor. This small feminist section has
grown enormously over the last ten years and now takes up a whole wall in
the middle of the shop, with sections on film studies, cultural studies and
media studies among many others. These include separate sections on black
and Third World women, which may or may not include film, cultural and
media studies books in any one instance. In turn writers such as Lola Young
or Jacqueline Bobo may or may not be included in film studies. When I go

to this shop I have to keep going up and down the stairs as what I want is in at least two places. Some feminist books are included in the basement, but you are usually more likely to find a particular text upstairs. On the other hand, I can't just stay upstairs because if I do I have no sense of what is being published in the field *generally*. 'Postcolonialism' is downstairs, but black feminist theory upstairs. Some authors have a split oeuvre: Ien Ang on *Dallas* is upstairs (1985), but Ien Ang's book of essays – which has a central section on feminism – is downstairs (1995a). These spatial arrangements fascinate me, for they offer a physical condensation of so many sets of relations, from the cost of space to the temporality of different identities, from the success of particular books to the ebbs and flows of political and intellectual fashion. They testify to the contradictory, mobile and unresolved relations between the academic literature of the new social movements and the mainstreams of disciplines. And one manifestation of these relations is what I have called academic parallel universes in which a space of difference is cultivated alongside, in opposition to and sometimes in dialogue with, the mainstream. So although there is an issue about the femininity of the focus of feminist media scholarship, there is also an issue about the impermeability of 'male' work to this scholarship. The work is constructed as not only by and about women, but also *for* – and only of relevance to – women. Meaghan Morris, in 1988, argued this point at some length in relation to the masculine-dominated construction of the field 'postmodernism'. She suggests that the issue is not whether feminists have written on postmodernism but under what conditions women's work 'can figure' in such debate (Morris 1988: 12). She also points out how difficult it is to make this type of point without becoming immediately inaudible as a dreary old-fashioned nag. The further point is that I have some doubt about whether work by feminists (or other politically claimed identities) that does not embrace the point of difference, in this case the feminine, is in fact *recognised* as feminist scholarship. So while I agree that there is an overdetermination in the femininity of feminist work, I don't agree that this is always self-imposed. I would rather see this subaltern field as a field in which feminist scholars are at least audible to each other, the very existence of which indicates the continuance of patterns of discrimination articulated through gender.

So if the first point is about the relationship between feminist work and what we might call the wider world, the second is about the substance of the concentration on femininity. Here again I think we find rather contradictory negotiations of power. For the dominant, valorised forms of femininity are clearly youthful heterosexual 'anglo' femininity. What in one incarnation is Pamela Anderson, in another, Barbie. And not only has feminist work repeatedly addressed the feminine spheres, it has also repeatedly addressed this dominant white/western femininity. Jacqueline Bobo and Ellen Seiter pointed this out in their discussion of the whiteness of nearly all feminist reception research (1991). Trinh T. Minh-ha made a related point in an international frame when she called her opening essay in the volume of the journal *Discourse* (8, 1986/7) that she edited, 'Difference: "A Special Third World Women Issue"'. Cathy Schwitchenberg has suggested that 'lesbians are the aporia of feminist audience research' (1994: 174), arguing that it is necessary for feminist research to pay attention to gender 'at the margins' (1994: 178). That is, the hegemony of white/western femininity is both addressed and reproduced in the historical emergence of feminist media scholarship. This much is clear in the bookshop arrangements I discussed above: the special labelled shelves in the women's section which are not for disciplines and topics such as 'literature' or 'therapy' are labelled with the identities of 'other women' – 'black women' 'Third World' – those who have challenged an inclusion in the unqualified 'feminism' with its historical assumptions. Judith Butler has argued that 'the premature insistence on a stable subject of feminism, understood as a seamless category of women, inevitably generates multiple refusals to accept the category' (1990: 4), and it is these refusals which have been most productive. For these refusals – among their many other effects – repeatedly reveal the point of privilege in the easy use of the term *feminist*, and the necessity of understanding this privilege historically and internationally. As Ien Ang (1995b) has suggested, perhaps feminism in the 1990s is useful only if understood as a partial and provisional identification in some circumstances for some women. If all usages are prefaced, 'I'm a feminist, but. . .'.

Chapter 11

Pedagogies of the feminine†

INTRODUCTION

When I told her the title of this essay, a friend said, 'You mean when you put lots of ribbons and bows in your hair before you go out and lecture.' She was, as usual, quite right, as I want to discuss practices of teaching, and to argue against some of the ways in which feminism seems to be appearing in film and media studies classrooms. It is the lurking opposition between the 'ribbons and bows' of femininity, and what is entailed in feminist teaching, which structures both this essay and the academic field which I discuss.

I want to reflect on a decade of teaching 'women's genres', the new feminist canons of femininity which have become partly institutionalised in the 1980s. My argument will be that there are features of the historically very rapid canon formation which lead to particular pedagogic problems. These can partly be understood as problems of tone and history, in that this field of study, which I outline in more detail below, has been mainly established through avowedly political criticism which has often had the implicit critique of conventional femininities installed as centrally as the more explicit critique of patriarchy. Much early feminist media criticism involved a passionate repudiation of the pleasures of consumption which, by extension, morally rebuked those who consumed.

The main theoretical issues in the teaching of 'women's genres', though, are the (historical) understanding of femininity, feminine cultures and gender identity, and the articulation of these identities and cultures with ideas of power. These are problems for both textual-institutional study and pedagogic practice, and can be posed as such simultaneously. For example, my teaching experience makes me very uneasy about the way in which gender identity can become 'renaturalised' in the classroom. That is, consciousness about the asymmetries of gendered experience (and divisions within the categories of gender), that every reader or viewer, for example, is not a 'he' or 'white', can boomerang, confining students, particularly female students, to a position

†First published in *Screen* 32, 4 (1991).

of difference which may be the more difficult to transcend or transgress for all the sophistication of its theorisation. Despite all those long battles to get 'women' on the syllabus, the benefits to female students can be rather mixed if it is only as a natural and self-evident pedagogic category that 'women' do appear. I wish finally to move from this discussion of identity politics in the classroom to suggest that some of these points have implications for feminism as we have known it in the 1970s and 1980s.

THE CANON IS COMING

Since the late 1970s it has been increasingly possible to design and teach courses which include some study of film melodrama, television soap opera and the 'woman's picture'. If early feminist work on the media concentrated on images *of* women, often focusing on advertising, as well as making reference to these genres, there is a shift in the later 1970s towards increased consideration of images *for* women.[1] The reasons for this shift are complex and various, but within the literature recurrent interest is expressed in: media genres and forms with mass appeal to women; the representation of, and identification with, central female protagonists; female desire; narrative modes and rhythms specific to femininity; and the position of the female spectator. The title of Annette Kuhn's article, 'Women's genres' (1984a), nicely catches the multiple inscription of women in, and in relation to, these films and television programmes.

There is now in existence a recognisable, if heterogeneous, feminist field of study, which, following Kuhn, we can call 'women's genres', with several different, traceable formations. It is not my purpose here to discuss the extent to which this cross-media field of study is, or should be, regarded as canonical, nor to discuss canon formation in general.[2] There does, however, seem now, in the 1990s, to be a *de facto* field of study that might be termed mass cultural fictions of femininity; and I want to reflect on the experience of teaching this material. To this end I will initially try to sketch the field from three different starting points: audiovisual texts; publications; and finally, through what I take to be the theoretical core of the field, the debates over the understanding of the female viewer. The three different starting points give different, but overlapping, outlines, which are offered as provisional – something to work with – rather than definitive.

Audio-visual texts

The term 'audiovisual' yokes together different disciplines and textualities. Thus the study of 'women's genres' on television has, until recently, effectively been the study of soap opera, which has a long history within mass communications with which the newer feminist work has hardly engaged.[3] The early feminist research on soap opera was often conducted in the context of inquiry into 'the housewife's day'. Thus Carol Lopate (1976) discusses US daytime soaps in a more general discussion of the rhythms and pre-occupations of daytime television, while Dorothy Hobson's 1982 work on *Crossroads* (Central, 1964–88) emerged from earlier research on the daily culture of young working-class women at home.[4] Concerns with domestic time, rhythm and the engaged role of the viewer recur in the work of Modleski (1979), Seiter (1982a) and Mattelart (1981). Kaplan (1987), indeed, to slightly different ends, uses Kristeva's periodisation of 'women's time' to structure her history of feminist television criticism. This initial focus, on ways and rhythms of viewing, rather than detailed textual analysis, could be seen to characterise feminist approaches to television domestic serial drama. Thus, although there is detailed work on *Coronation Street* (Granada, 1961–), *Dallas* (CBS/Lorimar, USA, 1978–), *Dynasty* (ABC/Aaron Spelling, 1981–), *General Hospital* (ABC, USA, 1963–) and *Brookside* (Channel 4, 1982–),[5] the overarching concerns do seem to have been more with the involvement and pleasures of female viewers in the patterns of domestic viewing. There is also a body of work on sit-coms which is rather less concerned with patterns of viewing, and includes Pat Mellencamp's 1986 work on Lucille Ball, Serafina Bathrick (1984) on Mary Tyler Moore and Lauren Rabinovitz (1984) on *Kate and Allie* (directed by Mort Lackman/Alan Landsburg, USA, 1984–). Although there are clear affinities with the soap work, these programmes seem rather more tangentially related to the core concerns of 'women's genres', basically because they offer laughter rather than tears.

In relation to the cinema, the field can be marked out through individual films, genres and various subgenres and cycles. Thus certain films have been the subject of particular debates, such as that about maternity and spectator-ship and the debate in subsequent issues of *Cinema Journal*, in relation to the 1937 version of *Stella Dallas* (directed by King Vidor) Kaplan (1983c), Williams (1984), or that about fantasy and the female consumer/spectator for *Now Voyager* (Irving Rapper, 1942) (Cowie (1984), LaPlace (1987) and Jacobs (1981)). Others, as with Mulvey (1977) on *All that Heaven Allows* (Douglas Sirk, 1959), have been used in influential theoretical formulations. Films such as *Mildred Pierce* (Michael Curtiz, 1945) and *Coma* (Michael Crichton, 1977), generically more hybrid, have long histories in debates about women protagonists, generic constitutions of femininity and the role of the melodramatic.[6] None of the quite extensive available material on *Mildred Pierce* discusses Lottie (Butterfly McQueen), which points to the problematic role of ethnicity in this corpus. The women of 'women's genres' are generally white women. Thus, for example, *Imitation of Life* (Douglas Sirk, 1959), clearly recognised on its release date as dealing with 'the colour problem', has until recently mainly been written about as 'mothers and daughters' within a 'Sirkian excess' framework.[7] Consciousness of the ethno-centricity of the canon leading, for example, to the rather ambiguous status of *Gone with the Wind* (Victor Fleming, 1939) has arguably led to the rather perverse addition of *The Color Purple* (directed by Steven Spielberg) to the list of frequently studied individual films, in that it is very often used in courses to raise issues of 'ethnic' voice (the film/book comparison), and, because of Jacqueline Bobo's work, issues of spectatorship.[8]

Thus, while one way of looking at the significant audiovisual texts of 'women's genres' produces a series of individual films as nodal points in a series of debates about spectatorship, consumption, identification and finally ethnicity, another way foregrounds the historical research on different genres and film cycles. This research, most of it listed below, or represented in Gledhill, has focused on US 1940s 'women's pictures'; British Gainsborough Studios; US 1930s 'fallen woman' cycle; US 1950s colour melodramas; and 1970s 'independent woman' films. With the historical work on the female spectator discussed below, this research is slowly transforming the wider historical field, as can be seen from recent histories of the Weimar cinema.[9] Similarly, feminist analyses of individual films such as *Letter from an Unknown Woman* (directed by Max Ophuls, 1948), *Caught* (Max Ophuls, 1949) and *Rebecca* (Alfred Hitchcock, 1940) alter the critical profile of their directors.[10]

Publications

Evidently, it is through publications that I construct both my first and third outlines of the field, in that it is through the reports of conference debates, journal articles and book reviews, that the changing contours of discussion can be traced. When addressed directly, Annette Kuhn's article (1984a), which surveys material on both film and television, appears formative. Since Kuhn surveyed the field in 1984, there has been a rapid expansion of work in this area, which is shown by the chronology of published books presented below. Listing only books creates various chronological distortions and omissions, but has some justification in terms of the availability necessary for canon formation. Kuhn could refer to only four books in this area, one of which – the British Film Institute dossier on Gainsborough melodrama – was not available for retail sale. Subsequently, Modleski's *Loving with a Vengeance*, at that stage published only in hardback by the Shoe String Press in the United States, was picked up by Methuen (now Routledge) in 1985, and there has been a considerable expansion of the literature on soap opera, including Ien Ang's book *Watching Dallas* (1985), translated from the Dutch and now in its second edition, Robert C. Allen's *Speaking of Soap Opera* (1985), David Buckingham's *Public Secrets* (1987) and, most recently, Christine Geraghty's *Women and Soap Opera* (1991). The late 1980s have seen the publication of several anthologies and collections of essays, such as those by Pribram (1988) and Gledhill (1987), both of which are now in their second editions. Gledhill in particular has consciously addressed herself to the issue of both feminist and film studies canons, arguing for the significance

BOOKS PUBLISHED IN THE FIELD OF WOMEN'S GENRES, 1981–90

1981
R. Dyer, C. Geraghty, M. Jordan, T. Lovell, R. Paterson and J. Stewart, *Coronation Street* (London: British Film Institute).

1982
Dorothy Hobson, *Crossroads: The Drama of a Soap Opera* (London: Methuen).
Tania Modleski, *Loving with a Vengeance* (Hamden, Conn.: Shoestring Press); includes Modleski's 1979 essay, 'The search for tomorrow in today's soap operas'.

1983
Sue Aspinall and Robert Murphy (eds), *Gainsborough Melodrama* (London: British Film Institute Dossier no. 18).
Muriel G. Cantor and Suzanne Pingree, *The Soap Opera* (Beverly Hills, Cal.: Sage).
Mary Cassata and Thomas Skill (eds), *Life on Daytime Television* (Norwood, NJ: Ablex).

1984
Peter Buckman, *All for Love* (London: Secker & Warburg).
Mary Ann Doane, Patricia Mellencamp and Linda Williams, *Re-Vision* (Los Angeles: American Film Institute); includes essays by Gledhill, Mayne and Doane.
Michael Intintoli, *Taking Soaps Seriously* (New York: Praeger).
Andrea S. Walsh, *Women's Film and Female Experience 1940–1950* (New York: Praeger).
[Janice Radway, *Reading the Romance* (Chapel Hill: University of North Carolina Press]
[Rosalind Coward, *Female Desire* (London: Paladin).]

1985
Ien Ang, *Watching Dallas: Soap Opera and the Melodramatic Imagination* (London: Methuen); trans. Della Couling; first published as *Het Geval Dallas* in 1982 (Amsterdam: Uitgeverij SUA).
Robert C. Allen, *Speaking of Soap Operas* (Chapel Hill: University of North Carolina Press).
Pam Cook (ed.), *The Cinema Book* (London: British Film Institute); section on melodrama.

1986
Michèle Mattelart, *Women, Media, Crisis* (London: Comedia); includes 1981–2 essays on telenovelas first published in French.
Charlotte Brunsdon (ed.), *Films for Women* (London: British Film Institute).
[Jean Radford, *The Progress of Romance: The Politics of Popular Fiction* (London: Routledge & Kegan Paul).]
[Cora Kaplan, *Sea Changes* (London: Verso); reprints essays on *The Thorn Birds* and *The Color Purple*.]

1987
Helen Baehr and Gillian Dyer (eds), *Boxed In: Women and Television* (London: Pandora).
David Buckingham, *Public Secrets: EastEnders and its Audience* (London: British Film Institute).
Mary Ann Doane, *The Desire to Desire: The Women's Film of the 1940s* (Bloomington: Indiana University Press).
Christine Gledhill (ed.), *Home Is Where the Heart Is: Studies in Melodrama and the Woman's Film* (London: British Film Institute).
[Janice Winship, *Inside Women's Magazines* (London: Pandora).]

[Rosemary Betterton (ed.), *Looking On: Images of Femininity in the Visual Arts and Media* (London: Pandora).]

[Janice Radway, *Reading the Romance* (British edition with new preface published by Verso).]

1988

Denise Mann and Lynn Spigel (eds), *Camera Obscura*, 16, 'Television and the Female Consumer'.

Lorraine Gamman and Margaret Marshment (eds), *The Female Gaze: Women as Viewers of Popular Culture* (London: The Women's Press).

Hilary Kingsley, *Soap Box* (London: Macmillan).

Marilyn Matelski, *The Soap Opera Evolution* (Jefferson, NC: McFarland).

E. Deidre Pribram (ed.), *Female Spectators* (London: Verso).

1989

Robert Lang, *American Film Melodrama* (Princeton: Princeton University Press).

Laura Mulvey, *Visual and Other Pleasures* (Basingstoke: Macmillan); reprints 'Visual pleasure and narrative cinema' (1975) and essays on melodrama.

Ellen Seiter, Hans Borchers, Gabriele Kreutzner and Eva-Maria Warth (eds), *Remote Control: Television, Audiences and Cultural Power* (London: Routledge).

Helen Taylor, *Scarlett's Women: Gone with the Wind and its Female Fans* (London: Virago).

[Ella Taylor, *Prime-Time Families* (Berkeley: University of California Press).]

1990

Janet Bergstrom and Mary Ann Doane (eds), *Camera Obscura*, nos 20–1, 'Special Issue on the Female Spectator: The Spectatrix' (dated 1989, published and copyright 1990).

Mary Ellen Brown, *Television and Women's Culture* (London and Newbury Park: Sage).

Jane Gaines and Charlotte Herzog, *Fabrications: Costume and the Female Body* (New York and London: Routledge).

Pribram reprinted.

Gledhill reprinted.

Notes

This is not an attempt to survey feminist film and television criticism generally but to give some sense of the publication of books in the area 'women's genres'. Thus most of the standard 'women and film' publications are omitted, as are works which concentrate on female authorship and other genres, such as science fiction. I have excluded most works, mainly on soap opera within US mass communications, which do not engage with feminist critical paradigms. However, I have included, in square brackets, feminist work about women's genres in other media, such as women's magazines and romance fiction.

Listing only book-length publications, which has some justification at the level of canon formation as well as because of the constraint of space, omits several key contributions, such as those of Elizabeth Cowie, E. Ann Kaplan and Annette Kuhn, and nearly all work on the lesbian spectator. It also seriously distorts the chronology of certain debates, in that many articles have their most formative impact before they appear in anthologies or 'collected works'. For example, as the anthology itself reveals, much of the groundwork for Gledhill's influential 1987 anthology is done in the late 1960s and early 1970s, particularly by Thomas Elsaesser. I have thus tried to indicate the original date of publication of key articles. There are extensive bibliographies in Allen (1985), Gledhill (1987) and *Camera Obscura* (1989), nos 20–1.

of the historical understanding of the melodramatic mode to both (1987). Arguably, however, the single most significant contribution to the field, apart from Christine Gledhill's explicit project of canon formation and Mary Ann Doane's 1987 study of women's films of the 1940s, has been Janice Radways's *Reading the Romance*, published in the USA in 1984, and in Britain, with a new introduction, in 1987. Although dealing with paperback fiction rather than film or television, the methodological breadth and its paradigmatic set of concerns (popular fiction – feminism – reading – ordinary women) has given this book an impact outside its original disciplinary home of American studies.

In the period of the chronology, the status of these genres in the academy has changed, and many film, television and media studies courses now deal with these and related media genres and forms such as girls' teenage comics, women's magazines and popular romance fiction. In the same period these genres have appeared elsewhere in the academy at all levels, from schools to universities, in 'decanonised' English and art history, 'modernising' European languages and history, as well as in the newer, more unstable, field of cultural studies.

In addition to the presence of these texts on an increasing number of syllabuses there have been clear shifts in the ways in which the object of study has been conceptualised which register both academic and political debates. The most noticeable moves, apart from the general, if fiercely contested, loosening and leavening of the canons of many disciplines within the humanities, are away from the study of text to the study of audience, within a general revaluation of cultures of consumption. It is on these grounds that I want finally to outline these fields of study through the emerging role of the female viewer in film and television studies since 1975.

The female viewer since 1975

The year 1975 is when Laura Mulvey's essay, 'Visual pleasure and narrative cinema' was first published; it thus forms a widely recognised 'inaugural moment' in the study of the female viewer.[11] To endorse the widely recognised significance of Mulvey's essay on the study of gendered spectatorship is not to collapse film and television viewing, and the paradigms within which they have been constituted, but to recognise that it was Mulvey's posing of the issue of gendered spectatorship in the cinema to which many subsequent scholars of film and television addressed themselves. To work here only with the recent period is also not to imply that there are no female viewers before 1975. Very briefly, using recent historical and theoretical feminist research we can construct two categories of female viewers before this period. There is the general, connotatively feminine category, the consumer of mass culture, whose gendering has recently been discussed by Andreas Huyssen (1986) and Patrice Petro (1986). This mainly evaluative category – passive victim of media manipulation – has specific manifestations in particular historical bodies of work on film and television. Thus we can distinguish female fans, mainly for the cinema – Kracauer's Little Shop Girls – from, in relation to the broadcast media, research subjects such as the radio-soap listeners investigated by Arnheim, Herzog and Kauffman in the late 1930s and early 1940s (Lazarsfeld and Stanton 1944). The second category of female viewer has been produced by post-1975 feminist research into historical cultures of femininity and media consumption, such as Petro's (1989) and Schlüpmann's (1991) work on Weimar cinema, Hansen's (1986) work on American silent cinema or Lynn Spigel's (1992) work on the installation of the television set.

To return, however, to 1975 and Laura Mulvey. Annette Kuhn uses Mulvey as a starting point in her discussion of feminist work on 'gynocentric' film and television – soap opera, melodrama and the 'woman's picture' – even though Mulvey herself is not particularly concerned with these genres. Kuhn argues that although all feminist critics agree that these gynocentric genres are 'aimed at a female audience', their understanding of what this means can be very different. She articulates the theoretical differences through a series of oppositions:

(textual) spectator	social audience
femininity as a subject position	femaleness as a social gender
textual analysis	contextual inquiry
cinematic (or televisual) institution as context	historical context of production and reception
sexual difference constructed through look and spectacle	sexual difference constructed through flow, address and rhythm

Although Kuhn is careful to characterise the ways in which individual writers lay differing emphases on different parts of these binaries, she also points out that there tends to be a patterning in which work which comes through film studies, particularly the engagement with psychoanalysis, tends to move through the categories on the left, whereas work through more institutionally sociological television studies tends to utilise the categories on the right. The crux of this difference could be characterised as the theoretical site of the 'engendering' of the spectator – is she already a woman when she comes to the text, or is it the text which constructs a feminine position for the viewer? Television scholars have tended to invoke already existing women, film scholars, the textual constitution of spectators. The theoretical problem of the relationship of these two is thus, arguably, displaced through disciplinary boundaries.

Since Kuhn wrote this piece, a good deal more feminist scholarship has been published, although some of these binary oppositions remain very much in place, if deployed over different terrain. Thus Linda Williams (1988) characterises a not dissimilar set of oppositions as constitutive of differences between textual and historical feminist film scholars in her discussion of *Mildred Pierce*. Christine Gledhill, too (1988), in her discussion of spectatorship, explicitly uses the concept of negotiation to bridge the dualism Kuhn identifies. Kuhn herself (1988), in her study of film censorship and sexuality in Britain in the 1910s and 1920s, argues that what she calls the text/context distinction is overcome in her specific historical inquiry.

There have been several recent surveys of research on the female viewer which have tended, through their disciplinary origins, to be located on one or other side of this divide, but which together give a relatively full picture of recent work. The special issue of *Camera Obscura* on 'The Spectatrix' (1989), which offers statements by individual scholars about the female spectator as well as some national surveys and a general introduction, is clearly, as the concern with the female spectator would suggest, formed within film studies. On the other hand, recent survey articles by Liesbet van Zoonen (1991), and Ien Ang and Joke Hermes (1991) concentrate on feminist approaches to the mass media and television. What I wish to pursue here is the 'television' work, for it is this area of work, along with print media, which has seen the noticeable expansion, in the 1980s, of ethnographic work. Thus while earlier work assumed or hypothesised the responses of female viewers and readers, there is now a distinct body of ethnographic work on the female audience. This work, by Dorothy Hobson (1989), Ien Ang (1985), Andrea Press (1990), the Tübingen project (Seiter *et al.* 1987), and Ann Gray (1992) has been concerned with the investigation of the media tastes and usages of 'ordinary women'. It is through a shared concern with ordinary women that Janice Radway's research, although not on television, is so important; *Reading the Romance* is the most extensive scholarly investigation of the act of reading, and of the qualitative criteria and interpretative strategies used by a particular group of women readers. The figure of the ordinary woman is now firmly installed in the classroom. Her likes and dislikes, her pleasures and fantasies are discussed in seminars and summarised in essays. The problem with this figure, though, is that she can lose the contours of her particularity in the classroom, and join that generalised other to feminism, 'the housewife'. This is both a theoretical and a pedagogic problem, in that, without the particularity of the original ethnographic enterprise, gender can be asked to explain both too little and too much. Femininity, instead of being a difficult and contradictory psychic, historical and cultural formation, to which feminists have been historically ambivalent, becomes an explanatory factor. Women like these texts because they (both the texts and the women) have feminine concerns. The categories of gender, constituted as pure as if persons are 'just' gendered, also begin to function in a theoretical short-circuit as explanatory. This can then make it very difficult, in the classroom, to avoid either celebrating or pathologising the pleasures of these gynocentric texts. Because much feminist media criticism so powerfully installs the figure of the ordinary woman as both the object of study and, in some ways, the person on whose behalf study is undertaken, and because, as I argue at more length in the final section, the identity 'feminist' has historically been constructed partly in contrast with 'ordinary women', this opposition is always potentially present in the classroom. It can be played out in various ways: students can focus on the way in which they are *not* like the women whose tastes are reported in the literature, *not* like the feminist critics they have to read, or *not* like their teacher. Or they can claim recognition and identification. It is this staking out of the different and overlapping identities and oppositions of woman and feminist in the classroom with which the next section is concerned.

THE THREE DS: DISRUPTION, DISAPPOINTMENT AND DEFERENCE

In this section I present some of the difficulties of teaching 'women's genres', drawing on several years of experience, mainly in British and US universities. I draw mainly on my teaching experience not because I consider it exemplary but out of necessity, in that there has been very little discussion of *pedagogies* of these genres, as opposed to the quite extensive literature on the texts, female spectators and women audiences.[12] Conversations with other feminist teachers in a range of contexts, and material I see as an external examiner, suggest that elements of this experience may be typical, and that other people working in the field face similar problems. I should also make clear that I am not talking about teaching in a 'women's studies' context, where the category woman is itself one of the main 'subjects' and where there is a much more extensive debate about, and literature on, pedagogy.[13]

Disruption seems the most straightforward problem with teaching women's genres. Other teachers have suggested 'derision' and 'dismissal' to describe student responses to some texts and classes. I use the term 'disruption' to designate the disruption of screenings, lectures and classes by some part of the student body on the grounds that the study material is 'stupid', 'ridiculous', and so on. Obviously this type of disruption does not take place only in response to 'women's genres'. Also, in certain contexts, it can be difficult to separate from the routinised sexual harassment of female teachers, the 'what she needs . . .' approach to women authority figures. It is a strategy I have seen deployed, sometimes apparently almost involuntarily, in a range of contexts. It is generally male students who behave in this way, apparently unable to sit quietly, to be complicit with femininity, for even the half hour of a soap opera; but in my experience feminist women can be pretty noisy too, providing 'active oppositional readings' throughout screenings. It is not here my purpose to analyse the range of defences and denials at stake, but minimally to suggest that there is here also a salutary dramatisation of social power in play. The study of 'women's genres' may have become more acceptable within the academy; but it has not yet become an acceptable part of hegemonic masculine identity. Nor, in complicated ways which I discuss at more length in the last section, is it compatible with some subcultural feminist identities. Aesthetic and social hierarchies in the wider social context underpin and reinforce these noisy repudiations of girls' things.

The very fact of the disruption can be an excellent starting point for discussion of aesthetic hierarchy, social statuses of audiences, gendered genres and subcultural readings; but it is also important to construct agendas for discussion that are not disruption-led, and to find a place from which 'those whose viewing has been disrupted' can speak. Otherwise work on the disrupted text focuses only on the important – but not all-consuming – issue of context/institution, and may be conducted mainly in defensive terms.

These noisy classrooms, however, can also be seen to signal the affect at stake with some of these texts. 'Weepies' are not so known for no reason. Teaching a class in which perhaps a majority were crying when the lights went up is different to, say, looking at the structure of television title sequences.[14] Passionate emotional investment in the fate of characters, or the outcome of stories, can be disruptive, in a different sense, of some academic habits. It can also put students in very vulnerable positions – particularly if a class is divided over the value of the study material. This leads me to another danger, in some ways the obverse of students groaning theatrically at a kiss: the problem of a sometimes rather paralysing 'niceness' in seminars on material in which many class members may have a very high personal investment. I have found that, despite taking for granted some things for which older feminists had to fight hard, most young female students still need a great deal of support to work confidently in critical and analytical ways. Pedagogically there seems a fine line between contexts which are supportive and confidence-building, and those in which disagreement is interpreted as disruptive and a problem in itself. The conciliatory element in many cultures of femininity can contribute to a much more congenial atmosphere than the cut and thrust of some academic modes; but it can also leave intellectual differences and disagreements uninterrogated. This tendency is experientially and theoretically complicated if questions of participants' very identity are always conceptually at stake. (This is not to deny that at some level all debate involves the fluctuating constitution and enactment of identities – but to argue that the threat of being found lacking as a woman because you do, or indeed don't, like *Neighbours* does not contribute to either the intellectual or the political project of feminism.)

This evocation of the disrupted classroom leads on to a series of relatively speculative points I would like to formulate about the experience of being taught this material. I should say at the outset that I am dwelling on the downside – there are many students for whom the study of this material is both illuminating and rewarding and it is certainly a corpus which I choose to teach.

If they have any choice, students choose to take courses on 'women's genres' for a variety of reasons. Often, of course, students encounter this material as part of a larger course on television or Hollywood cinema. In both cases, though, there is often a discernible excitement among young women at the prospect of studying material which they like, and on which they may be relatively expert. As is often the case in the teaching of popular culture, at least part of the classroom group is composed of individuals who are also fans. Without wishing to labour the point, I should make clear here that I am not suggesting that all young women naturally prefer, for example, romances to football – indeed, it is the increased tendency of media studies textbooks to assume this with which I am partly concerned. Under present cultural arrangements, nevertheless, they very often do, and it is clear that learning about, say, genre through case studies of horror and sci-fi, or television sport through coverage of the World Cup, often involves them in the study of material which they can find at best boring, at worst frightening and upsetting. The bedroom subcultures of femininity tend to give young women the skills of dress, gossip and romance rather than a fan's self-protective sense of the imminence of the next monstrous moment in a horror film. There is also the issue of the class provenance of clearly feminine media genres, often articulated with the extent to which academic success – being in tertiary education in the first place – has demanded the disavowal and relinquishing of these media skills and pleasures of femininity. This adds further poignancy to the dilemmas of these students. For the excited expectancy of studying – for a change something they like, of maybe finding grounds for the validation of these tastes, is disappointed by the very structure of the canon. For the canon of femininity is, precisely, a feminist canon. And herein lies both its justification and its crisis. Without feminism, when and where would these works have appeared on the syllabus? But through feminism, and that constitution of feminist identity as other than or opposed to conventional femininities (discussed at more length below) much of the available critical work can be described only, in Angela McRobbie's term, as 'recruitist' (McRobbie, 1982). Hence the disappointment. Because there are homologies between some feminist attitudes and the more general pejorative evaluation of cultures of femininity, too often, given the available reading material – and despite recent embraces of the pleasures of the popular – studying this material, as Judith Williamson observed in 1980, can actually confirm why it is stupid to like it (1981–2: 81). Bolstered by its institutional position in the formation of this canon, feminism begins to function as the politically correct form of femininity. And here we come to deference.

The problem of deference is not specific to this field. Students in many disciplines reproduce accounts and discussions of topics not of their choice, within parameters they may feel quite distanced from and bored by. The problem seems acute, though, when there is a very small critical literature, almost all of which inhabits the same paradigms. Take the example of British Gainsborough melodrama. All the substantial discussion of these films is within, or strongly influenced by, feminist paradigms.[15] It is very difficult for students who write on these films, and who may not have extensive know-ledge of postwar Britain or indeed of developments in feminist film criticism, to find other ways of writing about the films. They defer to feminist paradigms, not because they particularly agree but because that is the structure of the field. This again is not unique to this field, and indeed an ability to grasp the parameters and dominant paradigms of a discipline is an essential element in scholarship. The problem is that feminist paradigms, particularly in their more popular manifestations, include quite developed ideas about identity, about what women do and do not enjoy, and what is and is not in their interests. Although this can be challenging and thought-provoking, it can also be very undermining or alienating for female students, who can experience a pressure to defer to (feminist) definitions and accounts of their own identity and experience, or at least of the category – women – to which they think they belong. Again, this can be pedagogically productive, in that, if recognised, it poses all sorts of questions about identity, and particularly about the historical contestations for the category 'woman'. But it should also be recognised that being a good girl, which so many female students want to be, can be profoundly contradictory and stressful for women with feminist teachers.

THEORETICAL ISSUES

At a theoretical level, three different, but related, problems can be dis-tinguished. The first is formulated by Donna Haraway (1985) in her 'Manifesto for cyborgs', when she argues that 'feminisms have simultaneously natural-ized and denatured the category "woman" and consciousness of the social lives of "women"' (Haraway 1989: 199). She is particularly concerned in this essay to argue for political affiliations rather than a 'natural matrix of unity', and argues against the naturalisation of the category 'woman' which subtends some feminist ideas of unity. Although Haraway's essay is primarily directed towards the forging of political alliances, her theoretical point about the tendency towards the naturalisation of the categories of gender has relevance to practices of teaching. This theoretical tendency is accelerated in the classroom in the context of any pedagogical strategies – such as the use of everyday incidents as examples; or sentences which begin 'Women . . .' or 'Men . . .' – which attempt to articulate complex theoretical ideas initially in recognisable forms. This is clearly a controversial issue, and there are those who would argue that teachers who face these problems are in pits of their own excavation. However, this drift towards the naturalisation of the cat-egories of gender, for good historical reasons, pervades – indeed constitutes

– the terms of the debate, as the titles of recent anthologies illustrate: *The Female Gaze; Television and Women's Culture; Soap Opera and Women*. It is also within these terms, almost inevitably, that students first attempt to grasp ideas like gendered spectatorship.

The reason for this lies partly in the second theoretical issue, which is the inescapable historical and political imbrication of the category 'woman' in the (feminist) analysis of gender. It is not through theoretical naivety that the category 'woman' haunts the theoretical-intellectual field of gender, but because this field was constituted historically by political mobilisation through this identity, and those of homosexuality. Renascent feminism in the late 1960s was a movement for *women's* liberation. It is this political movement which has constructed the space which now allows me to raise these academic issues. Michele Barrett and Rosalind Coward offered a 1982 formulation of the issues at stake here in their disagreement with the editorial collective of *m/f* over the status of the categories 'women' and 'men', when they wrote 'We believe that you have mistakenly extended your challenge to the explanatory pretensions of these categories to a denial of their existence as categories at all' (Barrett and Coward 1982: 88). Denise Riley pushes the argument further in her historical analysis of the category 'woman', arguing that 'an active scepticism about the integrity of the sacred category "women" would be no merely philosophical doubt to be stifled in the name of effective political action in the world. On the contrary, it would be a condition *for* the latter.' She reaches this conclusion, however, in a context where she has argued for the simultaneous recognition of the historicity of the category 'woman' – 'women' don't exist – and the necessity of maintaining a politics 'as if they existed' (Riley 1988: 113). A different inflection of this issue – one taken up more widely in feminist media studies – is the distinction between 'woman' and 'women' proposed by Teresa de Lauretis (1984).[16] In this distinction 'woman' is an historical discursive construct, while 'women' are the real historical beings who cannot be defined outside discourses of 'woman', but who do nevertheless exist (de Lauretis 1984: 4). The problem, in the classroom, when the object of study is not feminist philosophy but *Coronation Street* or *Now Voyager*, is how to mobilise the necessarily contradictory accounts of the validity of the category 'woman', in conjunction with discussions of audiences which use 'women' as an explanatory category, in a way which is enabling rather than inhibiting for female students.

The third theoretical issue is that of the political agenda and status of 'second-wave' feminism itself. The most theoretically chic heritage of 1970s feminism is its contribution, with antiracist and anticolonialist movements, to the radical decentring of 'white male tradition'. Meaghan Morris (1988: introduction) has argued that this feminist contribution to the postmodern world is consistently ignored by those most empowered by the academic establishment. Stuart Hall (1987 and 1989) has testified to the paradoxes of the shifting locations of identity, now that, as Fusco (1988) suggests, 'the other is in'. However, this understanding of the theoretical heritage of 1970s and 1980s feminism, with its stress on the historicity and contingency of identifications of the self, obscures a strong countervailing feature of some feminist discourse of that period, its almost eschatological stance in relation to conventional femininities. In this discursive formation the identity 'feminist' would end sex-objecthood and housewifery for ever. Feminism was the enabling political project through which women's real potential could be liberated: the final femininity. This eschatological project is particularly clear in the feminist/sex-worker clashes of the 1970s and 1980s (themselves partly reminiscent of some of the social purity campaigns in the late nineteenth century)[17] documented in debates over sexuality in collections such as *No Turning Back* (Feminist Anthology Collective, 1981) and *Good Girls/Bad Girls* (Bell, 1987), and the way in which feminists were popularly regarded, and represented, as being 'antihousewife'. That individual feminists had no such understanding of themselves is not at issue; the point is that there are or were features of the feminist identity, and the discourses through which that identity was constituted, which were not compatible with other 'earlier' feminine identities – for example, being a mother of boys, to recall a notoriously divisive issue addressed by Hamblin (1982). Feminist identity was, in some ways, understood as an identity for women which transcended – and by implication, put an end to – traditional femininity. Laura Kipnis, in her video A *Man's Woman* (1988) produced in association with Channel 4, investigates the appeal of validations of conventional femininity in a period when feminist polemic threatened, paradoxically, to enable men, rather than women, to 'have it all'. Barbara Ehrenreich (1983) has traced the historical impact of these feminist discourses on US masculinity. This work, and that of Jacqueline Rose (1988) on Ruth Ellis and Margaret Thatcher, with its reinvestigation of the historical meanings of, and psychical investments in, femininity, works against feminist eschatology while at the same time allowing us to begin to locate it as a significant feminist discourse at a particular historical moment. It also reminds us that the issue of femininity is not easy, either for feminism or for women, as Rose (1986) has argued. When this element of feminist discourse is traced – and I would argue that it is perhaps more constitutive of second-wave feminism than it is currently comfortable to remember – it becomes clear that terms like *postfeminism* may, usefully, have a certain precision of historical reference. I would argue that we must at this stage recognise the historical specificity of 1970s–1980s feminism: see it, in its variousness, as just one of the discourses employed in the struggle for dominance over the meanings of femininity. This does not mean abandoning a feminist project; but it does mean jettisoning a certain kind of politically correct feminist identity which constructs other feminine identities as somehow 'invalid'. In the academic context with which I am concerned, this also means examining critically attitudes to 'ordinary women' in feminist media research, while, of course, in the true spirit of women's work, reminding the various dinosaurs in the field that feminist media research does exist.

Helpful reference points here are a 1985 article by Janice Winship, where she offers an analysis of the address and appeal of the new British young women's magazines like *Just Seventeen, Etcetera* and *Mizz*, and Ien Ang's 1988 review of Janice Radway's *Reading the Romance*. Winship uses an idea of 'marginality' in two senses to describe the concerns of these magazines and their young readership. Firstly, she suggests that this readership finds itself on the edges of the 'overpolished, complacent' address of the more established women's titles. Secondly, she shows how aspects of feminist culture form one of the take-for-granted aspects of the streetwise culture of these young women. So this readership is constructed as marginal to conventional femininity – but also as having gone beyond, assumed, some of the major concerns of 1970s feminism. In the context of this analysis, Winship argues for a revaluation of 'the stark confrontational style of feminism in the 1970s', arguing that the meanings of images, and indeed, what readers bring to them, has changed over the intervening period. This I understand to be an argument that the historical identity 'feminist' has proved less responsive to change than other feminine identities. I have no evidence apart from conversations with students and sessions with classes; but their experience of institutionally installed feminist texts is often one of faint perplexity at the evangelical tones in which what seem to them rather old-fashioned ideas are expounded. Andrea Stuart explores a similar sense of distance when she examines the difficulties that 'old' feminism is having with difference, pointing, in contrast, to the appeal of the magazine *Elle*: 'The assumption is that if you're an *Elle* girl you are already improved. Instead of reassuring us that we were all the same, with the same problems, *Elle* stressed difference' (1990: 31).

Ien Ang's review of *Reading the Romance* raises related issues, equally pressing in the classroom. Ang goes to considerable lengths to recognise the accomplishments of Radway's book, while also pointing to disagreements with elements of its overall project. Radway herself has offered several critical retrospectives on her research, including the generous methodological 'replacing' of the work in terms of British cultural studies in the Verso edition (Radway 1987 and 1988). I want to use Ang's review not as part of an attack on Radway but because it offers some formulations with which to pursue difficult disagreements in what I would hope could still be understood as a shared feminist project. It is issues of identity which I wish to pursue. Ang argues that, beyond a certain point in the research, the identities of the participants are fixed:

These are the theoretical terms in which Radway conceives the troubled relationship between feminism and romance reading. A common ground – the perceived sharing of the experiential pains and costs of patriarchy – is

analytically secured, but from a point of view that assumes the mutual
exteriority of the two positions. The distribution of identities is clearcut:
Radway, the researcher, is a feminist and *not* a romance fan, the Smithtown
women, the researched, are romance readers and *not* feminists. From such
a perspective, the political aim of the project becomes envisaged as one of
bridging this profound separation between 'us' and 'them'.

(Ang 1988: 183–4)

From this Ang goes on to argue that, for Radway, doing feminist research is
a matter of pedagogy: 'its aim is directed at raising the consciousness of
romance reading women' (184). Ang argues against this position as involving
a vanguardist idea of the relationship between 'feminism' and 'women', and
continues that this political predicament is the result of a failure to theorise
fantasy or pleasure in terms other than those of ideological function for non-
feminist women. She concludes by arguing for a different starting point for
the feminist researcher, one which attempts to overcome the opposition
between feminism and romance-reading through recognition of a shared
investment in fantasy, and therefore allows change in 'the sense of identity
that is constructed by feminism itself' (189).[18]

Ang's delineation of 'feminist desire' in this review essay seems relevant
to the teaching of the genres with which I have been concerned; indeed
feminist desire pervades the literature. This desire is to transform 'ordinary
women' into feminists. I have argued that these identities have been more
interdependent historically than is often recognised, and that a feminist
project can only gain from a rather more provisional, attentive, even ironic,
sense of self – and other. In the classroom I think this means increasing
attention to the historical construction of the personae and positions of
feminist criticism – the 'female spectator', 'reading as a woman', 'women of
colour', 'we', 'the ordinary women' – as, precisely, *historical* identities, the
contradictory sites and traces of political arguments and exclusions. Seeing
these identities and positions historically makes it more difficult to sustain a
recruitist pedagogy, and can perhaps facilitate discussion of what Kobena
Mercer (1990) has called the 'sheer difficulty of living with difference'.

Chapter 12

Identity in feminist television criticism†

INTRODUCTION

It is about fifteen years since the first feminist television criticism began to appear in Britain and the USA, and it is now possible to begin to construct a history of this criticism, and particularly, a history of its personae, of the characters who are specific to feminist television criticism: the feminist television critic and the female viewer. This pair, and the drama of their identity and difference, seem one of the most interesting productions of feminist television criticism, and in the contours of their relationships I think we can see patterns of feminist intellectual work which are not specific to the criticism of television.

My argument is briefly, that the formative stage of feminist television criticism extends from about 1976 to the mid-1980s, and that the key feature of this formative stage is the move from outside to inside the academy. While in 1976 the feminist critic writes with a primary address to her movement sisters, in a tone quite hostile to the 'mass media', yet concerned to justify her attention to television, by the mid-1980s she inhabits a more academic position, tends to address other scholars and is beginning to be anthologised in books used on both communications and women's studies courses (*Spare Rib* 1972 onwards; Butcher *et al.* 1974; King and Stott 1977; Tuchman *et al.* 1978; Kaplan 1983b; Masterman 1984; MacCabe 1986). There are a series of journal special issues in the 1980s through which it is also possible to chart a rather more confident engagement with television specifically.[1] Thus occasions such as the 'Console-ing Passions' conference held at the University of Iowa in 1992 and billed, correctly, as 'The first feminist conference on television and video', can properly be understood as one manifestation of the more academic second period of feminist television criticism, as can the recent rash of 'woman and television' books such as Mary Ellen Brown's *Television and Women's Culture* (1990), Christine Geraghty's *Women and Soap Opera* (1991), Andrea Press's *Women Watching Television* (1991),

†Written for the first 'Console-ing Passions' conference held at the University of Iowa, 1992. First published in *Media, Culture and Society* 15 (1993).

Lynn Spigel's *Make Room for TV* (1992), Ann Gray's *Video Playtime* (1992) and Julie D'Acci's *Defining Women: Television and the Case of Cagney and Lacey* (1994). If the formative period is marked, as I have suggested, at an institutional level, by a move from outside to inside the academy, it is also characterised, or perhaps I should say experienced, through the constitution of a new and, as we shall see, contradictory kind of individual, the feminist intellectual.

FEMINIST TELEVISION CRITICISM AND THE ACADEMY

One of the reasons for the shift from outside to inside the academy is that feminist concerns have had a particular impact in two critical areas in the study of television: firstly, in relation to the study of a genre, soap opera, and secondly, in relation to the study of the audience, a perennial concern for media studies and mass communications. This is not to suggest that there hasn't been substantial feminist work in other genres or fields (for example: Mellencamp 1986; Skirrow 1987; Holland 1991; or work collected in Mellencamp 1990; Tuchman, Daniels and Benét 1978; Creedon 1989) or to underestimate the attention to audiences and serial drama in existing research on television (Arnheim 1944; Herzog 1944), but to argue that it is in relation to soap opera and audience that feminist critical work on television has made a distinctive contribution which is recognised as such in the wider arena.

Thus Ien Ang (1985), Dorothy Hobson (1982), Michèle Mattelart (1986), Tania Modleski (1979), Ellen Seiter (1982a) and the London Women and Film Group (Dyer *et al.* 1981) all conducted research on soap opera in the late 1970s and 1980s, work which either hypothesised about the female audience or, in Ien Ang's case, actually investigated it. All this work forms part of a much larger body of feminist research, begun in the late 1970s, which re-evaluates traditional feminine genres and forms, like the women's picture, romantic fiction, the diary and the magazine, and, either by implication or directly, investigates audience engagement (Radway 1984; Gledhill 1987; Taylor 1989; Winship 1987).

Soap opera, as a genre, including US prime-time shows as well as much more localised national serials, has moved from being a ridiculed object of study to a mainstay of many syllabuses. Thus, in addition to the pioneering work mentioned above, there has been – and this is not an exhaustive list – the long Liebes and Katz *Dallas* project (1990), Robert Allen's *Speaking of Soap Operas* (1985), Sandy Flitterman-Lewis's work on commercials and seriality (1983; 1988), David Buckingham's study of *EastEnders* (1987), Christine Geraghty's comprehensive analysis of the genre (1991), Sonia Livingstone's pyschological study of audiences (1989) and the work of Kim Christian Schrøder (1988a), Jostein Gripsrud (1990), Jane Feuer (1984) and Mark Finch (1986) on the prime-time soap *Dynasty*.

In the same period there has been a general shift, across a whole range of social science and humanities disciplines, from a focus on the study of the text to an increased interest in the audience. In the study of television there has been a noticeable – if controversial – embrace of the virtues of qualitative methodology, a vogue for the work associated with the Centre for Contemporary Cultural Studies, and a series of detailed studies of particular audiences or audience sectors (Fiske 1987; 1990; Gillespie 1989; Grossberg *et al.* 1992; Seiter *et al.* 1989).

From its inception, this 'new' media ethnography has been marked by the problematic of gender in one of two ways. Either it has been mainly women who were the subject of the enquiry – as with the work of Hobson (1980), Ang (1985), Bobo (1988) and Radway (1984) or, because the focus of the work is domestic, as with the work of Morley (1986), Gray (1987), Moores (1991a) and Spigel (1992), gender (and generation) have been significant analytic and interpretative categories. Thus we could identify the feminist contribution to television research in the last fifteen years, in its most widely accepted form, to be the gendering of two key concepts, that of genre and that of audience. We now have gendered genres, and we also have gendered audiences. This shift can be exemplified quite simply in the differences between early textbooks of television studies, such as Fiske and Hartley's *Reading Television* (1978) and Len Masterman's *Teaching About Television* (1980), or textbook collections in communications such as Curran *et al.* (1977), and later books such as John Fiske's *Television Culture* (1987), Robert Allen's *Channels of Discourse* (1987) and Curran and Gurevitch's *Mass Media and Society* (1991), which pay more specific attention to issues of gender both as an analytic category and as an object of study.

EXISTING ACCOUNTS OF FEMINIST TELEVISION CRITICISM

There are several surveys of feminist media criticism, only one of which, by Ann Kaplan (1987), is specifically concerned with the study of television, although the introductions to the three collections on women and television – Baehr and Dyer (1987), Brown (1990) and Spigel and Mann (1992) – also offer some mapping of the field. What is striking about the more general surveys of feminism and the media such as those offered by Leslie Steeves (1987) and Liesbet van Zoonen (1991) is the similarity of the typologies used by both these authors and Kaplan (1987). In each case, the typologies are a variant of the familiar political distinctions between liberal, radical and socialist feminism. Thus Kaplan combines 'bourgeois, Marxist, radical and post-structuralist' feminism with the distinction between essentialist and non-essentialist approaches, while van Zoonen distinguishes between liberal, radical and socialist feminism in her analysis of the range of feminist media research. Both authors, with slightly different emphases and inflections, argue for the methodological and analytic significance of the tradition of British cultural studies to the feminist analysis of television, seeing this as one way of avoiding essentialism. The value of these typologies – the way in which they point to the differentiations within feminist thought, and the connection between media analyses and the analyses of wider social issues – should not obscure the fact that, as the authors themselves suggest, and Margaret Gallagher (1992) points out, very little criticism fits into only one category, and some work, such as Gallagher's own, is categorised differently in different schemas. Van Zoonen however, in a suggestive section entitled 'The audience and "US"' (1991: 43–4) raises issues about feminist research on popular culture which recur across all feminist work, and it is these ideas which I wish to explore in my own typology.

A DIFFERENT TYPOLOGY

I want to construct a typology which is based on the conceptualisation of the relationship between *feminism* and *women*, or the feminist and other women as inscribed within the critical text. I offer this categorisation most immediately as an heuristic, rather than an historical, typology. That is, I am not suggesting that feminist criticism has moved from stage one to stage three, although I would argue that there are discernible historical shifts in the type of paradigms that are dominant at any one moment. My three categories would be the following:

• Transparent – no others
• Hegemonic – non-feminist women others
• Fragmented – everyone an other

Each of these categories is defined through the relationship between the feminist and her other, the ordinary woman, the non-feminist woman, the housewife, the television viewer. It is this relationship, the way in which feminism constructs and has constructed itself in relation to the category 'woman', rather than the way in which women's subordination is theorised, which is essential to an understanding of feminist cultural criticism. That is, I am suggesting that feminist critical discourse itself constructs and produces, rather than simply analyses, a series of positions for 'women'.

Transparent

The positing of a transparent relationship between feminism and women is characteristic of the utopian, activist – and I think we could properly say formative – phase of post-1960s feminism. Although very rarely found without some articulation with the second 'hegemonic' relation, this utopian moment posits a shared sisterhood between all women, a consciousness of women as a gender group who are subject to a global patriarchal subordination and who thus have gender specific experiences in common. The dream, and the frequently asserted reality, of this moment is that all women are sisters, there is no 'otherness' between feminism and women, and that the appropriate pronoun of criticism is 'we'.

It is this consciousness that dominates media reviews in, for example, early British movement magazines like *Spare Rib* in the 1970s, and it is this consciousness, this 'we', which has been most vulnerable to attack for its political exclusions (which women?) and its epistemological assumptions (do women know differently?).

It is also, however, this notion of a shared gender experience which underpins part of the challenge that feminist work has offered to sociological and ethnographic research. Thus Dorothy Hobson's early research – which was scrupulous in its understanding of the complexity of the relationship between interviewer and interviewee, and which was consistently cautious about the class assumptions of the feminist 'we' – was not initially about the media but about the experience of *being* a young working-class housewife and mother, and she insists on the way in which reference to shared experience increased the richness of her interviews (Hobson 1978). Similarly, the work of the distinguished sociologist Ann Oakley offers some of its most radical challenges to existing social science methodologies in her consistent refusal to occupy conventional positions of neutrality in response to the questions of her 'interviewee mothers' (Oakley 1981). She adopts this strategy as a specific response to what she calls 'the dilemma of a feminist interviewer interviewing women' (Oakley 1981: 47), when the topic of the interviews is the frightening, but eagerly anticipated experience of a first baby.

Ironically, given that it has partly been the political attacks on the unthinking exclusions of this feminist 'we' that have marginalised it as an enunciative position, it is currently in response to the writing of women of colour that we most often find the assumption of transparency. Thus we find Jacqueline Bobo's work often characterised as 'what black women think' and as the site for the investigation of ethnicity – as if all those white audiences were without ethnic identity – and as if the articulation of ethnicity and gender here is not also historical, contradictory and sometimes provisional (Bobo 1988). Indeed, in less academic feminism, it could be argued that the acceptance of the political critique of the transparency of the straight white western feminist 'we' has led to a multiplication of special category, transparent, representative identities – older lesbians, working-class women, etc. – who are perhaps enabled to speak as a 'we' but also imprisoned by the inflexible demands of this identity fixing. This tendency is clearly represented by the British collection on women in the media, *Out of Focus* (Davies *et al.* 1987).

Hegemonic/recruitist[2]

What I am calling the hegemonic relationship between the feminist and the woman has been the most common position within feminist television criticism. It would also be possible to call this structure of relationship 'recruitist' to use Angela McRobbie's term (1982), the impulse to transform the feminine identifications of women to feminist ones. The construction of feminist identity through this relation involves the differentiation of the feminist from her other, the ordinary woman, the housewife, the woman she might have become, but at the same time, a compulsive engagement with this figure. The position is often profoundly contradictory, involving both the repudiation and defence of traditional femininity. In psychoanalytic terms we could hypothesise that the encounter between the feminist and the housewife – a very clear arena for early and proto-feminist work from the 1960s on (Friedan 1963; Gavron 1966; Oakley 1974, Hall 1980; Lowry 1980) – involves not just the construction of an identity 'independent woman' against another possible one 'dependent woman', but, specifically, an engagement with the mother.[3] In terms of feminist television criticism this usually meant the television viewer, in relation to whom much of the early writing is profoundly ambivalent.

A key rhetorical device here, one with which we are familiar from other traditions of anthropological and sociological work, is the introduction of a guide or intermediary, who gives instruction to the researcher about the pleasures and procedures of television viewing. These figures are often to be found in acknowledgements – for example, Carol Lopate, in one of the first feminist discussions of soap opera: 'I should like to thank Irena Kleinbort, whose insights were invaluable in helping me develop some of the ideas in this paper, and who furnished me with examples from her more extensive soap opera watching' (1977: 51). This disclaimer about soap expertise was anticipated by her earlier comment about learning how to watch, 'Until I got to know the stories, the afternoon felt like one long, complicated saga' (1977: 41). It is almost as if the researcher must prove herself not too competent within the sphere of popular culture to retain credibility within the sphere of analysis.

Tania Modleski's influential essay 'The search for tomorrow in today's soap operas' is marked by a similar ambivalence, particularly in its early version. For example:

> Clearly women find soap operas eminently entertaining, and an analysis of the pleasure that soaps afford can provide clues not only about how feminists can challenge this pleasure, but also how they can incorporate it. For, outrageous as this assertion may at first appear, I would suggest that soap operas are not altogether at odds with a possible feminist aesthetics.
>
> (1979: 18)

This passage displays a clear separation between the author and 'women', with the author explicitly addressing herself to 'feminists', a category in some

ways opposed to 'women'. The key words are 'clues' and 'outrageous'.
'Clues' reveals that this is an evangelical enterprise of detection, the analysis
of soap opera will render information about other pleasures – pleasures that
must be challenged. So the justification of the academic enterprise to other
feminists is through its gathering of politically useful knowledge. However
within this address to an imagined sceptical feminist audience, Modleski is
also making a polemical point: 'outrageous as this assertion may at first
appear'. This 'outrageous' marks the other element in what I am calling the
hegemonic relationship, the defence of 'women's culture'. In 1979 this
insistence is made against the grain of feminist attitudes to popular television,
insisting that there is something here to be taken seriously. Both 'clues' and
'outrageous' disappear from the rewritten book version of the essay, where
the two sentences are split.

> Clearly, women find soap operas eminently entertaining, and an analysis
> of the pleasure these programmes afford can provide feminists with ways
> not only to challenge this pleasure but to incorporate it into their own
> artistic practices.
>
> (Modleski 1982: 104)

and a page later:

> Indeed, I would like to argue that soap operas are not altogether at odds
> with an already developing, though still embryonic, feminist aesthetics.
>
> (Modleski, 1982: 105)

These rewritten versions, smoother, more confident, less embattled, also give
much less sense of that author as caught between the positions of 'woman',
'feminist' and 'intellectual'.

What we find, over and over again, in early feminist television criticism is
the complicated negotiation of the position from which the author writes.
There is a fleeting and fluctuating identification with a gender group (the
residue of 'we women') which is at the same time a disavowal of many of
the attributes of conventional femininity, crossed with the contradictory
demands of intellectual credibility, which is of course conventionally un-
gendered. The identity of the feminist intellectual, which strains to
combine these identities, is – necessarily – at this stage, profoundly unstable.
What I have called the hegemonic impulse within feminist criticism, apart
from its straightforward desire for a political mobilisation around the
inequities of gender, is also I think, an attempt to make the femininity/
feminism relationship less contradictory by recruiting the one to the other.

Fragmented

The third way of thinking about the relationship between feminism and
women I am calling 'fragmented' because it is founded on the possibility that

there is no necessary relationship between these two categories. This moment is constituted by the force of the critiques directed at what I have called the 'transparent' moment both politically and theoretically as the implications of what is normally called the 'essentialism' debate percolate through the academy. 'Woman' becomes a profoundly problematic category – and arguably and ironically – 'feminist' becomes rather more stable (Riley 1988; Haraway 1985; Spivak 1987). Franklin *et al.* (1991) have already offered one survey of the more general issues at stake here for cultural analysis in *Media Cutlure and Society*. I want to sketch briefly two distinct directions in current research work which share a radical particularism. One is towards 'historical autobiography', the other towards a stress on the contingency of gender identifications, and the significance of the articulation of these identifications with the whole range of other formative identifications. Valerie Walkerdine's work (1990) on the video-viewing of the *Rocky* films in the home of a working-class family can be understood in the context of a growing body of very sophisticated feminist autobiography (Heron 1985; Steedman 1986; Trinh 1989; Kuhn 1991; Lury 1991; Wallace 1990; Ware 1992), all of which can be understood as contributing to, or commenting on, the fragmentation of the 'transparent' relationship between feminism and women in their exploration of the constitutive dynamics of class, ethnicity, migration and gender in the story of each self. All of these accounts suggest the impossibility of telling stories in which individuals are 'just' gendered. The other thread, best exemplified by Ang and Hermes's radical review of the use of gender as an explanatory category in recent ethnographic projects, argues for the radical contingency of gender identifications, and against a research agenda which concentrates on 'women's culture' to the neglect of an articulation with ethnicity and class. The logic of Ang and Hermes's position is to jettison 'some fixed figure of "women"', and to argue that 'any feminist standpoint will necessarily have to present itself as partial, based upon the knowledge that while some women sometimes share some common interests and face some common enemies, such commonalities are by no means universal' (Ang and Hermes 1991: 324).

CONCLUSION

In summary, I have offered a typology of feminist television criticism in which the varying inscriptions of the relative identities 'feminist critic' and 'ordinary woman viewer' are seen as distinctive. I have suggested that the period (1975–84) of the institutional acceptance and development of feminist television criticism in the white anglophone academy (Britain, USA, Australia) is a period in which we see the professionalisation of the enunciative identity 'feminist critic'. I have tried to stress that I am offering an analytic, rather than an historical, typology, although Raymond Williams's distinction between residual, dominant and emergent modes of production might allow some mapping of these modes of feminist identity over both institutional changes in the academy and political changes in the feminist movements. I can offer here only the most blunt hypotheses. I could thus characterise the utopian, transparent moment, as dominant within the early days of second-wave feminism. There are also at this stage no scholars appointed to teach 'feminist theory' or 'gender studies' in universities and colleges. The unconscious class and ethnic identity of the 'we' of this moment has been extensively documented elsewhere. I suggest that the dominant mode of feminist critique in the period of academic institutionalisation is an hegemonic/recruitist one, hegemonic in the sense that this feminism has aspirations to dominate all accounts of the feminine. In this mode the feminist critic is distinguished from her other, the ordinary woman, and the complicated defence and repudiation of conventional feminine culture which characterises much feminist criticism of popular culture begins to be institutionalised. The pronouns here are 'we' and 'they', with the shifting referent of the 'we' being both 'feminists' and 'women', although the 'they' is always 'women'. The third moment is that in which the epistemological grounding of the political category 'woman' is thrown into crisis – engulfed in a sea of what Dick Hebdige has called 'the Posts' (Hebdige 1988). Here we have the confluence of the political critique of the 1970s with post-structuralist thought and the theorisation of the postmodern. Everyone here is an other – and there are no pronouns beyond the 'I' – but there are, relatively, lots of women teaching and writing books about these ideas.

It is customary, in topologies of this type, for the approach or position being advocated to come at the end. However, I am not sure that this type of theoretical clean get-away is either possible or desirable. Firstly, the logic of my own argument so far compels me to observe that my theoretically chic third category is itself dependent on its otherness from the first two categories. It too involves a repudiation of earlier femininities – in this case, feminisms. Indeed I would even venture that the fierce debate about essentialism which dominated feminist academic work in the later 1980s could be understood symptomatically as the repudiation of the 'transparent' and 'hegemonic' moments (de Lauretis, 1990b). Secondly – and this is a point which I can only make most tentatively – I think the apparent intellectual autonomy of the third category would reward sociological scrutiny. That is, I am interested by arguments made by feminist scholars such as Meaghan Morris that post-structuralism and postmodernism should partly be understood as responses to the political and epistemological challenges of feminism (Morris 1988). However, I also think this last position may be a much less conflictual one for *women* to inhabit *as intellectuals*, and it is to this end that I would, very crudely, point to the increasing dominance of this position as feminism becomes more academically visible outside the specialist enclaves of women's studies.

So if there are no theoretical clean get-aways, how can we reinterrogate

Notes

CHAPTER 1

1 For example, early research on American radio soaps either assumes a female audience or only investigates one. See Herzog (1944), Arnheim (1944) and Kauffman (1944). It is of course precisely the perceived 'feminine' appeal of the genre which has fuelled recent interest – see for example Dyer *et al.* (1981) and Modleski (1979).
2 See, for instance Neale (1977), Willemen (1978) and Morley (1980).
3 These notes are based on 1978 research when *Crossroads* was transmitted four evenings a week.
4 The production constraints of *Crossroads* are discussed by Brown (1978) and Miles (1980).
5 I am indebted to Lowe (1977) who originally discussed the other key British soap opera of this period, *Coronation Street*, in related terms.

CHAPTER 2

1 There has been a series of *Crossroads* novels authored by Malcolm Hulke, for example, *Crossroads: A New Beginning* (1974). Early *Coronation Street* novels were written by H. V. Kershaw. There are also a large number of supporting publications for *Crossroads*, such as the *Crossroads Cookbook* (1977), which appeared under the names of Hazel Adair and Peter Ling (originators of *Crossroads)* and *Crossroads Monthly*, 'The Official Magazine of the ATV Series', which was published from 1976 until the late 1970s. The *Birmingham Evening Mail* (the local paper for the region in which *Crossroads* was both produced and set) did a series of special issues to coincide with events in the serial. For example, a supplement entitled 'Meg's Memories' was produced in summer 1978 to coincide with the three-thousandth episode.
2 Brunt (1983) discusses press coverage of soap opera very interestingly.
3 (1996) It is properly salutary to point out here that I was wrong. Sheila Grant did have her baby, although the debate did follow the course here recorded. I point this out as too much teaching about soap opera proceeds with a rather general notion of the text – soap operas as serials in which certain *types* of narrative event occur.

CHAPTER 3

1 The recent Radio Rentals advertisement for a video tape recorder is a good example. 'It can take eight hours of *Crossroads* if you can.'

2 People involved in *Brookside* are a noticeable exception here. The *Soap City* day, organised by Dorothy Hobson as part of the 1985 Birmingham Film and Television Festival, demonstrated many of these attitudes.
3 Coward (1984) and Wilson (1985) take these issues on in different ways.

CHAPTER 4

1 hooks's challenge to the white feminist celebration of Madonna is the clearest instance here (hooks 1992: 157–164).
2 See also *Journal of Communication Inquiry* 11, 1 (1987).
3 Krishnan and Dighe (1990) discuss the sacred serials based on the *Ramayana* and *Mahabharata* epics. They use a mixture of traditional content analysis and much broader specific contextual analysis, which Gallagher (1992: 4–5) argues is exceptional among current feminist analysis of television in its attention to the political.
4 See Mellencamp (1986: 80–98), Bathrick (1984) and D'Acci (1987: 203–25). There is an extensive feminist literature on *Cagney and Lacey* which D'Acci (1994) references.
5 See Rabinovitz (1984) and Flitterman-Lewis (1993).
6 *Prime Suspect*, written by Lynda La Plante and starring Helen Mirren as a senior policewoman investigating serial killing of women, attracted enormous popular and critical acclaim when shown on British television in 1991. Skirrow (1987: 164–83) wrote on an earlier La Plante series, *Widows*. See also Chapter 6.
7 McCormack (1983: 273–83) offers a feminist critique of assumptions about female audiences in mass communications research.
8 See also Allen (1985).
9 For example, essays in Frentz (1992) use data about male and female audiences, although this is not the object of investigation in most cases.
10 Allen (1989) discusses the lack of precision in the use of 'soap opera' from a slightly different angle.

CHAPTER 5

1 *Girlfriends* was independently produced, and then distributed, by Warners.
2 It might be more appropriate to see *Goodbar* in relation to *Coma* and *The Eyes of Laura Mars* with a much less specifically feminine address.
3 Coward (1978) discusses some of these factors in a more extended way.
4 The 1970s films are discussed as a group by Davidson (1978), Mellen (1978) and Burstyn (1981). On the individual films see Geraghty (1976), and Cowie (1979) on *Coma*.
5 I would understand women's subordination as an oppression constituted around a gender category which is complexly articulated with categories of class and ethnicity. Barrett (1980) provides a useful discussion, as does Coward (1980).
6 See Williams (1977).
7 *Norma Rae* (directed by Martin Ritt, *USA*, 1979) is the obvious exception here.
8 See Cowie (1979) for an attack on the notion of the 'progressive' text, and Macpherson and Williamson (1981) for a discussion of 'repressive' film criticism.
9 Cook and Johnston (1974) discuss the 'danger' of the sexual woman, as do several of the essays in Kaplan (1978). Theresa in *Looking for Mr. Goodbar* would be an example of a character who is 'desirable but a mess'. Julia in *Julia*, a competent, political woman, is mainly off-screen and progressively physically mutilated as the film progresses.

10 The 'unfemininity' of the 'liberated woman' is discussed by Baehr (1980).
11 Steve Neale (1980: 59) points out that westerns as a genre, function precisely to 'privilege, examine and celebrate the body of the male', but that the erotic component of this look is consistently rendered innocent, as part of a relay of looks at the female body. It is in this sense that I use the term 'legitimate'.
12 Although I have no space to discuss the *mise-en-scène* in class terms, I would like to comment on the mode of Erica's undress. She wears white bikini knickers, white T-shirt and long white socks at several points in the early part of the film. It is particularly the girlish socks and the whiteness of the garments that connote a nice clean innocent (married) sexuality.
13 This is not to suggest that the 'cracks and fissures' visible to us now in the reading of a 1950s melodrama tell us much about its putative 'ideological effectivity' in the decade. However, this critical work has opened up the study of melodrama (1996). Barbara Klinger (1994) offers an illuminating account of the different historical meanings of the films of Douglas Sirk.

CHAPTER 6

1 For an early example of the first approach see King and Stott (1977); Kuhn (1985) provides examples of the latter.
2 Feminist film criticism has been much concerned with the question of the gendering of the gaze. See 'Is the gaze male?' in Kaplan (1983a), and the essays by Doane and Williams in Doane, Mellencamp and Williams (1984). Kuhn (1984a) provides a very useful summary of theorisation of the female spectator. See also Flynn and Schweikart (eds) (1986) in relation to feminist literary criticism.
3 For a preliminary discussion of gender and genre see Batsleer *et al.* (1985). With specific reference to television, see Curti (1986) and Deming (1986).
4 'In the old days evildoers were always seen to be punished. But times have changed and it would not surprise me if the widows get away with it in next week's final instalment' (Herbert Kretzmer, *Daily Mail*, 14 April 1983).
   'What's more, they get away with it. Dolly and her gang lifted £700,000. They stashed £600,000 behind the lockers in the convent school and last night we saw them get away clean scotfree to Rio with a cool thou.
   I always thought there was some law about crime not being seen to pay on the telly' (Stanley Reynolds, *'Widows'* in *The Guardian*, 21 April 1983).
5 See Chapter 5.
6 This, and the later quotation from this research, are taken from the transcripts of Morley's interviews, which were conducted while *Widows* was being broadcast.
7 The report in *The Voice* (23 February 1983) was the exception to the general 'Eva's web of tragedy' tone. *The Voice* defines itself as a black newspaper.
8 The second series of *The Bill*, transmitted in the autumn of 1985, featured the rather low-key introduction of an Afro-Caribbean police constable. He partly functions to reveal the racism of some of his colleagues.
9 Eva Mottley received considerable publicity in March 1983, just after the first series started, which included a profile in the *Sunday Telegraph Magazine* (26 April 1983). 'Black beauty' and 'Black widow' seem to have been irresistible headlines.
10 British racism reserves a special place for rich South Americans and the sort of women who marry them. The rather embarrassed press coverage in 1986 of the fact that the mother of Sarah Ferguson (who was about to marry into the British

royal family) was married to not just a South American but an Argentinian provides one example, as does the plot and particularly the sex scenes in Jill Tweedie's novel *Bliss* (1984). I would want to argue that *only* Bella, of the four women, could 'plausibly' fall in love with a South American.

11 See Morley (1986) and Ann Gray (1987).
12 There has been extensive discussion of 'endings' in relation to film melodrama. See Gledhill (1987).

CHAPTER 7

I am grateful to Ginette Vincendeau and Ellen Seiter for comments on this essay. Julia Roberts's next film, *Sleeping with the Enemy*, has an equivalent trying-on-hats sequence.

2 For example, in the London reviews, Phillip French observed, 'Directed by Mike Nichols from a screenplay by Kevin Wade, the highly enjoyable *Working Girl is Wall Street* remade in the style of a 1930s screwball comedy, and something of a cross between Nichols' blue-chip fantasy *The Graduate* and his blue-collar tragedy *Silkwood*' ('Marnie grows up', *Sunday Telegraph*, 2 April 1989: 41). Margaret Walters wrote in *The Listener*, 'Mike Nichols hasn't made a movie this good since *The Graduate* (1967) or *Carnal Knowledge* (1971)' ('The office copier', *The Listener*, 6 April 1989: 41). Pauline Kael offered the most substantial negative review of the film in *The New Yorker*, 9 January 1989: 80–1.

3 For example, Melanie Griffith was described as 'bimbo-voiced' by Derek Malcolm ('Working the system for all it's worth', *The Guardian*, 30 March 1989: 25), while Lorraine Gamman referred to her 'squeaky little girl voice' (review in *Spare Rib* 200 (April 1989): 31–2).

4 Elizabeth Traube has the most extended discussion of the 'bony ass' insult, with reference to a script scene cut from the movie (Traube 1992: 113).

5 *Cinderella* was mentioned in many reviews of both films. Examples include: Sue Heal in the British newspaper *Today*, 'Take Cinderella in thigh-length boots, a pinch of Pygmalion and mix in the glossy air of corporate greed and you have *Pretty Woman*' (11 May 1990: 20) and Amy Taubin in *The Village Voice*, 'Cinderella with the niceties of royal blood replaced with the not-yet-fallen-dollar' (*Film Special*, December 190: 11).

6 See part (iii) of *Films for Women* (Brunsdon 1986b) for documentation of feminist responses to 1970s films. Lesage (1982) writes on *An Unmarried Woman* as an example of 'hegemonic female fantasy'.

7 The substantial exceptions here are Taubin (1990), Hallam (1994) and Radner (1993). Hallam and Radner, which I discuss at more length below, are however, both concerned with what is different about these films in their relation to femininity and feminism. Thus the general point remains true – it is just that Taubin, Hallam and Radner don't write off the films – and indeed, as I do, seem to quite enjoy them.

8 Frank Mort, in his *Cultures of Consumption* (1996), traces the complex articulation of masculinities and consumption in this period.

9 Jane Gaines, introducing a 1990 feminist collection on fashion, gives an extremely evocative account of these shifts, including a mention of a group called 'Lesbians for Lipstick' (1990a: 5–6).

10 Teresa de Lauretis (1990a) discusses *Black Widow* (directed by Bob Rafelson, 1987) as exemplifying 'the narrative images and trajectories typical of the woman's film in the age of post-feminism'. My own interest here is in rather more

girly films and heroines. Walters (1995: 116–42) discusses *Pretty Woman* within a more general context of post-feminism but understands what she calls 'popular post-feminism' as simply negative.

11 Julia Hallam (1994) discusses the generic origins of *Working Girl* with particular reference to the work of Mary Beth Haralovich (1990) on proletarian women's pictures.

12 As many commentators have recognised, the final image of the film is ambivalent. On the one hand, as I have here discussed, we have Tess with a room of her own. On the other, as the camera recedes and 'The New Jerusalem' swells in volume, Tess's room is shown to be one of many hundreds in her block, again shown to be one of many.

13 Williamson developed her analysis of the single working woman in Hollywood cinema across a number of film review columns in *The New Statesman* in the 1980s. Her well-indexed collection (1993) reprints all the key articles.

14 John Updike, discussing the difficulty of writing about sex in the 1990s, points to this periodisation: 'One of the things that interested me was that the mid-Seventies were a kind of window of sexual opportunity between the invention of the pill and the onset of Aids' (John Updike interviewed by Mark Lawson, 'Sex and the rabbit man', *Independent on Sunday Magazine*, 27 February 1993: 33–6, p 36). There are objective reasons why sexual experimentation – as used for example in *An Unmarried Woman* – is a 1970s, rather than a 1990s, metaphor for female self-discovery.

CHAPTER 8

1 The following have addressed these issues: Caughie (1985: 53–66 and 1984: 109–20); Williamson (1986: 14–15).

2 There are many accounts of the *Dallas* project available, for example Katz and Liebes (1985) and Liebes and Katz (1990). The Tübingen project is reported in Seiter *et al.* (1989).

3 This is, in Britain, inextricable from the image of BBC and ITV. Taylor and Mullan (1986) provide some interesting insights on channel image, and Buckingham (1987) also discusses the issue in terms of the *Jewel in the Crown/Thornbirds* controversy.

4 *The Listener*, which was established as a magazine dealing only with the radio output of the BBC addressed the output of the commercial television companies from March 1988 until its demise in January 1991.

5 The problems of the legitimation of video art as an art form are to some extent explored in Hanhardt (1987). See also O'Pray (1988).

6 The following provide useful surveys of television criticism in Britain and the USA: Poole (1984); Caughie (1984); Newcomb (1986).

7 See particularly Chapter 10. Robert Allen (1985: 222–3) has argued that Newcomb is over-dependent on British television to exemplify his point. This would be significant in the context of my argument because of the way in which the art/entertainment axis is also inscribed over British/American television. See also Allen (1985: chapter 4).

8 The 1982 British Film Institute Summer School course 'Who Does Television Think You Are?' co-ordinated by David Lusted and held at Stirling University, attempted to work through some of the issues involved in conceptualising television through notions of mode of address.

9 I don't want to underestimate the role of industry spectaculars, Emmy nights, etc.,

but in Britain, at least, these are radically separate from any type of endorsement of television as 'legitimate' culture – that one can, for example, gain instruction in at universities. The more practice- and industry-oriented courses in broadcast media at North American universities may make any generalisation about this point quite improper.

10 See also Simon Frith (1983: 101–23) for a discussion of the making of BBC light entertainment.

11 Williams (c. 1991), *Writing in Society*.

12 I was a member of the organising committee of the 1986 ITSC, and a discussant in 1984.

13 See Kaplan (1978), Nowell-Smith (1977), *Screen Education* 20 and Dyer *et al.* (1981).

14 See Jameson (1984) and Grossberg (1987).

15 Allen also provides an extensive bibliography.

16 A restricted set of references here would include Seiter (1982a), Hobson (1982), Brunsdon (1981), Dyer *et al.* (1981), Ang (1985), Gledhill (1987), Radway (1984) and Radford (1986).

17 See, for example, Coward and Spence (1986: 24–39) and McCarthy (1986: 134–41).

18 See Gray (1987) and Morley (1986).

CHAPTER 9

1 See, for example, Hansard (1989); Broadcasting Research Unit (1989); the leaflets and advertisements (national press, week beginning 12 June 1989) of the Campaign for Quality Television; Douglas Hurd's address to the Royal Television Society convention in Cambridge, 12 September 1989, and the subsequent coverage of this event – e.g. *The Guardian*: 'Hurd denies TV quality faces threat', G. Henry, (22 September 1989); 'TV chiefs jockey for a lead in Hurd's big race', M. Leapman, *The Independent*, (27 September 1989).

2 King (1989) and Collins (1989). See also Stuart Prebble, 'White lies', *The Listener* (17 November 1988: 4–6), and Philip Whitehead, 'Farewell Auntie', *New Statesman and Society* (ll November 1988: 37–8); Christopher Dunkley, 'More and more ways of communicating less', *The Financial Times* (9 November 1988: 31); Alan Peacock, 'Laying the foundations of consumer-driven broadcasting', *The Independent* (9 November 1989) and Brian Wenham, 'Any questions?', *The Listener* (6 April 1989).

3 See Blanchard (1982) and Lambert (1982).

4 'Quality' has had a slightly polemical generic usage within television studies, as in the title of the book edited by Feuer *et al.* (1984): *MTM 'Quality Television'* where the quotation marks indicate a certain self-consciousness about the usage on the part of the authors. This was clearly picked up in reviews, with *The Times* giving Brian Appleyard's review of the book and accompanying season the subhead 'Channel Four and the NFT are taking mass American TV seriously' (1 December 1984: 11), and Susan Boyd Bowman's 1985 review providing one of the few instances of the discussion of quality in *Screen*.

5 Frank Kermode (1988) offers a generous discussion of the literary canon and 1930s writing. The debate in the USA over the canon and the humanities which has been partly provoked by by Allan Bloom's 1987 *The Closing of the American Mind* continues. See Levin *et al.* (1988).

6 With cinema, for example, the canons deducible from works like Christopher

Lyons, *International Dictionary of Films* (1984) are part print availibility, part technological or industrial history, part stars, directors, producers, studios, etc. See also Staiger (1985).

7   The history this article needs is perhaps, above all, the history of the changing attitudes to, and meanings of, television in Britain. Most obviously relevant is the introduction of commercial television in 1955, and the preceding campaigns such as those of the Popular Television Association and the National Television Council. Particularly interesting are the clear splits in the establishment attested to by all commentators, for example: Wilson (1961) and Black (1972). *The Independent* reminded its readers of this history in a leader, 'Maintaining quality television' (18 June 1989), but generally the debates of the 1950s have not been much referenced. Charles Barr (1986) traces changing attitudes to commercial television in the late 1950s and early 1960s, also arguing that the Pilkington report of 1962 (which led to the establishment of BBC2) was crucial in recruiting commercial television to the public service ethos.

8   See Garnham and Williams (1986) and Frow (1987).

9   Recent relevant discussions of the issue of value in television include: Thorburn (1987), Deming (1988), Caughie (1985) and Schrøder (1988b).

10 Wolff (1983) provides a lucid summary of the range of positions on transcendent and contingent value.

11 Nearly all the recent ethnographic work with female audiences about their television watching reveals this awareness of taste hierarchies, and the clear assignment of their own personal taste to a very lowly position, one which is inhabited in ways ranging from the defiant to the self-ridiculing. See, for example, Seiter *et al.* (1989).

12 Clyde Taylor (1989) provides a trenchant critique of the aesthetic enterprise as such in relation to the Afro-American tradition.

13 Ellis (1978) provides a particularly interesting tracing of traditional aesthetic criteria and the cinema in the 1940s, in which 'quality' figured significantly.

14 For the institutional evaluative codes of the BBC see Burns (1977); for Channel 4 much material is broadcaster-authored, as in Ellis (1983). Andrew Higson (1989) discusses the relationship of professionalism and innovation in a review of books on Channel 4. Programme studies often provide examples of 'professional aesthetics', for example Alvarado and Buscombe (1978).

15 See Pateman (1974).

16 Melvyn Bragg, 'Closedown for the golden age', edited text of Channel 4 *Opinions* (9 March 1989), printed in *The Guardian*, 9 March 1989: 25–7; 'Theory and practice', Charles Wood, Linda Agran, Melvyn Bragg, Tim Delaney, Alan Yentob and Aubrey Singer on the White Paper in *The Listener*, 17 November 1988; Anna Home, 'The wolf at the door of children's television', *The Independent*, 19 July 1989.

17 I do not discuss realist paradigms fully here, but see Lovell (1980).

18 Geraghty (1983) provides an interesting discussion of soap opera and realist conventions.

19 Ellis (1978: 28) discusses the moral resonance of realist arguments, the way in which 'the real . . . is primarily a moral imperative' in British critical discourse in the 1940s.

20 See also Gardner and Wyver (1983: 127) who make the point, which seems relevant now, that what they see as the rapid collapse of the principles of public broadcasting, 'leaves left critics in the curious position of having to defend and fight to retain a television system which they have spent years attacking for its elitism, paternalism, class-specificity and inaccessibility'.

21 Ellis (1978) discusses 'restraint' as a key element in ideas of quality in the 1940s.

It recurs quite noticeably in the Broadcasting Research Unit pamphlet (1989: 17) on *Quality in Television* in a way that is relevant to my point here: 'High production values are not necessarily the same thing as precise and elaborate sets and costumes, clever lighting and expensive original scores. . . . In the pursuit of excellence inexpensive simplicity may be the best bet. This also requires craftsmanship or high production values.'

22 Rupert Murdoch, 14th James McTaggart Memorial Lecture, 1989 Edinburgh Television Festival, quoted in *Broadcast* 1 (September 1989): 8.

23 See essays by Richard Paterson and David Lusted in Paterson (ed.) (1984). The way in which the popular resonance of particular programmes and catchphrases, which arguably point to sites of 'everyday aesthetics', is ignored in discussions of 'quality' once again indicates the importance of the written over the oral in the construction of legitimate judgements.

CHAPTER 10

References to newspaper articles are given in full in the text.

1 See, for example Gray (1987); Seiter *et al.* (1989); Morley and Silverstone (1990); Moores (1991a and b).

2 The key titles here are Hall and Jefferson (1976) and Hebdige (1979). However, it is the media studies take-up of these paradigms, rather than the initial subcultural formulations, which seem more indifferent to content.

3 My argument should be understood, if I may phrase it this way, as 'post Clifford and Marcus' (1986). That is, I am not pointing out that power is always inscribed within the ethnographic enterprise, etc., and would here follow Geertz (1988) in his response to postcolonial and epistemological critiques: 'The moral asymmetries across which ethnography works and the discursive complexity within which it works make any attempt to portray it as anything more than the representation of one sort of life in the categories of another impossible to defend' (144). Within this recognition he does, however, strongly defend the ethnographic enterprise. I am concerned with how, if you like, cultural power is spoken and circumscribes speech.

4 See also the review of this book, Ien Ang (1988).

5 BARB figures, Socio Economic Breakdown of Satellite Viewers, week ending 10 June 1990. Published in *Broadcast* 11 (August 1990): 10–11.

6 The merger of BSB with Sky was announced on 2 November 1990 with little warning. See appendix to the chapter for comment.

7 Thorstein Veblen's classic notion of 'conspicuous consumption' provides one obvious possible approach to the acquisition of satellite dishes (Veblen 1899). Another is offered by Alfred Gell, who discusses the (hard-earned) purchase of television sets by Catholic Sri Lankan fishermen. He argues that for these poor hardworking people the (electrically unconnected) television set functions like a work of art to negate or transcend the real world. He argues that this is 'adventurous consumerism' 'which struggles against the limits of the known world', rather than dull unimaginative consumerism which reiterates the class habitus. Attractive as this argument is, and it would obviously form one direction for future research, I think it would be more tenable in the case of satellite dishes if they did not in fact receive satellite television (Gell 1988). The Algerian film *From Hollywood to Tamanrasset* (directed by Mahmoud Zemmouri, 1990), a comedy of dish-passion in Algiers, posits the anarchy of satellite reception against the staid state channel.

8 Television ownership and rental increased very rapidly in Britain in the 1950s. Calculated from the number of sound and television licences issued, the increase is from 763,941 in 1951 to 9,255,422 in 1959. Figures from Montgomery (1965).

9 'The elected representatives of the villagers say they do not want these unsightly dishes everywhere,' he said. 'It is not that they dislike satellite television. We already have a strict rule of indoor aerials only.' Mr Cedric Dennis, director of housing, New Earswick, Yorkshire, *Daily Telegraph*, 4 December 1989: 5.

10 A *Daily Telegraph* story, 'Camouflage designed to hide eyesore dishes' featured Mr Peter Plaskett, photographed painting a dish in a leafy pattern. Mr Plaskett is marketing individually designed dishes and 'said he was being kept busy by people who are concerned about the neighbourhoods' (8 December 1989: 9). Another *Daily Telegraph* story, with a guest writer from *Electronics Weekly*, Leon Clifford, featured a similarly posed 'man and dish' photograph of Mr Stan Bacon who has made a satellite receiver from a dustbin lid. The Sky spokesperson commented that this method was used for reception of Superchannel in Poland (13 April 1989: 23).

11 It is this I understand John Fiske (1990) to be specifying in his use of the *langue/parole* distinction in a discussion of taste, or Lull (1988) in his notion of cultural extension.

12 John Wyver made a feature for the Channel 4 arts programme, *Without Walls* (shown 17 October 1990) which had several wonderful examples of satellite dishes in secluded spots.

13 In the letters to the national press following the merger Dr Michael Ward commented, 'My family's decision to buy a "squarial" was a considered one because we believed the quality and variety of the programmes on offer to be appropriate to our viewing needs. We had no wish to receive Sky transmission as we felt the transmission to be largely inane' (letter to *The Independent*, 5 November 1990). The following day Mr Warren Newman wrote, 'Above all, we will miss the high quality of digital stereo sound and picture from the MAC satellite. We will miss the compact aerials which will have to be replaced by ASTRA monsters' (letter to *The Independent*, 6 November 1990). Apart from the intriguing unanimity of the 'we' of each letter from a paterfamilias, we see here also the uphill struggle of 'quality' television taste.

14 See, for example, Anthony Simonds-Gooding 'When the sky fell in'. 'My week' feature in *The Independent*, 14 November 1990; Maggie Brown, 'Murdoch takes his revenge', *The Independent*, 7 November 1990; Georgina Henry, 'A deal that dishes the law-makers', *The Guardian*, 5 November 1990. The report in *The Times* the day after the merger maintains a fifty-fifty interpretation ('Bitter baffle ends as Sky and BSB become one', 3 November 1990). while *Today*, which greeted the news with a front page headline 'TV THRILLER', scrupulously points out that News International owns *Today* as well as Sky.

15 Immediately after the merger shares rose for BSB backers, Granada Group, Pearson and Reed International, as well as for News International and News Corporation (*Financial Times*, Share Index, 6 November 1990). Bronwen Maddox of Kleinwort Benson Securities estimated that Sky had lost £95m in the year to June 1990, while BSB would lose more than £330m in 1990. Maddox was quoted with (approximately) these figures in all the quality press on 3 November 1990. I have taken the conservative estimate of BSB's losses quoted by *The Independent*. *The Times* quoted £400m for 1990.

16 At the time of the merger, Sky claimed reception in 1.5m homes (including Eire), while BSB claimed 600,000 (Nisse and Fagan, 'BSB to merge with Sky', *The Independent*, 3 November 1990).

CHAPTER 11

Many students have helped me to think about these ideas. I should like to thank those on my 'Melodrama and Soap Opera' course at Duke University (1987), Special Topic 'Femininity and Genre' at Warwick University (1989–90), and CA613 'Feminism, Film and Television' at the University of Wisconsin–Madison (1991), particularly the Madison students from Women's Studies.

1 A comparison of one of the earliest 'women and media' anthologies, Tuchman *et al.* (1978) with later collections such as Brown (1990) makes this point.
2 Staiger (1985) offers discussion of the role of feminist criticism in canon formation.
3 Allen (1985) surveys some of the mass communications research on soap opera.
4 A report on the earlier research can be found in Women's Studies Group (ed.) (1978: 79–95).
5 Dyer *et al.* (1981); Feuer (1984); Finch (1986); Flitterman-Lewis (1988) and Geraghty (1983).
6 Gledhill (1988) indicates that she has chosen to offer an anlysis of *Coma* because it has already been substantially discussed by other feminist critics.
7 Aniko Bodroghozy (1991) has demonstrated that Universal marketed the film in 1959 with clear consciousness of the 'race' angle, offering different advertising campaigns in the US south. More recent work includes Heung (1987) and Flitterman-Lewis (1991).
8 Bobo (1988) and Stuart (1988).
9 Petro (1990) has recently argued for the importance of feminist textual analysis in the project of film history.
10 See Cowie (1984); Modleski (1987) and (1988) and Doane (1981–2).
11 Gaines (1991) in a review of Mulvey's collection *Visual and Other Pleasures* (1989) listed six other reprintings of this article.
12 Judith Williamson, in one of the few relevant discussions of pedagogy, observed in 1981 that 'teaching in *Screen Education* is like sex – you know other people do it, but you never know exactly what they do or *how* they do it' (Williamson 1981–2: 83). See also Penley (1986) and Walkerdine (1990).
13 See Culley and Portuges (1985); hooks (1989: chapters 6–11) and Treichler (1986) who provides an extensive bibliography.
14 Franco Moretti recognises the disruptive effect of tears in academic study when he constructs his corpus of 'moving literature': 'But why precisely this group of texts and not others? Because – let theory addicts try to stay calm at this point – only those texts have made me cry' (Moretti 1983: 158).
15 Aspinall and Murphy (1983); Aspinall (1983); Durgnat (1985); Richards (1985); Harper (1985); Petley (1986); Harper (1987); Murphy (1989) and Cook (1990). The Durgnat and Richards articles are most distanced from feminist arguments but, arguably, would not have been commissioned without them, as they form part of the *Monthly Film Bulletin* re-reviewing of Gainsborough films in 1985. (1996) This point is rather confirmed by the publication of Harper 1994 and Cook 1996.
16 D'Acci (1987) also uses this distinction, as does Mayne (1988).
17 DuBois and Gordon (1984) and Bland (1991).
18 (1996) See also Radway's own retrospective critique of her own work (1994a).

CHAPTER 12

1 For example: *Women's Studies International Quarterly* (1980) 3, 1; *Communica-*

tion (1987) 9, 3–4; *Journal of Communication Inquiry* (1987) 11, 1; *Camera Obscura* (1988) 16.

2 Jostein Gripsrud has argued that my use of 'hegemonic' in this context is misleading. His argument is that, certainly within a cultural studies context, the term 'hegemonic' has a specific, Gramscian lineage, and is thus associated with ruling classes and class fractions. To use hegemonic in relation to femininity would invoke the dominant white western femininities which shape our under-standing of acceptable femininities, rather than any kind of feminism. Julia Lesage (1982) uses hegemonic in this way in her discussion of *An Unmarried Woman*. I was trying to describe a certain attitude within feminism to conventional femininity which often involves a determination to lead the benighted to the light (of feminism). Although I would stand by my argument, I do now accept that my usage may be confusing and the 'recruitist' might have been clearer. I have retained the terminology as debate has already commenced in these terms.

3 Janice Winship, whose work van Zoonen selects as not producing a tension between 'us' feminists and 'them', makes this point explicit in her dedication of her book on women's magazines to 'My mother and . . . myself' (Winship 1987: v).

Bibliography of works cited

Abrahamsson, U. and Kleberg, M. (eds) (1981 – continuing) *Newsletter: Gender and Mass Media*, Stockholm: Department of Journalism, Media, and Communication, Stockholm University, and Audience and Programme Research Department, Swedish Broadcasting Corporation (between 1981 and 1988 this publication was called *Newsletter: Sex-Roles and Mass Media*).

Adams, P. and Cowie, E. (eds) (1990) *The Woman in Question: m/f*, London: Verso.

Allen, R. C. (1985) *Speaking of Soap Operas*, Chapel Hill: University of North Carolina Press.

—— (ed.) (1987) *Channels of Discourse*, Chapel Hill: University of North Carolina Press.

—— (1989) 'Bursting bubbles: "soap opera", audiences, and the limits of genre', in E. Seiter *et al.* (eds) *Remote Control*, London: Routledge.

—— (ed.) (1995) *To be Continued . . . Soap Operas Around the World*, London: Routledge.

Alvarado, M. and Buscombe. E. (1978) *Hazell: The Making of a TV Series*, London: British Film Institute/Latimer.

Alvarado, M. and Stewart, J. (eds) (1985) *Made For Television: Euston Films Limited*, London: British Film Institute.

Amos, V., Lewis, G., Mama, A. and Parmar, P. (eds) (1984) *Many Voices, One Chant: Black Feminist Perspectives, Feminist Review* 17.

Ang, I. (1982) *Het Geval Dallas*, Amsterdam: Uitgeverij SUA.

—— (1985) *Watching Dallas: Soap Opera and the Melodramatic Imagination*, London: Methuen.

—— (1988) 'Feminist desire and female pleasure: on Janice Radway's *Reading the Romance*', *Camera Obscura* 16 (January): 179–92.

—— (1990) 'Melodramatic identifications: television fiction and women's fantasy', in M. E. Brown (ed.) *Television and Women's Culture*, London: Sage.

—— (1990) *Desperately Seeking the Audience*, London: Routledge.

—— (1995a) *Living Room Wars*, London: Routledge.

—— (1995b) 'I'm a feminist but . . . ."Other" women and postnational feminism', in B. Caine and R. Pringle (eds) *Transitions*, St Leonards: Allen & Unwin.

Ang, I. and Hermes, J. (1991) 'Gender and/in media consumption', in J. Curran and M. Gurevitch (eds) *Mass Media and Society*, Sevenoaks: Edward Arnold.

Arnheim, R. (1944) 'The world of the daytime serial', in P. Lazarsfeld and F. Stanton (eds) *Radio Research 1942–3*, New York: Duell, Sloane & Pearce.

Aspinall, S. (1983) 'Women, realism and reality in British films 1943–1953', in J. Curran and V. Porter (eds) *British Cinema History*, London: Weidenfeld & Nicolson.

Aspinall, S. and Murphy, R. (1983) *Gainsborough Melodrama* (BFI Dossier no. 18), London: British Film Institute.

Attfield, J. (1989) 'Inside pram town: a case study of Harlow house interiors, 1951–1961', in J. Attfield and P. Kirkham (eds) *A View from the Interior*, London: Virago.

Attfield, J. and Kirkham, P. (eds) (1989) *A View from the Interior*, London: Virago.

Baehr, H. (1980) 'The "liberated woman" in television drama', *Women's Studies International Quarterly* 3, 1: 29–39.

Baehr, H. and Dyer, G. (eds) (1987) *Boxed In: Women and Television*, London: Pandora.

Baehr, H. and Spindler-Brown, A. (1987) 'Firing a broadside: a feminist intervention in mainstream TV', in H. Baehr and G. Dyer (eds) *Boxed In: Women and Television*, London: Pandora.

Barr, C. (1986) 'Broadcasting and cinema: 2: screens within screens', in C. Barr (ed.) *All Our Yesterdays*, London: British Film Institute.

Barrett, M. (1980) *Women's Oppression Today*, London: Verso.

Barrett, M. and Coward, R. (1982) 'Letter to the editors of *m/f*', *m/f* 7: 88.

Barrett M. and Phillips, A. (1992) 'Introduction', in M. Barrett and A. Phillips (eds) *Destabilizing Theory*, Cambridge: Polity.

Bathrick, S. (1984) '*The Mary Tyler Moore Show:* women at home and at work', in J. Feuer, P. Kerr and T. Vahimagi (eds) *MTM: 'Quality Television'*, London: British Film Institute.

Batsleer, J., Davies, T., O'Rourke, R. and Weedon, C. (1985) *Rewriting English*, London: Methuen.

Bausinger, H. (1984) 'Media, technology and daily life', *Media Culture and Society*, 6, 4: 343–51.

Beasley, M. and Silver, S. (1977) *Women in Media: A Documentary Sourcebook*, Washington DC: Women's Institute for Freedom of the Press.

Bell, L. (ed.) (1987) *Good Girls/Bad Girls: Sex Trade Workers and Feminists Face to Face*, Toronto: The Women's Press.

Belsey, C. (1980) *Critical Practice*, London: Methuen.

Bennett, T., Boyd-Bowman, S., Mercer, C. and Woollacott, J. (eds) (1981) *Popular Television and Film*, London: British Film Institute and Open University Press.

Bennett, T. and Woollacott, J. (1987) *Bond and Beyond: The Political Career of a Popular Hero*, Basingstoke: Macmillan.

Betterton, R. (1987) *Looking On: Images of Femininity in the Visual Arts and Media*, London: Pandora.

Black, P. (1972) *The Mirror in the Corner*, London: Hutchinson.

Blanchard, S. (1982) 'Where do new channels come from?', in S. Blanchard and D. Morley (eds) *What's This Channel Four?*, London: Comedia.

Bland, L. (1991) 'Feminist vigilantes of late Victorian England', in C. Smart (ed.) *Regulating Womanhood: Historical Essays on Marriage, Motherhood and Sexuality*, London: Routledge.

—— (1995) *Banishing the Beast: English Feminism and Sexual Morality*, London: Penguin.

Bloom, A. (1987) *The Closing of the American Mind*, New York: Simon & Schuster.

Bobo, J. (1988) '*The Color Purple:* black women as cultural readers', in E. D. Pribram (ed.) *Female Spectators*, London: Verso.

—— (1995) *Black Women as Cultural Readers*, New York: Columbia University Press.

Bobo, J. and Seiter, E. (1991) 'Black feminism and media criticism: *The Women of Brewster Place*', *Screen* 32, 3: 286–302.

Boddy, W. (1985) '"The shining centre of the home": ontologies of television in the

"Golden Age"', in P. Drummond and R. Paterson (eds) *Television in Transition*, London: British Film Institute.

Bodroghozy, A. (1991) *'Imitation of Life* in black and white: marketing strategies and reception of the 1959 version', unpublished paper, University of Madison-Wisconsin.

Bordwell D. and Thompson, K. (1979) *Film Art*, Massachusetts: Addison-Wesley.

Bourdieu, P. (1979) *Distinction*, trans. R. Nice (1984), London: Routledge & Kegan Paul.

Boyd-Bowman, S. (1985) 'The *MTM* phenomenon', *Screen* 26, 6 (Nov.–Dec.): 75–87.

Brandt, G. W. (1981) *British Television Drama*, Cambridge: Cambridge University Press.

—— (1993) *British Television Drama in the 1980s*, Cambridge: Cambridge University Press.

Briggs, A. (1985) *The BBC: The First Fifty Years*, Oxford: Oxford University Press.

Broadcasting Research Unit (1989) *Quality in Television*, London: John Libbey & Co.

Bromley, R. (1978) 'Natural boundaries: the social function of popular fiction', *Red Letters* 7: 34–60.

Brown, G. (1978) 'I'm worried about chalet nine', *Time Out* 449, 24–30 November: 14–15.

Brown, M. E. (1986) 'The politics of soaps: pleasure and feminine empowerment', *Australian Journal of Cultural Studies* 4, 2: 1–25.

—— (ed.) (1990) *Television and Women's Culture*, London and Newbury Park: Sage.

—— (1994) *Soap Opera and Women's Talk*, Thousand Oaks: Sage.

Brunsdon, C. (1981) *'Crossroads*: notes on soap opera', *Screen* 22, 4: 32–7.

—— (1982) 'A subject for the seventies', *Screen* 23, 3–4: 20–9.

—— (1986a) 'Women watching television', *Mediakultur* 4: 100–6.

—— (ed.) (1986b) *Films for Women*, London: British Film Institute.

—— (1989) 'Text and audience', in E. Seiter, H. Borchers, G. Kreutzer and E.-M. Warth (eds) *Remote Control*, London: Routledge.

—— (1990a) 'Television: aesthetics and audiences', in P. Mellencamp (ed.) *Logics of Television*, Bloomington and London: Indiana University Press and the British Film Institute.

—— (1990b) 'Problems with quality', *Screen* 31, 1: 67–90.

—— (1991) Pedagogies of the feminine: feminist teaching and women's genres', *Screen* 32, 4: 364–81.

—— (1993) 'Identity in feminist television criticism', *Media, Culture and Society* 15: 309–20.

Brunsdon, C. and Clarke, J. (1980) 'The big frame', *Red Rag* 12: 34–40.

Brunsdon, C. and Morley, D. (1978) *Everyday Television: Nationwide,* London: British Film Institute.

Brunt, R. (1983) 'Street credibility', *Marxism Today*, December: 38–9.

Buckingham, D. (1987) *Public Secrets: EastEnders and its Audience*, London: British Film Institute.

—— (1997) 'Normal science? Soap studies in the nineties', *Cultural Studies* 11 (forthcoming).

Buckman, P. (1984) *All For Love*, London: Secker & Warburg.

Burns, T. (1977) *The BBC: Public Institution and Private World*, London and Basingstoke: Macmillan.

Burstyn, V. (1981) 'Sex and class in the Hollywood cinema', *Canadian Women's Studies* 3, 2: 22–8.

Butcher, H., Coward, R., Evaristi, M., Garber, J., Harrison, R. and Winship, J. (1974) *Images of Women in the Media*, Birmingham: Stencilled Occasional Paper no. 31, Centre for Contemporary Cultural Studies, University of Birmingham.

Butler, J. (1990) *Gender Trouble*, New York: Routledge.

Cagan, E. (1978) 'The selling of the Women's Movement', *Social Policy* 8 (May/June): 4–12.

Cahiers du Cinéma (eds) (1970) 223: 'Young Mr. Lincoln', reprinted in translation in B. Nichols (ed.) (1976) *Movies and Methods I*, Berkeley: University of California Press.

Camera Obscura (1989) Special Issue: *The Spectatrix*: 20–1.

Cantor, M. G. and Pingree, S. (1983) *The Soap Opera*, Beverly Hills: Sage.

Carby, H. (1982) 'White woman, listen!' in Centre for Contemporary Cultural Studies, University of Birmingham, *The Empire Strikes Back*, London: Hutchinson.

Cassata, M. and Skill, T. (1983) *Life on Daytime Television*, Norwood, NJ: Ablex.

Caughie, J. (1977) 'The "world" of television', in C. Johnston (ed.) *History, Production, Memory*, special issue of *Edinburgh Film Festival Magazine*.

—— (1984) 'Television criticism: a discourse in search of an object', *Screen* 25, 4–5: 109–20.

—— (1985) 'On the offensive: television and values', in D. Lusted and P. Drummond (eds) *Television and Schooling*, London: British Film Institute and the Institute of Education.

Centre for Contemporary Cultural Studies (1975) 'Working papers in cultural studies 7/8', reprinted as S. Hall and T. Jefferson (eds) (1976) *Resistance Through Rituals*, London: Hutchinson and the Centre for Contemporary Cultural Studies.

Chaney, D. (1979) *Fictions and Ceremonies*, London: Edward Arnold.

Clayton, S. (1982) 'Cherchez la femme', *City Limits*, 30 April–6 May: 44–5.

Clifford, J. and Marcus, G. E. (1986) *Writing Culture: The Poetics and Politics of Ethnography*, Berkeley: University of California Press.

Clover, C. (1992) *Men, Women and Chainsaws*, London: British Film Institute.

Collins, J., Radner, H. and Collins, A. P. (eds) (1993) *Film Theory Goes to the Movies*, New York: Routledge.

Collins, R. (1989) 'The White Paper on broadcasting policy', *Screen* 30, 1–2: 6–23.

Collins, R., Curran, J., Garnham, N., Scannell, P., Schlesinger, P. and Sparks, C. (eds) (1986) *Media, Culture and Society: A Critical Reader*, London: Sage.

Comolli, J.-L. and Narboni, J. (1969) 'Cinema/ideology/criticism', *Cahiers du Cinema* 216. Reprinted in translation in B. Nichols (ed.) (1976) *Movies and Methods I*, Berkeley: University of California Press.

Cook, P. (1985) *The Cinema Book*, London: British Film Institute.

—— (1990) 'Gainsborough Studios', in A. Kuhn (ed.) *The Women's Companion to International Film*, London: Virago.

—— (1996) *Fashioning the Nation*, London: British Film Institute.

Cook, P. and Johnston, C. (1974) 'The place of women in the cinema of Raoul Walsh', in C. Johnston and P. Willemen (eds) *Raoul Walsh*, London: British Film Institute.

Corner, J. (ed.) (1991a) *Popular Television in Britain*, London: British Film Institute.

—— (1991b) 'Meaning, genre and context', in J. Curran and M. Gurevitch (eds) *Mass Media and Society*, Sevenoaks: Edward Arnold.

—— (1995) *Television Form and Public Address*, London: Edward Arnold.

Corner, J., Harvey, S. and Lury, K. (1994) 'Culture, quality and choice: the re-regulation of TV 1989–91', in S. Hood (ed.) *Behind the Screens*, London: Lawrence & Wishart.

Coward, R. (1978) 'Sexual liberation and the family', *m/f* 1: 7–24.

—— (1980) 'Socialism, feminism and socialist feminism', *Gay Left* 10: 8–11.

—— (1981) 'Underneath we're angry', *Time Out* 567 (27 February–5 March): 5–7.

—— (1984) *Female Desire*, London: Paladin.

Coward, R. and Spence, J. (1986) 'Body talk', in P. Holland, J. Spence and S. Watney (eds) *Photography Politics: Two*, London: Comedia.

Cowie, E. (1979) 'The popular film as progressive text', m/f 3: 59–81 (1980, 4: 57–69).

—— (1984) 'Fantasia', *m/f* 9: 70–105.

Cowie, E., Kaplan, C., Kelly, M., Rose, J. and Yates, M. (1981) 'Representation vs. communication', in Feminist Anthology Collective (ed.) *No Turning Back*, London: The Women's Press.

Creedon, P. (ed.) (1989) *Women in Mass Communication*, Newbury Park: Sage.

Culley, M. and Portuges, C. (eds) (1985) *Gendered Subjects: The Dynamics of Feminist Teaching*, London: Routledge & Kegan Paul.

Cullingworth, J. B. (1964), tenth edition 1988, *Town and Country Planning in Britain*, London: Unwin.

—— (1979) *Peacetime History of Environmental Planning Vol. III 1939–1969, New Towns Policy*, London: HMSO.

Curran, J., Gurevitch, M. and Woollacott, J. (eds) (1977) *Mass Communication and Society*, London: Edward Arnold.

Curran, J. and Gurevitch, M. (1991) *Mass Media and Society*, Sevenoaks: Edward Arnold.

Curti, L. (1986) 'Genre and gender', paper presented to the second International Television Studies Conference, London.

D'Acci, J. (1987) 'The case of *Cagney and Lacey*', in H. Baehr and G. Dyer (eds) *Boxed-In: Women and Television*, London: Pandora.

—— (1994) *Defining Women: Television and the Case of Cagney and Lacey*, Chapel Hill: University of North Carolina Press.

Davidson, J. (1978) 'So long, buddy, it's back to the woman's movie', *Cosmopolitan*, September: 128–31.

Davies, K., Dickey, J. and Stratford, T. (eds) (1987) *Out of Focus*, London: The Women's Press.

de Lauretis, T. (1984) *Alice Doesn't*, London: Macmillan.

—— (1988) *Technologies of Gender: Essays on Theory, Film and Fiction*, Indianapolis: Indiana University Press.

—— (1990a) 'Guerilla in the midst: women's cinema in the 1980s', *Screen* 31, 1: 6–25.

—— (1990b) 'Upping the anti (sic) in feminist theory', in M. Hirsch and E. Fox Keller (eds) *Conflicts in Feminism*, New York: Routledge.

Deming, C. (1986) 'Gender and genre: the criticism of television melodrama', paper presented to the International Communications Association Conference, Chicago.

—— (1988) 'The feminization of television criticism', in J. Anderson (ed.) *Communication Yearbook. no. 11*, Newbury Park: Sage.

Doane, M. A. (1981–2) '*Caught* and *Rebecca:* the inscription of femininity as absence', *enclitic* 5, 2 and 6, 1: 75–89.

—— (1987) *The Desire to Desire: The Women's Film of the 1940s*, Bloomington: Indiana University Press.

Doane, M., Mellencamp, P. and Williams, L. (eds) (1984) *Re-Vision*, Los Angeles: American Film Institute.

Downing, M. (1974) 'Heroine of the daytime serial', *Journal of Communication* 24, 2: 130–9.

Drummond, P. and Paterson, R. (1985) *Television in Transition*, London: British Film Institute.

DuBois, E. C. and Gordon, L. (1984) 'Seeking ecstasy on the battlefield: danger and pleasure in nineteenth century feminist sexual thought', in C. S. Vance (ed.) *Pleasure and Danger: Exploring Female Sexuality*, London: Routledge & Kegan Paul.

Durgnat, R. (1985) 'Gainsborough: the times of its time', *Monthly Film Bulletin* 52, 619: 259–61.

Dyer, R. (1973) *Light Entertainment* (BFI Television monograph no. 2), London: British Film Institute.

—— (1985) 'Taking popular television seriously', in D. Lusted and P. Drummond (eds) *Television and Schooling*, London: British Film Institute and Institute of Education.

Dyer, R., Geraghty, C., Jordan, M., Lovell, T., Paterson, R. and Stewart, J. (1981) *Coronation Street*, London: British Film Institute.

Dyer, R., Lovell, T. and McCrindle J. (1977) 'Soap opera and women', *Edinburgh International Television Festival Official Programme*, free supplement to *Broadcast 926*, 22 August: 24–8.

Eagleton, T. (1983) *Literary Theory*, Oxford: Basil Blackwell.

Ehrenreich, B. (1983) *The Hearts of Men: American Dreams and the Flight from Commitment*, New York: Anchor Doubleday.

Ehrenstein, D. (1978) 'Melodrama and the New Woman', *Film Comment* 14, 5: 59–62.

Ellis, J. (1978) 'Art, culture and quality – terms for a cinema in the forties and the seventies', *Screen* 19, 3: 9–14.

—— (1982) *Visible Fictions*, London: Routledge.

—— (1983) 'Channel Four – working notes', *Screen* 24, 6: 37–51.

Elsaesser, T. (1972) 'Tales of sound and fury', *Monogram* 4: 2–15, reprinted in C. Gledhill (ed.) (1987) *Home Is Where the Heart Is*, London: British Film Institute.

Elsaesser, T., Simons, J. and Bronk, L. (eds) (1994) *Writing for the Medium*, Amsterdam: Amsterdam University Press.

Feminist Anthology Collective (ed.) (1981) *No Turning Back: Writings from the Women's Liberation Movement 1975–80*, London: The Women's Press.

Feminist Review (1984) *Manv Voices, One Chant: Black Feminist Perspectives* 17.

Feuer, J. (1984) 'Melodrama, serial form and television today', *Screen* 25, 1: 4–16.

—— (1986) 'Reading *Dynasty*: television and reception theory', paper presented to the International Television Studies Conference, London.

—— (1994) 'Feminism on Lifetime: Yuppie TV for the nineties', *Camera Obscura* 33–4: 133–45.

—— (1995) *Seeing Through the Eighties: Television and Reaganism*, Durham, NC: Duke University Press.

Feuer, J., Kerr, P. and Vahimagi, T. (eds) (1984) *MTM* 'Quality Television', London: British Film Institute.

Finch, M. (1986) 'Sex and address in *Dynasty*', *Screen* 27, 6: 24–42.

Fiske, J. (1987) *Television Culture*, London: Routledge.

—— (1990) 'Ethnosemiotics: some personal and theoretical reflections', *Cultural Studies* 4, 1: 85–99.

Fiske, J. and Hartley, J. (1978) *Reading Television*, London: Methuen.

Flitterman, S. (1983) 'The real soap opera: TV commercials', in E. A. Kaplan (ed.) *Regarding: Television*, Los Angeles: American Film Institute.

Flitterman-Lewis, S. (1988) 'All's well that doesn't end: soap operas and the marriage motif':, *Camera Obscura* 16: 119–29.

—— (1991) 'Discourses of desire and difference', paper presented to the Screen Studies Conference.

—— (1993) 'The production of social reality and the reality of social production: the pre-Quayle *Murphy Brown*', paper presented to 'Console-ing Passions' Conference, Los Angeles.

Flynn, E. and Schweikart, P. (eds) (1986) *Gender and Reading*, Baltimore: Johns Hopkins University Press.

Franklin, S., Lury, C. and Stacey, J. (1991) 'Feminism and cultural studies: pasts, presents and futures', *Media, Culture and Society* 13, 2: 171–92.
—— (eds) (1991) *Off-Centre: Feminism and Cultural Studies*, London: Harper-Collins Academic.
Fraser, N. (1992) 'The uses and abuses of French discourse theories for feminist politics', *Theory, Culture and Society* 9, 1: 51–72.
Frentz, S. (ed.) (1992) *Staying Tuned: Contemporary Soap Opera Criticism*, Bowling Green, OH: Bowling Green State University Press.
Friedan, B. (1963) *The Feminine Mystique*, New York: Dell Publishing Company.
Frith, S. (1983) 'The pleasures of the hearth', in *Formations of Pleasure*, London: Routledge.
—— (1988a) *Music for Pleasure*, Cambridge: Polity.
—— (1988b) 'Towards an aesthetic of popular music', in R. Leppert and S. McClary (eds) *Music and Society*, Cambridge: Cambridge University Press.
Frow, J. (1987) 'Accounting for tastes: some problems in Bourdieu's sociology of culture', *Cultural Studies* 1, 1: 59–73.
Fuchs, C. (1989) *'Working Girl'*, *Cinéaste* 17, 2: 50–1.
Fusco, C. (1988) 'The other is in', in *ICA Documents 7: Black Film British Cinema*, London: ICA.
Gaines, J. (1990a) 'Introduction: fabricating the female body', in J. Gaines and C. Herzog (eds) *Fabrications: Costume and the Female Body*, New York and London: Routledge.
—— (1990b) 'Costume and narrative: how dress tells the woman's story', in J. Gaines and C. Herzog (eds) *Fabrications: Costume and the Female Body*, New York and London: Routledge.
—— (1991) Review of Mulvey, Penley and Fischer, *Screen* 32, 1: 109–19.
Gaines, J. and Herzog, C. (eds) (1990) *Fabrications: Costume and the Female Body*, New York and London: Routledge.
Gallagher, M. (1981) *Unequal Opportunities: The Case of Women and the Media*, Paris: UNESCO.
—— (ed.) (1987) *Women and Media Decision Making: The Invisible Barriers*, Paris: UNESCO.
—— (1992) 'Women and men in the media', *Communication Research Trends* 12, 1: 1–15.
Gamman, L. and Marshment, M. (eds) (1988) *The Female Gaze*, London: the Women's Press.
Gardner, C. and Wyver, J. (1983) 'The single play: from Reithian reverence to cost-accounting and censorship', *Screen* 24, 4–5: 114–29.
Garnham, N. and Williams, R. (1986) 'Pierre Bourdieu and the sociology of culture', in R. Collins, J. Curran, N. Garnham, P. Scannell, P. Schlesinger and C. Sparks (eds) *Media, Culture and Society: A Critical Reader*, London: Sage.
Gavron, H. (1966) *The Captive Housewife*, London: Routledge & Kegan Paul.
Geertz, C. (1988) *Works and Lives: The Anthropologist as Author*, Cambridge: Polity Press.
Gell, A. (1988) 'Newcomers to the world of goods: consumption among the Muria Gonds', in A. Appadurai (ed.) *The Social Life of Things*, Cambridge: Cambridge University Press.
Geraghty, C. (1976) *'Alice Doesn't Live Here Anymore'*, *Movie* 22: 39–42.
—— (1983) *'Brookside* – no common ground', *Screen* 24, 4–5: 137–41.
—— (1991) *Women and Soap Opera*, Cambridge: Polity Press.
—— (1992) 'British soaps in the 1980s', in D. Strinati and S. Wragg (eds) *Come On Down? Popular Media Culture in Post-war Britain*, London: Routledge.
—— (1996) 'Feminism and media consumption', in J. Curran, D. Morley and V. Walkerdine (eds) *Cultural Studies and Communications*, London: Arnold.

—— (1997) 'Women and sixties British Cinema: the development of the "Darling" girl', in R. Murphy (ed.) *Sixties British Cinema* (forthcoming).
Gillespie, M. (1989) 'Technology and tradition: audio-visual culture among South Asian families in West London', *Cultural Studies* 3, 2: 226–39.
Gitlin, T. and Wolman, C. (1978) *'An Unmarried Woman'*, *Film Quarterly* 32, 1: 55–8.
Gledhill, C. (ed.) (1987) *Home Is Where the Heart Is: Studies in Melodrama and the Woman's Film*, London: British Film Institute.
—— (1988) 'Pleasurable negotiations', in E. Deidre Pribram (ed.) *Female Spectators*, London: Verso.
—— (1992) 'Speculations on the relationship between soap opera and melodrama', *Quarterly Review of Film and Video* 14, 1–2: 103–24.
Gray, A. (1986) 'Women's work and boys' toys', paper presented to the International Television Studies Conference, London.
—— (1987) 'Behind closed doors: video recorders in the home', in H. Baehr and G. Dyer (eds) *Boxed-In*, London: Pandora.
—— (1992) *Video Playtime: The Gendering of a Communications Technology*, London: Comedia/Routledge.
Greer, G. (1971) *The Female Eunuch*, London: Paladin.
Gripsrud, J. (1988) 'Watching vs. understanding *Dynasty*', paper presented to the International Television Studies Conference, London.
—— (1989) '"High culture" revisited', *Cultural Studies* 3, 2: 194–207.
—— (1990) 'Towards a flexible methodology in studying media-meaning: *Dynasty* in Norway', *Critical Studies in Mass Communication* 7: 117–28.
—— (1995) *The Dynasty Years*, London: Routledge.
Grossberg, L. (1987) 'The in-difference of television', *Screen* 28, 2: 28–45.
Grossberg, L., Nelson, C. and Treichler, P. (eds) (1992) *Cultural Studies*, New York: Routledge.
Hall, C. (1980) 'The history of the housewife' in E. Malos (ed.) *The Politics of Housework*, London: Allison & Busby.
Hall, S. (1973) 'Encoding and decoding in television discourse', *Stencilled Occasional Paper no. 7, University of Birmingham: Centre for Contemporary Cultural Studies*.
—— (1987) 'Minimal selves', in *ICA Documents 6: Identity*, London: ICA: 44–6.
—— (1989) 'Cultural identity and cinematic representation', *Framework* 36: 68–81.
—— (1998) *Early Writings on Television*, London: Routledge.
Hall, S., Hobson, D., Lowe, A. and Willis, P. (eds) (1980) *Culture, Media, Language*, London: Hutchinson.
Hall, S. and Jefferson, T. (1976) *Resistance Through Rituals*, London: Hutchinson.
Hall S. and Whannel, P. (eds) (1964) *The Popular Arts*, London: Pantheon Books.
Hallam, J. (1994) *'Working Girl*: a woman's film for the eighties', in S. Mills (ed.) *Gendering the Reader*, Hemel Hempstead: Harvester.
Hallam, J. and Marshment, M. (1995) 'Framing experience: case studies in the reception of *Oranges Are Not The Only Fruit*', *Screen* 36, 1: 1–15.
Halliday, J. (1971) *Sirk on Sirk*, London: Secker & Warburg.
Hamblin, A. (1982) 'What can one do with a son? Feminist politics and male children', in S. Friedman and E. Sarah (eds) *On the Problem of Men*, London: The Women's Press.
Hanhardt, J. (1987) *Video Culture*, New York: Visual Studies Workshop Press.
Hansard 8 (1989) Debate on the White Paper *Broadcasting in the 90s*, House of Commons, February.
Hansen, M. (1986) 'Pleasure, ambivalence, identification: Valentino and female spectatorship' *Cinema Journal*, 25, 4: 6–32.
Haralovich, M. B. (1990) 'The proletarian woman's film of the 1930s: contending with censorship and entertainment', *Screen* 31, 2: 172–87.

Haraway, D. (1985) 'A manifesto for cyborgs: science, technology and socialist feminism in the 1980s', *Socialist Review* 15, 80: 65–107 (reprinted in L. J. Nicholson (ed.) (1989) *Feminism/Postmodernism*, New York: Routledge).

Harper, S. (1985) 'What's in a costume?', *Monthly Film Bulletin* 52, 621: 324–7.

—— (1987) 'Historical pleasures: Gainsborough costume melodrama', in C. Gledhill (ed.) *Home Is Where the Heart Is*, London: British Film Institute.

—— (1994) *Picturing the Past*, London: British Film Institute.

Hebdige, D. (1979) *Subculture: The Meaning of Style*, London: Methuen.

—— (1981) 'Towards a cartography of taste', *Block* 4: 39–56.

—— (1988) *Hiding in the Light*, London: Comedia/Routledge.

Herrnstein Smith, B. (1984) 'Contingencies of value', in R. von Halberg (ed.) *Canons*, Chicago: University of Chicago Press.

Heron, L. (1985) *Truth, Dare or Promise*, London: Virago.

Herzog, H. (1944) 'What do we really know about daytime serial listeners?' in P. Lazarsfeld and F. Stanton (eds) *Radio Research 1942–3*, New York: Duell, Sloane & Pearce.

Heung, M. (1987) '"What's the matter with Sara Jane?"' *Cinema Journal* 26, 3: 21–43.

Higson, A. (1989) 'A wee trendy channel', *Screen* 30, 1–2: 80–91.

Hill, J. (1986) *Sex, Class and Realism*, London: British Film Institute.

HMSO (1986) *Report on the Financing of the BBC* (Cmnd 9824) (Peacock Report), London.

—— (1988) *Broadcasting in the '90s: Competition, Choice and Quality* (Cmnd 517), London.

Hobson, D. (1978) 'Housewives: isolation as oppression', in Women's Studies Group, CCCS (ed.) *Women Take Issue*, London: Hutchinson.

—— (1980) 'Housewives and the mass media', in S. Hall, D. Hobson, A. Lowe and P. Willis (eds) *Culture, Media, Language*, London: Hutchinson.

—— (1982) *Crossroads:* The Drama of a Soap Opera, London: Methuen.

—— (1989) 'Soap operas at work', in E. Seiter *et al.* (eds) *Remote Control*, London: Routledge.

Holland, P. (1991) '*This Week:* moments of crisis', paper presented to the 1991 International Television Studies Conference, London.

Holmlund, C. (1991) 'When is a lesbian not a lesbian: the lesbian continuum and the mainstream femme film', *Camera Obscura* 25–6: 145–78.

—— (1993) 'A decade of deadly dolls: Hollywood and the woman killer', 127–51 in H. Birch (ed.) *Moving Targets: Women, Murder and Representation*, London: Virago.

Hood, S. (1980) *On Television*, London: Pluto Press.

—— (ed.) (1994) *Behind the Screens*, London: Lawrence & Wishart.

hooks, b. (1981) *Ain't I a Woman? Black Women and Feminism*, Boston, Mass.: South End Press.

—— (1989) *Talking Back*, Boston: South End Press.

—— (1992) *Black Looks*, Boston: South End Press.

Hurd, G. (1981) 'The television presentation of the police', in T. Bennett, S. Boyd-Bowman, C. Mercer and J. Woollacott (eds) (1981) *Popular Television and Film*, London: British Film Institute and Open University Press.

Hurtado, A. (1989) 'Relating to privilege: seduction and rejection in the subordination of white women and women of color', *Signs* 14, 4: 833–55.

Huyssen, A. (1986) 'Mass culture as woman: modernism's other', in *After the Great Divide*, Bloomington: Indiana University Press.

Independent Broadcasting Authority (1979) *Television and Radio 1979*, London: IBA.

Intintoli, M. (1984) *Taking Soaps Seriously*, New York: Praeger.

Jacobs, L. (1981) 'Now Voyager: some problems of enunciation and sexual difference', Camera Obscura 7: 89–104.

James, C. (1983) Glued to the Box, London: Picador.

Jameson, F. (1984) 'Postmodernism, or, the cultural logic of Late Capitalism', New Left Review 196: 53–92.

Janus, N. (1977) 'Research on sex-roles in the mass media: towards a critical approach', Insurgent Sociologist 7, 3: 19–32.

Jayamanne, L. (1995) Kiss Me Deadly: Feminism and Cinema for the Moment, Sydney: Power Publications.

Jermyn, D. (1996) 'Re-reading the "bitches from hell": a feminist appropriation of the female psychopath', Screen 37, 3: 251–67.

Julien, I. and Mercer, K. (1988) 'De margin and de centre', introduction to 'The last "special issue" on race?', Screen 29, 4: 2–10.

Kaplan, C. (1986) Sea Changes, London: Verso.

Kaplan, E. A. (ed.) (1978) Women in Film Noir, London: British Film Institute.

—— (1983a) Women and Film, New York: Methuen.

—— (ed.) (1983b) Regarding Television, Los Angeles: American Film Institute.

—— (1983c) 'The case of the missing mother: maternal issues in Vidor's Stella Dallas', Heresies 16: 81–5.

—— (1987) 'Feminist criticism and television', in R. C. Allen (ed.) Channels of Discourse, Chapel Hill: University of North Carolina Press.

Katz, E. and Liebes, T. (1985) 'Mutual aid in the decoding of Dallas: preliminary notes from a cross-cultural study', in P. Drummond and R. Paterson (eds) Television in Transition, London: British Film Institute.

Kauffman, H. (1944) 'The appeal of specific daytime serials', in P. Lazarsfeld and F. Stanton (eds) Radio Research 1942–43, New York: Duell, Sloane & Pearce.

Kermode, F. (1988) History and Value, Oxford: The Clarendon Press.

Kerr, P. (1982) 'Classic serials – to be continued', Screen 23, 1: 6–17.

—— (1989) 'Quality control', New Statesman and Society, 21 July: 36–7.

Kilborn, R. (1992) Television Soaps, London: Batsford.

King, B. (1989) 'Introduction', Screen 30, 1–2: 2–5.

King, J. and Stott, M. (eds) (1977) Is This Your Life?: Images of Women in the Media, London: Virago.

Kingsley, H. (1988) Soap Box, London: Macmillan.

Klinger, B. (1994) Melodrama and Meaning, Bloomington: Indiana University Press.

Krishnan, P. and Dighe, A. (1990) Affirmation and Denial: the Construction of Femininity on Indian Television, New Delhi: Sage.

Kuhn, A. (1984a) 'Women's genres', Screen 25, 1: 18–28.

—— (1984b) 'Dear Linda', Feminist Review 18: 112–20.

—— (1985) The Power of the Image, London: Routledge & Kegan Paul.

—— (1988) Cinema, Censorship and Sexuality 1909–1925, London: Routledge.

—— (1991) 'Remembrance' in J. Spence and P. Holland (eds) Family Snaps: The Meanings of Domestic Photography, London: Virago.

—— (1992) 'Mandy and possibility', Screen 33, 3: 233–43.

Lambert, S. (1982) Channel Four – Television with a Difference?, London: British Film Institute.

Lang, R. (1989) American Film Melodrama, Princeton: Princeton University Press.

LaPlace, M. (1987) 'Producing and consuming the woman's film: discursive struggle in Now Voyager', in C. Gledhill (ed.) Home Is Where the Heart Is, London: British Film Institute.

Lazarsfeld, P. and Stanton, F. (eds) (1944) Radio Research 1942–43, New York: Duell, Sloan & Pearce.

Leal, O. F. (1990) 'Popular taste and erudite repertoire: the place and space of television in Brazil', *Cultural Studies* 4, 1: 19–29.

Lesage, J. (1982) 'The hegemonic female fantasy in *An Unmarried Woman* and *Craig's Wife*' *Film Reader* 5: 83–94.

Levin, G., Brooks, P., Culler, J., Garber, M., Kaplan, E. A. and Stimpson, C. R. (1988) *Speaking for the Humanities*, Occasional paper no. 7, New York: American Council of Learned Societies.

Lewis, L. (1990) 'Consumer girl culture: how music video appeals to girls', in M. E. Brown (ed.) *Television and Women's Culture*, London: Sage.

Liebes, T. and Katz, E. (1990) *The Export of Meaning: Dallas*, Oxford: Oxford University, Press.

Livingstone, S. (1989) *Making Sense of Television: The Psychology of Audience Interpretation*, Oxford: Pergamon.

Lodziak, C. (1986) *The Power of Television*, London: Francis Pinter.

Lopate, C. (1976) 'Daytime television: you'll never want to leave home', *Feminist Studies* 3, 3–4: 69–82. Reprinted in *Radical America* 11, 1 (1977): 33–51.

Lovell, T. (1980) *Pictures of Reality*, London: British Film Institute.

—— (1981) 'Ideology and *Coronation Street*', in R. Dyer, C. Geraghty, M. Jordan, T. Lovell, R. Paterson and J. Stewart *Coronation Street,* London: British Film Institute.

—— (1987) *Consuming Fiction*, London: Verso.

Lowe, A. (1977) 'Narrative spaces and closure', unpublished paper, Media Group, Centre for Contemporary Cultural Studies, University of Birmingham.

Lowry, S. (1980) *The Guilt Cage*, London: Elm Tree Books.

Lubiano, W. (1993) 'Black ladies, welfare queens and state minstrels: ideological war by narrative means', in T. Morrison (ed.) *Race-ing, Justice, En-gendering Power*, London: Chatto & Windus: 323–63.

Lull, J. (1988) 'Constructing rituals of extension through family television viewing', in J. Lull (ed.) *World Families Watch Television*, Newbury Park: Sage.

—— (1990) *Inside Family Viewing: Ethnographic Research on Television's Audiences*, London: Routledge/Comedia.

Lury, C. (1991) 'Reading the self: autobiography, gender, and the institution of the literary' in S. Franklin, C. Lury and J. Stacey (eds) *Off-Centre*, London: Harper Collins.

Lyons, C. (1984) *International Dictionary of Films*, London: Firethorn Press [Waterstone's].

McArthur, C. (1980) 'Point of review: television criticism in the press', *Screen Education* 35: 59–61.

MacCabe, C. (1974) 'Realism and the cinema: notes on some Brechtian theses', *Screen* 15, 2: 7–27.

—— (ed.) (1986) *High Theory, Low Culture*, Manchester: Manchester University Press.

McCarthy, S. (1986) 'Autobiographies', in P. Holland, J. Spence and S. Watney (eds) *Photography Politics: Two*, London: Comedia.

McCormack, T. (1983) 'Male conceptions of female audiences: the case of soap operas', in E. Wartella *et al.* (eds) *Mass Communication Review Yearbook*, Beverly Hills: Sage.

Macpherson, D. and Williamson, J. (1981) 'A sense of outrage', *Time Out* 566 (20–6 February): 14–15, reprinted as 'Prisoner of love' in Williamson (1993) *Deadline at Dawn*, London: Marion Boyers.

McRobbie, A. (1982) 'The politics of feminist research: between talk, text and action', *Feminist Review* 12: 46–57.

—— (ed.) (1989) *Zoot Suits and Second Hand Dresses*, London: Macmillan.

—— (1991) *Feminism and Youth Culture*, London: Macmillan.

—— (1994) *Postmodernism and Popular Culture*, London: Routledge.
—— (1996) 'Body, space and capitalism', paper presented to 'Dialogue with Cultural Studies' Conference, Tokyo University, March 1996.
Maio, K. (1991) *Popcorn and Sexual Politics*, Freedom, CA: The Crossing Press.
Masterman, L. (1980) *Teaching About Television*, London: Macmillan.
—— (ed.) (1984) *Television Mythologies*, London: Comedia.
Matelski, M. (1988) *The Soap Opera Evolution*, Jefferson, NC: McFarland.
Mattelart, A., Delcourt, X. and Mattelart, M. (1984) *International Image Markets*, London: Comedia.
Mattelart, M. (1981) 'Women and the cultural industries', trans. Keith Reader, *Media Culture and Society* 4, 4: 133–51.
—— (1986) *Women, Media, Crisis*, London: Comedia.
Mayne, J. (1988) '*LA Law* and prime-time feminism', *Discourse* 10, 2: 30–47.
Mellen, J. (1978) 'The return of women to seventies films', *Quarterly Review of Film Studies* 3, 4: 525–43.
Mellencamp, P. (1986) 'Situation comedy, feminism and Freud: discourses of Gracie and Lucy', in T. Modleski (ed.) *Studies in Entertainment*, Bloomington: Indiana University Press.
—— (ed.) (1990) *Logics of Television*, Bloomington and London, Indiana University Press and the British Film Institute.
—— (1995) *A Fine Romance: Five Ages of Film Feminism*, Philadelphia: Temple University Press.
Mepham, J. (1990) 'The ethics of quality in television', in G. Mulgan (ed.) *The Question of Quality*, London: British Film Institute.
Mercer, K. (1990) 'Welcome to the jungle', in J. Rutherford (ed.) *Identity*, London: Lawrence & Wishart.
Miles, R. (1980) 'Everyday stories, everyday folk', MA Dissertation, University of Leicester.
Miller, N. (1993) 'Decades', in G. Greene and C. Kahn (eds) *Changing Subjects*, New York: Routledge: 31–47.
Modleski, T. (1979) 'The search for tomorrow in today's soap operas', *Film Quarterly* 33, 1: 12–21.
—— (1982) *Loving With a Vengeance*, Hamden, Ct: Shoe String Press.
—— (1987) 'Time and desire in the woman's film', in C. Gledhill (ed.) *Home Is Where the Heart Is*, London: British Film Institute.
—— (1988) *The Women Who Knew Too Much*, New York: Methuen.
Moi, T. (1994) 'Psychoanalysis, feminism and politics: a conversation with Juliet Mitchell', *The South Atlantic Quarterly* 93, 4: 925–49.
Montgomery, J. (1965) *The Fifties*, London: George Allen & Unwin.
Moore, S. (1989) 'The real McCoy', *New Statesman and Society*, 7 April: 49–50.
Moores, S. (1991a) 'Dishes and domestic cultures: satellite TV as household technology', paper presented to International Television Studies Conference, London.
—— (1991b) 'Satellite TV as cultural sign: consumption, embedding and articulation', *Media, Culture and Society* 15, 4: 621–40.
—— (1993) *Interpreting Audiences*, London: Sage.
—— (1996) *Satellite Television and Everyday Life*, Luton: John Libbey Press.
Moretti, F. (1983) 'Kindergarten', trans. D. Forgacs, in F. Moretti, *Signs Taken for Wonders*, London: Verso.
Morley, D. (1980) *The Nationwide Audience*, London: British Film Institute.
—— (1986) *Family Television: Cultural Power and Domestic Leisure*, London: Comedia.
—— (1992) *Television, Audiences and Cultural Studies*, London: Routledge.

Morley, D. and Robins, K. (1989) 'Spaces of identity: communications technologies and the reconfiguration of Europe', *Screen* 30, 4: 10–34.

Morley, D. and Silverstone, R. (1990) 'Domestic communication: technologies and meanings', *Media, Culture and Society* 12, 1: 31–55.

Morris, M. (1988) *The Pirate's Fiancée*, London: Verso.

—— (1990) 'Banality in cultural studies', in P. Mellencamp (ed.) *Logics of Television*, Bloomington and London: Indiana University Press and BFI (first published in *Discourse* 10, 2 (1988).

Mort, F. (1996) *Cultures of Consumption*, London: Routledge.

Mulgan, G. (ed.) (1990) *The Question of Quality*, London: British Film Institute.

Mulvey, L. (1975) 'Visual pleasure and narrative cinema' *Screen* 16, 3: 6–18.

—— (1977) 'Notes on Sirk and melodrama', *Movie* 25: 53–7.

—— (1989) *Visual and Other Pleasures*, Basingstoke: Macmillan.

Mumford, L. S. (1995) *Love and Ideology in the Afternoon*, Bloomington: Indiana University Press.

Murphy, R. (1989) *Realism and Tinsel*, London: Routledge.

Muthesius, S. (1982) *The English Terraced House*, New Haven and London: Yale University Press.

Myers, K. (1984) 'Television previewers – no critical comment', in L. Masterman (ed.) *Television Mythologies*, London: Comedia.

Nava, M. (1984) 'Karen Alexander: video worker (interview)', *Feminist Review* 18: 28–34.

Neale, S. (1977) 'Propaganda', *Screen* 18, 3: 9–40.

—— (1980) *Genre*, London: British Film Institute.

Newcomb, H. (1974) *TV: The Most Popular Art*, New York: Anchor Doubleday.

—— (ed.) (1976) *Television: The Critical View*, Oxford and New York: Oxford University Press, 2nd edition, 1979; 3rd edition, 1982; 4th edition, 1987; 5th edition, 1995.

—— (1986) 'American television criticism 1970–1985', *Critical Studies in Communication* 3: 217–28.

Newcomb, H. and Hirsch, P. (1983) 'Television as a cultural forum', *Quarterly Review of Film Studies*, summer 1983, reprinted in H. Newcomb (ed.) (1987) *Television: the Critical View*, New York: Oxford University Press.

Nochimson, M. (1992) *No End to Her*, Berkeley and Los Angeles: California University Press.

Nowell-Smith, G. (1977) 'Minnelli and melodrama', *Screen* 18, 2: 113–18.

O'Connor, A. (ed.) (1989) *Raymond Williams on Television*, London and New York: Routledge.

O'Pray, M. (1988) 'Shows, schisms and modernisms', *Monthly Film Bulletin* 55, 649: 57–9.

O'Sullivan, T. (1991) 'Television memories and cultures of viewing, 1950–1960', in J. Corner (ed.) (1991) *Popular Television in Britain*, London: British Film Institute.

Oakley, A. (1974) *Housewife*, London: Allen Lane.

—— (1981) 'Interviewing women: a contradiction in terms', in H. Roberts (ed.) *Doing Feminist Research*, London: Routledge & Kegan Paul.

Pateman, T. (1974) 'Ideological criticism of television technical manuals', *Screen Education* 12: 37–45.

Paterson, R. (1980) 'Planning the family: the art of the schedule', *Screen Education* 35 (summer): 79–85.

—— (ed.) (1984) *Boys from the Blackstuff* (BFI Dossier no. 20) London: British Film Institute.

Pearce, L. and Stacey, J. (eds) (1995) *Romance Revisited*, London: Lawrence & Wishart.

Penley, C. (1986) 'Teaching in your sleep: feminism and psychoanalysis', in C. Nelson (ed.) *Theory in the Classroom*, Urbana and Chicago: University of Illinois Press.
—— (1992) 'Feminism, psychoanalysis, and the study of popular culture', in L. Grossberg, C. Nelson and P. Treichler (eds) *Cultural Studies*, New York: Routledge.
Petley, J. (1986) 'The lost continent', in C. Barr (ed.) *All Our Yesterdays*, London: British Film Institute.
Petro, P. (1986) 'Mass culture and the feminine: the "place" of television in film studies', *Cinema Journal* 25, 3: 5–21.
—— (1989) *Joyless Streets*, Princeton: Princeton University Press.
—— (1990) 'Feminism and film history', *Camera Obscura* 22: 9–26.
Pines, J. (1989) 'Introduction to part two', in T. Daniels and J. Gerson (eds) *The Colour Black: Black Images in British Television*, London: British Film Institute.
Poole, M. (1984) 'The cult of the generalist: British television criticism 1936–83', *Screen* 25, 4–5: 41–61.
Press, A. L. (1990) 'Class, gender and the female viewer: women's responses to *Dynasty*', in M. E. Brown (ed.) *Television and Women's Culture*, London: Sage.
—— (1991) *Women Watching Television*, Philadelphia: University of Pennsylvania Press.
Pribram, E. D. (ed.) (1988) *Female Spectators*, London: Verso.
Probyn, E. (1993) *Sexing the Self*, London: Routledge.
Punter, J. (1984 and 1985) *A History of Aesthetic Control I: The Control of the External Appearance of Development in England and Wales 1909–1947* (1984); 1947–1985 (1985), Reading: Department of Land Management, University of Reading.
Rabinovitz, L. (1984) 'Sit-coms and single moms: representations of feminism on American TV', *Cinema Journal* 29, 1: 2–27.
Radford, J. (ed.) (1986) *The Progress of Romance: The Politics of Popular Fiction*, London: Routledge.
Radner, H. (1993) 'Pretty is as pretty does: free enterprise and the marriage plot', in J. Collins *et al.* (eds) *Film Theory Goes to the Movies*, New York: Routledge.
—— (1995) *Shopping Around*, New York: Routledge.
Radway, J. (1984) *Reading the Romance*, Chapel Hill: University of North Carolina Press.
—— (1987) 'Reading *Reading the Romance*' in *Reading the Romance*, London: Verso.
—— (1988) 'Reception study: ethnography and the problem of dispersed audiences and nomadic subjects', *Cultural Studies*, 2, 3: 359–76.
—— (1994a) 'Romance and the work of fantasy: struggles over feminine sexuality and subjectivity at century's end', in J. Cruz and J. Lewis (eds) *Viewing, Reading, Listening*, Boulder, Co: Westview.
—— (1994b) 'On the gender of the middle-brow consumer and the threat of the culturally fraudulent female', *The South Atlantic Quarterly* 93, 4: 871–93.
Rakow, L. F. (1986) 'Re-thinking gender research in communication', *Journal of Communication* 36, 4: 11–26.
—— (ed.) (1992) *Women Making Meaning: New Feminist Directions in Communication*, New York: Routledge.
Richards, J. (1985) 'Gainsborough: maniac in the cellar', *Monthly Film Bulletin* 52, 620: 291–4.
Riley, D. (1988) *Am I That Name? Feminism and the Category of 'Women' in History*, London: Macmillan.
Root, J. (1986) *Open the Box*, London: Comedia.
Rose, J. (1986) 'Femininity and its discontents', in J. Rose, *Sexuality in the Field of Vision*, London: Verso.

—— (1988) 'Margaret Thatcher and Ruth Ellis', *New Formations* 6: 3–29.

Ross, A. (1989) *No Respect: Intellectuals and Popular Culture*, New York: Routledge.

Rowbotham, S. (1973) *Woman's Consciousness, Man's World*, Harmondsworth: Penguin.

Scannell, P. (1988a) 'Radio Times: the temporal arrangements of broadcasting in the modem world', in P. Drummond and R. Paterson (eds) *Television and Its Audience*, London: British Film Institute.

—— (1988b) 'The communicative ethos in broadcasting', paper presented to the International Television Studies Conference, London.

Schlesinger, P., Dobash, R. E., Dobash, R. P. and Weaver, C. K. (1992) *Women Viewing Violence*, London: British Film Institute.

Schlüpmann, H. (1991) 'Melodrama and social drama in the early German cinema', *Camera Obscura* 22: 73–88.

Schrøder, K. C. (1988a) 'The pleasure of *Dynasty*: the weekly reconstruction of self-confidence', in P. Drummond and R. Paterson (eds) *Television and its Audience*, London: British Film Institute.

—— (1988b) 'Cultural quality: search for a phantom?' paper presented to the International Television Studies Conference, London.

Schudson, M. (1987) 'The new validation of popular culture: sense and sentimentality in academia', *Critical Studies in Mass Communication* 4: 51–68.

Schwitchenberg, C. (ed.) (1993) *The Madonna Connection*, Boulder: Westview.

—— (1994) 'Reconceptualising gender: new sites for feminist audience research', in J. Cruz and J. Lewis (eds) *Viewing, Reading, Listening*, Boulder: Westview.

Screen Education (1976) 20 (special issue on *The Sweeney*).

Seiter, E. (1982a) 'The role of the woman reader: Eco's narrative theory and soap opera', *Tabloid* 6: 35–43.

—— (1982b) 'Promise and contradiction: the daytime television serials', *Film Reader* 5: 150–63 (Evanston, Ill.: Northwestern University).

—— (1989) '"To teach and to sell": Irna Phillips and her sponsors, 1930–54', *Journal of Film and Video* 40, 1–2: 223–47.

—— (1990) 'Making distinctions in TV audience research: case study of a troubling interview' *Cultural Studies* 4, 1: 61–84.

Seiter, E., Borchers, H., Kreutzner, G. and Warth, E.-M. (1987) 'Don't treat us like we're so stupid and naive', *Re-thinking the Television Audience*, symposium at the University of Tübingen, Tübingen, West Germany, February; also in E. Seiter *et al.* (eds) (1989) *Remote Control: Television Audiences and Cultural Power*, London: Routledge.

Seiter, E., Borchers, H., Kreutzner, G. and Warth, E.-M. (eds) (1989) *Remote Control: Television, Audiences and Cultural Power*, London: Routledge.

Sendall, B. (1982) *Independent Television in Britain*, vol. 1, *Origin and Foundation 1946–62*, London: Macmillan.

Skirrow, G. (1985) 'Widows', in M. Alvarado and J. Stewart (eds) (1985) *Made For Television: Euston Films Limited*, London: British Film Institute.

—— (1987) 'Women/acting/power', in H. Baehr and G. Dyer (eds) *Boxed-In*, London: Routledge.

Smith, M. C. (1989) 'Women's Movement media and cultural politics', in P. Creedon (ed.) *Women in Mass Communication*, Newbury Park: Sage.

Spigel, L. (1986) 'Ambiguity and hesitation: discourse on television and the housewife in women's homes magazines, 1948–1955', paper presented to the second International Television Studies Conference, London.

—— (1992) *Make Room for TV*, Chicago: University of Chicago Press.

Spigel L. and Mann, D. (eds) (1992) *Private Screenings*, Minneapolis: University of Minnesota Press.

Spivak, G. (1987) *In Other Worlds*, London: Methuen.
Stacey, J. (1993) 'Textual obsessions: methodology, history and researching female spectatorship', *Screen*, 34, 3: 260–74.
—— (1994) *Stargazing*, London: Routledge.
Staiger, J. (1985) 'The politics of film canons', *Cinema Journal* 24, 3: 4–23.
Steedman, C. (1986) *Landscape for a Good Woman*, London: Virago.
Steeves, H. L. (1987) 'Feminist theories and media studies', *Critical Studies in Mass Communication* 4, 2: 95–135.
Steiner, L. (1992) 'The history and structure of women's alternative media', in L. Rakow (ed.) *Women Making Meaning*, New York: Routledge.
Stern, L. (1978) 'Oedipal opera: *The Restless Years*', *Australian Journal of Screen Theory* 4: 39–48.
Stevenson, N. (1995) *Understanding Media Cultures*, London: Sage.
Stuart, A. (1988) '*The Color Purple*: in defence of happy endings', in L. Gamman and M. Marshment (eds) *The Female Gaze*, London: The Women's Press.
—— (1990) 'Feminism, dead or alive?', in J. Rutherford (ed.) *Identity*, London: Lawrence & Wishart.
Swanson, G. (1981) '*Dallas*', *Framework* 14: 32–5.
Taubin, A. (1990) 'Stocks and bonds that tie', *Village Voice: Film Special*, December 1990: 11–12.
Taylor, C. (1989) 'Black cinema in the post-aesthetic era', in J. Pines and P. Willemen (eds) *Questions of Third Cinema*, London: British Film Institute.
Taylor, E. (1989) *Prime-Time Families*, Berkeley: University of California Press.
Taylor, H. (1989) Scarlett's Women: *Gone With the Wind and its Female Fans*, London: Virago.
Taylor, L. and Mullan, B. (1986) *Uninvited Guests*, London: Chatto.
Television and Radio 1979 (1979) London: Independent Broadcasting Authority.
Theroux, P. (1988) '*Coronation Street*', *The Listener*, 31 March: 50.
Thomas, L. (1995) 'Feminist researchers and "real women": the practice of feminist audience research', *Changing English* 2, 2: 113–29.
Thorburn, D. (1987) 'Television as an aesthetic medium', *Critical Studies in Mass Communication* 4: 161–73.
Toynbee, P. (1978) 'Feminist chic', *What's On in London*, 4 August.
Traube, E. (1992) *Dreaming Identities*, Boulder: Westview.
Treichler, P. A. (1986) 'Teaching feminist theory', in C. Nelson (ed.) *Theory in the Classroom*, Urbana and Chicago: University of Illinois Press.
Treichler, P. A. and Wartella, E. (eds) (1986) *Communication* 9, 1.
Trinh, T. M. (1986) 'Difference: "A Special Third World Women Issue"', *Discourse* 8: 11–37.
—— (1989) *Woman, Native, Other*, Bloomington: Indiana University Press.
Tuchman, G. (1978) 'The symbolic annihilation of women', in G. Tuchman, A. K. Daniels and J. Benét (eds) *Hearth and Home*, New York: Oxford University Press.
Tuchman, G., Daniels, A. K. and Benét, J. (eds) (1978) *Hearth and Home: Images of Women in the Mass Media*, New York: Oxford University Press.
Tulloch, J. (1989) 'Approaching the audience: the elderly', in E. Seiter *et al.* (eds) (1989) *Remote Control*, London: Routledge.
Tulloch, J. and Moran, A. (1986) *A Country Practice: Quality Soap*, Sydney: Currency.
Tweedie, J. (1984) *Bliss*, London: Penguin.
Veblen, T. (1899) *The Theory of the Leisure Class*, New York: Macmillan.
Walker, A. (1982) 'A letter of the times, or should this sado-masochism be saved?', in *You Can't Keep a Good Woman Down*, London: The Women's Press.
Walkerdine, V. (1990) *Schoolgirl Fictions*, London: Verso.

Wall, I. and Chater, L. (undated, *c.* 1990) *British Satellite Broadcasting: Study Material*, London: BSB and Media Education.
Wallace, M. (1973) *Black Macho and the Myth of Superwoman*, New York: The Dial Press.
—— (1990) *Invisibility Blues*, London: Verso.
Walsh, A. (1984) *Women's Film and Female Experience*, New York: Praeger.
Walters, S. (1995) *Material Girls*, Berkeley and Los Angeles: University of California Press.
Ware, V. (1992) *Beyond the Pale*, London: Verso.
White, M. (1989) 'Representing romance: reading/writing/fantasy and the "liberated" heroine of recent Hollywood films', *Cinema Journal* 28, 3: 41–57.
Wicke, J. (1994) 'Celebrity material: materialist feminism and the culture of celebrity', *The South Atlantic Quarterly* 93, 4; 751–78.
Willemen, P. (1978) 'Notes on subjectivity: on reading Edward Branigan's "Subjectivity under siege"', *Screen* 19, 1: 41–69.
Williams, L. (1984) 'Something else besides a mother', *Cinema Journal* 24, 1: 2–27.
—— (1988) 'Feminist film theory: *Mildred Pierce* and the Second World War', in E. D. Pribham (ed.) *Female Spectators*, London: Verso.
Williams, R. (1960) 'Advertising: the magic system', reprinted in R. Williams (1980) *Problems of Materialism and Culture*, London: Verso.
—— (1961) *The Long Revolution*, London: Chatto & Windus.
—— (1974) *Television: Technology and Cultural Form*, London: Fontana.
—— (1977) 'A lecture on realism', *Screen* 18, 1: 61–74.
—— (1980) *Problems in Materialism and Culture*, London: Verso.
—— (1981) 'Crisis in English Studies', reprinted in *Writing in Society*, London: Verso, *c.* 1991.
—— (1983) 'Cambridge English past and present', 'Beyond Cambridge English', reprinted in *Writing in Society*.
—— (undated – *c.* 1991) *Writing in Society*, London: Verso.
Williamson, J. (1981–2) 'How does girl number twenty understand ideology?', *Screen Education* 40: 80–7.
—— (1986) 'The problems of being popular', *New Socialist* 41: 14–15.
—— (1991) '"Up where you belong": Hollywood images of big business in the 1980s', in J. Corner and S. Harvey (eds) *Enterprise and Heritage*, London: Routledge.
—— (1993) *Deadline at Dawn: Film Criticism 1980–1990*, London: Marion Boyers.
Willis, P. (1977) *Learning to Labour*, Farnborough: Saxon.
Willis, S. (1993) 'Hardware and hardbodies, what do women want?: a reading of *Thelma and Louise*', in J. Collins, H. Radner and A. P. Collins (eds) *Film Theory Goes to the Movies*, New York: Routledge.
Wilson, E. (1985) *Adorned in Dreams*, London: Virago.
Wilson, H. (1961) *Pressure Group*, London: Weidenfeld and Nicolson.
Winship, J. (1981) 'Handling sex', *Media, Culture and Society* 3, 1: 25–41.
—— (1985) '"A girl needs to get streetwise": magazines for the 1980s', *Feminist Review* 21: 25–46 (reprinted in R. Betterton (ed.) (1987) *Looking On: Images of Femininity in the Visual Arts and Media*, London: Pandora).
—— (1987) *Inside Women's Magazines*, London: Pandora.
Winston, B. (1994) 'Public service in the "New Broadcasting Age"', in S. Hood (ed.) *Behind the Screens*, London: Lawrence & Wishart.
Wolff, J. (1983) *Aesthetics and the Sociology of Art*, London: George Allen & Unwin.
Women's Studies Group (ed.) (1978) *Women Take Issue*, London: Hutchinson.
Wood, R. (1985) *Hollywood from Vietnam to Reagan*, New York: Columbia University Press.

Wright, P. (1985) *On Living in an Old Country: The National Past in Contemporary Britain*, London: Verso.

Young, L. (1995) *Fear of the Dark: 'Race', Gender and Sexuality in the Cinema*, London: Routledge.

Zoonen, L. van (1991) 'Feminist perspectives on the media', in J. Curran and M. Gurevitch (eds) *Mass Media and Society*, Sevenoaks: Edward Arnold.

—— (1994) *Feminist Media Studies*, London: Sage.

Index